D0867341

Yale Western Americana Series, 29

Blacks in Gold Rush California

Rudolph M. Lapp

New Haven and London, Yale University Press, 1977

Designed by John O. C. McCrillis and set in Baskerville type.
Printed in the United States of America by The Vail-Ballou Press, Inc., Binghamton, N.Y.

Published in Great Britain, Europe, Africa, and Asia (except Japan) by Yale University Press, Ltd., London. Distributed in Latin America by Kaiman & Polon, Inc., New York City; in Australia and New Zealand by Book & Film Services, Artarmon, N.S.W., Australia; and in Japan by Harper & Row, Publishers, Tokyo Office.

Library of Congress Cataloging in Publication Data

Lapp, Rudolph M
Blacks in Gold Rush California.

(Yale Western Americana series ; 29)
Bibliography: p.
Includes index.
1. Afro-Americans–California–History.
2. California–Gold Discoveries. 3. Slavery in the United States–California. 4. Gold mines and mining–California–History. I. Title.
II. Series.
E185.93.C2L36 979.4′004′96073 76-30534
ISBN 0-300-01988-2

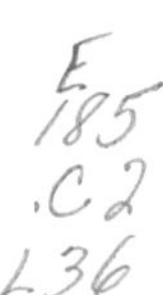

Contents

Illustrations

Following page 48

Preface

The true function of scholarship as of society is not to stake out claims on which others must not trespass, but to provide a community of knowledge in which others may share.

F. O. Matthiessen

I first became aware of the long history of blacks in the West in the late 1950s, through the coincidence of preparing to teach at the same time courses in California history and Afro-American history. It was then that I discovered blacks as miners in the California gold country. From the census I came to realize that the scattered references to blacks in contemporary journals and diaries represented more than just a small group of individuals. I soon learned, however, that research on the Negro in California was not bonanza mining. I was like the miner who panned only a few ounces a week and had to wash out tons of earth to get it. California journalism in this period was not paying much attention to blacks. Neither were the contemporary recorders of the period. The larger minority group of color, the Chinese, was much more observed by contemporaries. And, as researchers in Afro-American history well know, primary material written by blacks in this period was scant and survived in uneven amounts. The one book written on the subject of Negroes in the gold rush, Delilah Beasley's *Negro Trail Blazers of California*, published in 1919, bears so many of the characteristics of the county history "mug" book that it must be read with extreme care. It must be read, because Miss Beasley was able to interview old-timers who still had some memory of the gold rush period, but it suffers from the deficiencies that are always part of oral history derived from very old people.

As I continued to pursue this subject, I became aware of two things. First, the story of blacks in California has all of the dimensions of Eastern black history heightened by the dramatic character of the gold rush. Second, contemporary black and white Americans of all classes and stations in life were almost completely ignorant of this facet of Western history.

While the thousands of blacks who came west comprised in the early years only one percent of the California population, they made history. In proper perspective one sees that this was not a major movement of black peoples in the nineteenth century. The exodus to Canada that occurred almost simultaneously because of the Fugitive Slave Law of 1850 was larger, and of course the mass movement of slaves with their masters from the older slave states to the Deep South and Southwest was even greater, but neither of those was entirely voluntary. Of course, slaves were also brought to California, but the free Negroes were the larger group and their migration was almost completely by choice. In fact this nineteenth-century free Negro migration was unique in that blacks for the first time were not forced to migrate as slaves or to flee a return to slavery, but were voluntarily seeking a new region without being forced to leave the one from which they came. Most of these blacks were like most of the whites who migrated to California; they were not leaving a condition of unbearable economic depression but were simply seeking quick prosperity. It is their activities in the new environment that best reveal the westward extension of nineteenth-century black thought. This is not to say that slaves did not leave their mark on the period. Those who chose to make their strike for freedom also left an impression on the historical landscape of the gold rush decade.

The gold rush background also served to dramatize the essential Americanism of black aspirations. Nineteenth-century notions of progress and material wealth were as much the possession of the blacks as of the most upward-striving white Americans. These notions were most clearly apparent in the activities of the transplanted Eastern free Negro group. Their attachment to mainstream nineteenth-century values was expressed in the demands and the rhetoric of the civil-rights movements they led in California.

Most readers will be surprised to learn that thousands of Negroes worked at mining gold and had their proportion of lucky strikes. I hope that I have made that point most evident in the work that follows. I hope too that a certain Yale letter-writer, who asked caustically some years ago in his alumni paper whether anyone had ever heard of a Negro mining gold in California, will read this book. He had much to do with my desire to complete this study; I have meant this book for the general reader as much as for the professional historian.

Readers will note that I have used the words *black, Afro-American,* and *Negro* interchangeably. This requires an explanation. I am aware of the thrust to give dignity to the word *black* and heartily support the effort to wipe out the derogatory uses of that word which have long been a part of our language. However, I do not feel that this must destroy the dignity of the word *Negro.* To discredit the word *Negro* is to me a denial of all those remarkable and courageous blacks who laid their lives and careers on the line as proud men and women, proud of being "Negroes." When I think of this question, I think of a Negro hero of my youth named Paul Robeson.

I hope that this study will help to remove the stereotype of the whiteness of the Far West and that of the unambitious black; and by so doing this work may also throw a bit more muscle into the process of democratizing race relations in the United States. This last must happen if we are to succeed in removing the effects of one of the deepest flaws in the historical development of this country.

Acknowledgments

In the research and writing of this book I have received help in many ways. Financially I have been aided by grants from the American Philosophical Society and a fellowship from the National Endowment for the Humanities. Two sabbatical leaves granted by the Board of Trustees of the College of San Mateo provided me with much-needed time and funds to unearth this story. My colleagues at the College of San Mateo were most supportive in their encouragement of this research endeavor.

Library staffs have been of great assistance to me, and particular notice must be given to the wonderfully cooperative personnel of the staffs of the Bancroft Library of the University of California and the Beinecke Library of Yale University. Equally cooperative have been the staffs of the California Historical Society Library and the Society of California Pioneers Library in San Francisco. Dr. William N. Davis, Jr., California State Archivist, was helpful beyond the call of duty. Aid was given to me in southern California by the staffs of the Huntington Library and the manuscripts division of the library at the University of California, Los Angeles. Last, but hardly least, thanks go to the library staff of the College of San Mateo, who worked tirelessly to obtain materials for me through interlibrary loan. Here I must also mention James Abajian, who was kind enough to share with me some of the results of his bibliographical research in gold rush era blacks.

Many individuals have played some part in helping me to complete this study; among them are Professors Leon F. Litwack, Moses L. Rischin, and Roger Lotchin, as well as Dorothy Porter, John B. Tompkins, Earl Ramey, Julio L. Bortolazzo, Samuel Dickson, Lynn Cortopassi, Elizabeth

K. Gudde, Margaret F. Atkinson, and typists Phyllis Hechim and Ruth Rouse. Gerald Wheeler of San Jose State University deserves thanks for encouraging me to present my first research efforts on this subject as a scholarly paper. Robert A. Becker of Bancroft Library was an invaluable helper in guiding me through materials in that great Western collection. In the days of final writing, Robert E. Burke of the University of Washington was a great friend when I needed improvement in the stylistic condition of the manuscript. And Beverly Cayford, Yale Press copy editor, lent a powerful hand in the last stages of editing this book.

Some of the material in this volume appeared previously in the *Journal of Negro History* (April 1964; October 1968), the *California Historical Society Quarterly* (March 1966), and in *Archy Lee* (The Book Club of California, 1969).

My wife, Patricia Teeling Lapp, is the sine qua non of this work. She cheerfully read manuscript and newspaper material with me, and her prior professional editing experience was invaluable to the final completion of this book.

1 Before the Gold Rush

The first blacks came to western America with the Spanish thrust for empire in the new world. In the age of Columbus, free blacks and slaves served in the Spanish navy and merchant marine, thereby becoming participants in Spain's exploration and conquest in the western hemisphere.[1] While they did not come in sufficient numbers to form black communities, these men and women shared in an exciting period, and they are worthy of note. Their experiences testify to the little-known black presence in many of the distant corners of Western history.

In recorded history the first Negro to land within the present boundaries of the United States was Estebanico, or "Black Stephen." A Spanish shipwreck in 1527 or 1528 deposited the survivors, including Estebanico and a white sailor, Cabeza de Vaca, on what is now the shore of western Florida. The two men wandered from there through the South and Southwest for seven years. Eventually Estebanico found his way to New Spain (Mexico), where his knowledge of the Southwest and his tales of cities of gold encouraged further Spanish exploration. The most notable consequence of his reports was the organization of the Coronado expedition of 1540, which discovered the Colorado River.[2] A prelude to further exploration in the direction of California, this expedition—which turned east rather than west from the Colorado River—contributed its own footnote to black history. Two Negroes who had been serving with the expedition's priest stayed behind in Kansas with him when he decided to remain there to work for the church.[3]

About the time of the shipwreck of Estebanico, other Spanish ships began carrying African slave laborers to New Spain to exploit the country's soil and mineral resources.

This importation of Africans continued over the next 200 years and brought nearly a quarter of a million blacks to Mexico. With the passage of time these black men and women were absorbed into the Indian and Spanish populations. When the Jesuits settled Baja California in the seventeenth century, they brought along many of these racially mixed peoples to be among the first settlers. By the next century at least 20 percent of the Spanish in Baja had some African ancestry.[4]

Four Negroes with Sir Francis Drake in 1579 were probably the first blacks to touch land in present-day California. They apparently had been captured from the Portuguese or Spanish in the Caribbean and South America during Drake's famous global voyage. It is known that these three men and one woman were with Drake when he stopped near the San Francisco Bay area. However, they continued on with Drake when he crossed the Pacific.[5]

When the Portola and De Anza expeditions of the eighteenth century laid the basis for firm Spanish settlement in California, blacks were again part of the story. Many poor people of mixed ancestry from the Sonora and Sinaloa provinces of New Spain were members of the 1775 De Anza expedition. Black men and women were among the first citizens of the city of Los Angeles when it was founded in 1781; one authority surmised that more than half of the founders had African ancestry. Some of the most important leaders of Mexican California in the nineteenth century, including the prominent Pico and Tapia families, derived from this mixed group.[6] However, these two California families perceived themselves as primarily of Mexican ancestry and made no point of their African heritage. While color distinctions were less abrasive in Mexico, it was still a mark of status to be considered "Mexican" rather than "mulatto" or "Negro." This may explain why Mexican-Californians with some African heritage never alluded to it.

In the early part of the nineteenth century, Californians

occasionally showed hostility to those of unmistakable African ancestry. When the French adventurer Bouchard raided the coast of California in 1818, he was driven off, but several of his associates, among them some blacks, were captured. It is reported that one California woman thought they possibly had tails and wanted to burn them alive. Historian Hubert Howe Bancroft believed that the unpopular California governor Manuel Victoria was socially ostracized because he was clearly of African ancestry. According to Bancroft, Californians at this time were accustomed to seeing Negroes only in menial capacities.[7]

During the first decade of the nineteenth century, Mexico's already strained ties with Spain weakened even more when the mother country became absorbed in the Napoleonic wars in Europe. The resultant administrative confusion during that decade and the next provided the opportunity for Mexican nationalists to achieve a successful revolution. By 1823 California was the northernmost part of the new Mexican Republic. The constitution of the new nation abolished Negro slavery. It was in this period that increasing numbers of ships with multi-racial crews came to California's shores. Among them were American ships from which a small number of seafaring blacks and an even larger number of whites deserted and entered the California population. In the years between 1823 and the American conquest of 1846, California with its antislavery Mexican constitution, its great open spaces, and its sparse population of usually friendly, brown-skinned peoples must have looked attractive to North American blacks.

The distinction of being the first American slave to achieve freedom, Catholicism, and citizenship in California belongs to a man who was born in Africa. The Santa Barbara Mission records show that Father Ripoll baptized twenty-year-old Juan Cristobal in 1819. The two blacks who fell into the hands of the Californians in 1818 as a result of the ill-fated Bouchard raid and who nearly came to an unhappy end agreed to adopt the religion of the country and become citizens. About the rest of their lives so far nothing is known. Another early black citizen, William Warren, lived eighteen years in California under Mexican rule and twenty-nine under American. Most likely a runaway seaman, he arrived in California in 1828 and mined for gold in the first year of the gold rush twenty years later. Warren was known as "Uncle Billy" when he died in San Jose in 1875.[8]

In the 1830s the number of American ships, especially those from New England, that touched the California coast increased, and so did the number of black and white deserters. An intriguing case is that of John Caldwell, a black cook on the frigate *California,* who deserted in Monterey. The ship's captain asked the Monterey authorities to seize Caldwell. The official request suggested that he was hiding out at the San Jose home of a former Massachusetts ship's captain named John Burton. Burton had married a member of the Galindo family and was now a farmer. Was Caldwell, a Massachusetts black man, perhaps a former acquaintance of Burton in that state with its antislavery tradition?[9]

Possibly the most prestigious American black of the thirties in California was Allen Light, better known as "Black Steward" among his contemporaries. He sailed as a crew member on the *Pilgrim* while Richard Henry Dana was aboard gathering material for *Two Years Before the Mast.* Light deserted the *Pilgrim,* presumably in Santa Barbara in 1835, and soon became a leading otter hunter in the Santa Barbara area. By residence he also automatically became a citizen. For several years he worked with some of the most famous licensed otter hunters of the California coast. In the course of this work he became proficient in the techniques of fighting illegal otter hunters, who were most often Russians. In 1839 Governor Alvarado commissioned Allen Light to halt illegal otter hunting in the Santa Barbara coastal regions.[10]

During the 1840s, the decade approaching the conflict

with Mexico, American warships became more numerous in the California waters. They too made their contribution to the number of black deserters. One case had some interesting consequences. In 1843, Anderson Norris, a black cook on the U. S. warship *Cyane*, decided to desert while in Sausalito. From there he headed towards the upper Napa Valley and joined a group of white hunters around Calistoga. He was pursued there by Salvador Vallejo, brother of the better known Mariano Vallejo, who, instead of capturing him, killed him. Present at the killing of Norris was a well-known former mountain man, Ezekiel Merritt. He voiced his objection to the killing and was rewarded with a beating by Salvador Vallejo. As a consequence, he hated all Vallejos and became a leader a few years later in the Bear Flag revolt which briefly imprisoned these native California leaders.[11]

Just prior to the American conquest of California, black men appear momentarily in the records of the period, but so fragmented is the information one can learn little about them. Charles Brown, an early white deserting sailor, had gone into the lumbering business at the southern end of what is now San Mateo county. He had two black sawyers working for him in 1842, Jorge Willan (probably George Williams) and "Freeman." Blacks were at Sutter's Fort before American occupation. When Sutter went to Monterey in 1844 to seek skilled workmen for the community he was building in the Sacramento Valley, he brought back with him two black men. One was a cook and the other a cooper. Five years later, H. D. Pierce, a gold hunter, recalled that he had stopped for a meal at Sutter's Fort. He noted, "We took a cup of coffee and three small cakes each and paid one dollar, in the fort of an old Negro." This could well have been the same black man that Sutter hired in 1844.[12]

Until the middle of the 1840s the thin trickle of white and black men who came to California arrived by sea. Between 1841 and 1846 the number of whites coming into the territory increased, but they were coming from another direction. Wagon trains began to arrive in the Sacramento Valley after crossing the Sierra Nevada. But blacks are not known to have come with this movement.

The mountain fur trade and John C. Frémont's western explorations brought some unusual black men into California. The fur trade flourished during the second quarter of the nineteenth century and brought some men of African ancestry to the Far West at an early date. Black Peter Raney was an associate of Jedediah Smith, perhaps the best known of the fur-hunting mountain men. They both came to California in 1826 but did not stay long. Like Smith, Raney died in the mountains, a victim of conflict with the Indians.[13]

One Afro-American who made an indelible impact on California history was another mountain man, James Beckwourth. Beckwourth worked for the Rocky Mountain Fur Company in the 1820s, as did Jedediah Smith. He made several visits to California prior to the American conquest. When the dramatic overland migration to the California gold rush began in 1849, Beckwourth guided several groups of migrants. It was in 1851, while Beckwourth was exploring the Pit River Valley, that he discovered the pass that now bears his name. Beckwourth Pass became one of the important overland wagon routes to the upper Sacramento Valley. Beckwourth settled in a small valley, which also bears his name, at the mouth of his pass. Here he resided for a number of years, raising cattle and trying to promote a wagon road through his pass to Marysville. What appears to have been his last effort at obtaining financial aid for his road was a letter to the *Marysville Herald* in August 1853. Complainingly he wrote, "I intend to start today to the forks of the road at the sink of the Humboldt, to induce emigrants to travel this road—although the citizens of Marysville do not think it worthwhile to pay me for my trouble, or even pay me the amount I have paid out to get the road though it is more to their advantage than to mine." By 1858 Beckwourth was in Colorado conducting a variety of businesses around Denver as well as acting as government agent in Indian negotiations during the Civil War. In 1864, at the age of sixty-six, he was killed by Indians.[14]

Jacob Dodson came from Washington, D.C., where he had been a free Negro. He was employed by the Senator Thomas Hart Benton family. When Benton's son-in-law, John C. Frémont, went on his second Western expedition in 1843, he took along young Dodson, then eighteen. Dodson accompanied Frémont again on his third expedition, which also went to California. Shortly after the expedition arrived, the American occupation of California took place. Frémont soon thereafter became involved in a conflict of command with General Kearny which led to a need for a meeting between the two officers. This required that Frémont make a dramatic, eight-day, eight-hundred-mile trip overland by horseback from Los Angeles to Monterey and return. Jacob Dodson and one other man made this spectacular ride with Frémont. Shortly after this, when Frémont was brought East under arrest, Dodson accompanied him and returned to his own home in Washington, D.C.[15]

After hostilities between the United States and Mexico became official in 1846, and word reached the East that California had fallen easily into United States hands, migration from the States rose sharply. After the conquest of California, the very presence of military and naval units helped to swell the population. Many of the men chose to be demobilized in California. It was not long before merchants and professionals from various parts of the United States followed them to California seeking material gain. This pre-gold rush growth of population brought with it a few more black men, as well as black women for the first time.

One source of this small black population growth was military men who brought blacks with them either as personal servants or as service personnel for a military unit. When Lieutenant Archibald Gillespie came to California, he brought with him a body servant who is known only as "Ben."[16] William Tecumseh Sherman, a junior officer at this time, wrote home from Monterey in 1847, "I keep a house, and three officers mess with me. . . . A widow Spanish woman is the housekeeper, and an Indian man kind of cook, and a black boy we brought out with us is the servant." A year later, when Sherman had occasion to set up camp near Sutter's Fort, he noted that the cook, a black man named Aaron, was the personal servant of Colonel Richard B. Mason.[17] Walter Colton, who became the First American *alcalde* (mayor) in Monterey after the conquest, had in his jail a black man who had been working in some capacity in Frémont's battalion. Colton freed him and then hired him as prison cook. As such he became one of the alcade's most trusted employees.[18]

A jail break and subsequent tragedy revealed the presence of a black named John Edwards who had been sentenced to three years' hard labor in the Monterey jail in 1846. Because Edwards could speak Spanish, a white fellow inmate prevailed upon him to break jail and flee into the California countryside near Salinas. Pursuers caught up with them. Edwards was mortally wounded by someone described as a "hothead" and then left to die. One white man in the pursuit party was so upset by this that he turned back to try to carry Edwards so that he could at least be buried properly, but the rising Salinas River made this impossible. The newspaper *Californian* lamented this tragedy in its columns.[19]

A woman known only as "Mary" may have been the first black woman from the States to come to California, as well as the first slave to achieve freedom through the courts in the West. Her Missouri master brought her to California in 1846. They settled in San Jose, where she evidently decided that she should be a free person. She may have been advised that Maxican law forbade slavery and that the Americans had made a commitment to respect Mexican law. Her litigation took place before a justice of the peace. It seems her master decided not to fight to keep her a slave, but he did make a successful claim for what he said were his expenses in bringing Mary to California. An intriguing feature of this case is the fact that the justice of the peace, John Burton, is the same John Burton who was believed in 1832 to be harboring a deserting black American sailor, John Caldwell.[20]

Not all whites were as agreeable as Mary's master to parting with their human property. In the 7 October 1847 issue of the *Californian*, there appeared an advertisement for a "runaway" black from the bark *Tasso*, then anchored in San Francisco. He described as a "buck negro about 5 feet 6 inches . . . and a full head of wool running up above each ear like a ram's horn." A reward of twenty-five dollars was offered for his capture, by H. Lindsey. There is no indication that the Negro was ever caught, and this black man may be the first successful runaway slave in American California.[21]

By 1847 there were 9 black men and 1 black woman, probably the stewardess brought by the Mormons,[22] in a San Francisco population of 459. Unfortunately, no occupational breakdown of this group has ever been given, but they were described as the best of the free Negro class. They most likely worked in the service trades or maritime occupations.[23] The most prominent Afro-American at this time was William A. Leidesdorff, a well-to-do businessman whose contemporaries considered him white.

Leidesdorff was a West Indian of Danish-African ancestry. After leaving the West Indies as a young man, he made a successful career as a merchant captain in New York and then New Orleans. It is believed that an unhappy love affair in New Orleans caused him to leave a prosperous business in that city and move on to California. Legend has it that at the point of matrimony he revealed the African side of his ancestry to his betrothed and that ended the relationship. Soon after he arrived in California in 1841, he began shipping runs between Honolulu and California with his schooner, the *Julia Ann.* In 1844 he became a naturalized Mexican citizen and was granted 35,500 acres along the American River where Folsom now stands.

He settled in San Francisco, then called Yerba Buena, and became a leader and prominent businessman in this growing community. In the course of his business ventures he introduced the first steam vessel, the *Sitka,* into Bay waters. While he was, at this point, a Mexican citizen, his warm feelings for the United States were well known in this decade of approaching crisis. As a result he was appointed an American vice-consul in 1845 by President Polk, a Tennessee Democrat, who surely knew nothing of Leidesdorff's ancestry.

As a San Franciscan Leidesdorff was always a central figure in the life of the young city. He was elected in 1847, after the American conquest, to the town council, receiving the third highest vote. He was active in getting a school system started, and in 1848 he became the town treasurer. He lived through the transition period from the easy-going Mexican ways to the more hectic pace of the American lifestyle. He never saw the hysteria of the gold rush at its height, nor did he live long enough to see the 1849 California constitution with its nineteenth-century American racist features.[24]

When Leidesdorff died on 18 April 1848, he was honored to the fullest extent. As the *California Star* described the funeral in its obituary notice:

> One of the largest and most respectable assemblages ever witnessed in this place, followed the deceased from his late residence to the place of interment, and everything was done on the part of the community to evince its deep feeling for the loss it has sustained. All places of business and public entertainment were closed, the flags of the garrison and the shipping were flying at half-mast, and minute guns were discharged

> from the barracks and the shipping as the procession moved from town. . . . It is no injustice to the living, or unmeaning praise for the dead, to say that the town has lost its most valuable resident. . . . [25]

After Leidesdorff's death, General Folsom began negotiations to purchase his lands along the American River. These protracted negotiations led Folsom's lawyer to the Danish West Indies in order to clear the title of purchase by making proper payment to the members of the Leisdesdorff family. There they met Leidesdorff's mother, and it then became known that this early leader of San Francisco had African ancestry.[26]

Jacob W. Harlan, who arrived in California from Indiana several years before the gold rush, had come to know Leidesdorff very well in the course of business dealings. He thought that Leidsdorff was one of the finest men he had ever known and was deeply shocked when he learned of his friend's death. In his recollections, written many years later and with full knowledge of Leidesdorff's ancestry, he wrote, "He was a good and fair man and a good citizen. Instead of having his name given to the little street which bears it, he deserved to have one of the chief streets named for him."[27]

There is no indication that the ten blacks noted in 1847 were still in San Francisco when Leidesdorff died. It is doubtful that they developed any community life, since only one was a woman. Few of the Afro-Mexicans were still identifiable as such by this time. Black community life would come only with a much larger migration of Afro-Americans from the United States, the West Indies, and South America. That migration was taking form in the eastern United States, for by the end of 1848 the gold fever was in full swing. By the beginning of 1849 ships bearing gold hunters were already leaving from Eastern ports for California, and the gathering flood of overland migrants was merely waiting for the first signs of good spring weather.

2 Blacks Join the Gold Rush

On a September day in 1848 a black man was walking near the San Francisco docks, when a white man who had just disembarked from a ship called to him to carry his luggage. The black cast him an indignant glance and walked away. After he had gone a few steps, he turned around and, drawing a small bag from his bosom, he said, "Do you think I'll lug trunks when I can get that much in one day?" The sack of gold dust that he displayed was estimated by the white man to be worth more than one hundred dollars.[1]

By December 1848, this story had found its way into the newspapers of New York City and New Bedford, Massachusetts, where there were large, well-organized, and highly literate free Negro communities. It was read by black people to whom the notion of travel on the high seas and to far-away places was neither strange nor frightening, for many of them were seamen or had seafaring men in their families. The pull of the West for blacks could only have been intensified when, in January 1849, a New York newspaper reprinted a letter, written by an army officer stationed in California, in which he said, "The merest Negro could make more than our present governor."[2]

Through reports like this the California gold fever spread throughout the nation and gripped black men as well as white. The fever was sustained through 1849 and 1850 by the continued enticing press reports that reached the free black communities of the North. Even the abolitionist press, normally negative about the West, carried stories of lucky strikes by Negroes in the mines. Frederick Douglass, the famous black abolitionist, reinforced the impression of black luck with gold when he reprinted in his *North Star* a letter written by a Southerner that stated, "The whole country . . . is filled with gold," and that "there are but three classes of individuals that can even work these mines, the Negro, Indian and Irish."[3]

California became irresistible for many when the anti-slavery press noted that groups of black men were already there in the early phases of the gold rush and to all appearances were surviving successfully. Early in 1850, the anti-slavery *Liberator* published a letter from San Francisco sent by thirty-seven black men in which they announced the organization of a mutual-aid society. They noted that it was not just for themselves, but also for "new comers." Their letter reported that they were earning from $100 to $300 a month. Of special interest is the fact that they appended all their names. This was a notice to their friends of their whereabouts and their well-being. Black readers could see the preponderance of New Englanders; they could also note that members came from towns all along the Atlantic seaboard. A black subscriber to the same paper could also read Frederick Douglass's proud report that forty New Bedford black citizens were already in California.[4] In the Eastern newspapers black men read glowing accounts of success in the Mother Lode and such hopeful remarks as, "There are no gentlemen here. Labor rules Capital. A darkey is just as good as a polished gentleman and can make more money."[5] In addition to all the published comments on Negroes in California, there must have been much word-of-mouth information making its rounds in the Eastern black communities.

New York Negroes who were considering going to California might have been encouraged by the public notice that preparing to sail for the gold fields was an all-black mining company, whose members included several who were well-known and politically prominent. Among them were Jonas H. Townsend, a journalist, and Newport Henry, a well-known employee of the business firm of the anti-slavery Tappan brothers.[6] This group, which left New York in November 1849, was in turn undoubtedly encouraged by a story in the *New York Tribune* reporting the gold-hunting success of a black man, Reuben Ruby, a familiar name to them and to antislavery circles in general. Ruby, of Portland, Maine, a friend of white abolitionist William Lloyd Garrison and supporter of the first black newspaper, *Freedom's Journal,* raced from Maine to New York in time to catch a ship to Panama and arrive in California early in 1849. By April he had acquired six hundred dollars from four weeks' digging on the Stanislaus River.[7]

The pre-Civil War image of the West did not hold the same attraction for black men that it did for whites. In the first half of the nineteenth century the "free" West was Ohio, Indiana, and Illinois in the minds of most Americans. The anti-Negro laws of these Western free states were no secret to the free blacks of the North.[8] They had read about the constitutions which denied to blacks the rights of suffrage, equal testimony rights in the courts, and education for black children. The lower Mississippi Valley slave states held only dread for blacks and were rarely a destination for free Negroes. Being "sold down the river" was the nightmare for blacks of the older slave states. (Texas may have been an exception, because from there slaves did, from time to time, escape into Mexico.)[9] Furthermore, the black and white antislavery press, which had kept blacks informed about these older Western states, continued to be negative about the West when California became the center of national interest after the Mexican War.

Until October 1849, when California declared itself a free state, abolitionist journalists were almost certain that this far western acquisition would be open to slavery. Up to that time they saw the departure of every Southerner for California as further proof of their belief. Even after slavery was ruled out by California's first Constitutional Convention, the white abolitionist papers continued to describe the gold rush in the bleakest of terms. Their columns were full of depressing commentary about sickness and death on the journey. The disgusted reports of those who returned home in mid-journey were often noted. San Francisco weather and health conditions were described in most unflattering terms.[10] The following gallows humor in one antislavery paper is typical:

> A Nantucket Yankee has been shipping a
> load of tombstones to California all marked
> "Sacred to the memory of ——
> erected by his brother ——" and etc.
> He sagaciously concluded that the demand for
> this article must increase.[11]

In a gentler vein, some antislavery papers presented editorials and poetry that lamented the follies of avarice. A typical piece is the following:

Lament of the Gold-Digger

> Tis Evening and I stand alone
> On San Francisco's desert shore
> The wandering night winds sadly moan
> And shrieking sea birds round me soar
> The weary sun had sunk to sleep
> Beyond the great Pacific's wave
> While here I stand and Idly weep
> That I have been to gold a slave![12]

But blacks, like whites, saw what they wanted to see. With all of the racism in the western free states, now for the first time there was news from a western region holding material promise for Negroes. The reports of the social fluidity of the California frontier environment perhaps suggested racial equality to some blacks. Furthermore, one of the aggravations to free Negroes at this time, the laws of the western states that barred or created financial hurdles for free Negroes who wished to migrate to those states, did not materialize in California. When Fred Douglass reported in his *North Star* that the 1849 California Constitutional Convention had defeated an attempt to adopt such a provision, blacks who were wrestling with themselves about going to California were encouraged.

Of paramount importance in weighing the pros and cons of going to California was the personal makeup of each potential black argonaut. The more aggressive and daring preferred to see opportunity in this adventure. Mifflin Wistar Gibbs, the black abolitionist from Philadelphia whose entire life represented the achievement-oriented Negro, recalled hearing both negative and positive reports and then deciding that, in his own words, "Fortune . . . may sometimes smile on the inert, but she seldom fails to surrender to pluck, tenacity and perseverance."[13]

In these years the American Colonization Society, detested by antislavery workers, was working to send slaves and free Negroes to Liberia. Douglass dared the Colonization Society to use their funds to send blacks to California instead of Liberia.[14] There is no evidence that the society ever took up his challenge, but the attraction of California was evidently reaching some of the American Colonization Society recruits for Liberia and giving them second thoughts. As early as 5 February 1849, a Virginia Colonization Society agent complained that one of his emigration prospects, Samuel Frog, was catching the "California Fever." Douglass's challenge to the Colonization Society reflected a change of position from his earlier attitude toward black migration to California. Through most of 1849 his newspaper, the *North Star,* printed uniformly unfavorable coverage of the gold rush.[15] In December, the *North Star* started to run positive comment on blacks going to California. By the end of 1849 Douglass's position stood in sharp contrast to that of the white abolitionist journalists. The high ground they took condemning this hunger for gold and criticizing materialism revealed their myopic perception of the thoughts and feelings of blacks. Douglass understood that the American Negro had to seize any opportunity that arose in order to reach the same economic starting point as the lowliest upward-striving white American. It was unreasonable to expect that black Americans would reject any possible economic springboard in order to measure up to the standards of the more financially secure, idealistic white abolitionists.

While the aspiring black argonaut received little encouragement from the white antislavery press, he was heartened by the example of prominent white abolitionists. He read about them leaving for the gold fields and he noted that many were openly carrying the antislavery banner to the Pacific coast. As early as 1848, the son of a prominent abolitionist was reported to be in California. Edward Gould Buffum, son of Arnold Buffum, the great Quaker abolitionist, wrote glowing reports of gold prospects in California that year. He also proclaimed, in a letter printed in a New England newspaper, that "a few of us, ardent and strong, have pledged ourselves to labor against tyranny."[16] In 1850, the senior Buffum opened a New York office for passenger service to California, further encouraging a favorable image of California for eager but understandably apprehensive black men. He reinforced this positive feeling by publishing in his subsequent advertisements the names of Thaddeus Stevens, Horace Mann, and William Seward, two antislavery congressmen and an antislavery senator, as his references.[17]

When a group of white Bostonians departed for the gold fields in January of 1849, the press notice identified their captain, Hiram Cummings, as an antislavery lecturer.[18] Captain George Randall of the New Bedford ship *Mayflower* publicly described his California-bound company, in March 1849, as "having no narrow feelings of caste. The descendants of Africa and the sons of New England and Pennsylvania . . . [the *Mayflower*] bears them all to one fortune and one fate."[19] When later that year a *New York Tribune* correspondent wrote, with some exaggeration, that in California one could see "the Southern slaveholder beside the swarthy African, now his equal,"[20] the prospective black emigrant could hope that racial democracy was truly emerging in the Far West.

A considerable number of eastern urban Negroes were optimistic and daring enough to come to the new land in the face of the dire predictions of the antislavery press. While hard documentation is not available, some must have been encouraged by the knowledge of the hundreds of New Englanders already in California as well as the large numbers continuing to depart for the gold fields. Of special comfort to blacks may have been the information that many of these New Englanders were from New Bedford, Massachusetts, a city with a relatively progressive attitude toward its black citizens.

It was also known that crew members from New Bedford whalers who had jumped ship in California in favor of gold mining included New England Negroes.[21] Black seamen, especially those from New England sailing ships, were among the first men in the gold fields. They were part of the mass desertions affecting scores of East Coast commercial ships. Ship captains unwittingly sailed into San Francisco Bay in 1848, only to find that their crews became infected by the gold hysteria.

There is irony in the probability that some Americans followed the American Dream because as ex-slaves they had to flee the slave-hunter. New England and upper New York State had a considerable number of black residents who had fled slavery in the South and lived many years in comparative security until the passage of the Fugitive Slave Law of 1850. Many Northern Negroes who now felt threatened went to Canada. However, some families had second thoughts, and by 1852 they were on their way from Canada to California.[22] There were also those who came directly to California. There is some evidence that white abolitionists tried to help send to California blacks who were threatened by the Fugitive Slave Law. The clue to this is a letter received by Samuel J. May, a vigorous opponent of the law. Evidently May was soliciting funds to finance the passage of black men to California. The letter he received in 1852 was a refusal of his appeal.[23]

New Bedford, Massachusetts, had a considerable number of long-settled fugitives. By 1851 the panic over hunters of fugitive slaves reached Massachusetts and the *New Bedford Mercury* openly advised its black readers to consider California as a place of refuge. It further suggested that single men consider employment on one of the many New Bedford whaling ships.[24] At the time of the gold rush New Bedford led New England in number of whalers to the Pacific Ocean.

Circumstantial evidence suggests that T. E. Randolph, who in later years became a Baptist minister for the Marysville, California, Negro community, may have heeded the "go west" advice of the *New Bedford Mercury*. He had fled slavery in Virginia in December 1848 and settled the next year in New Bedford. By 1851, he was in California, having arrived by way of Cape Horn, the route of the New Bedford whalers.[25] Gilbert Carter may have done likewise. He had lived in New Bedford before going to California. A report that he had been murdered in Marysville for his money was carried in a New Bedford newspaper. The newspaper reported that he was in California "endeavoring to secure a sufficient sum to purchase his children who are held in slavery."[26]

James R. Starkey, a North Carolina black, moved to New York City shortly after purchasing his freedom. There he felt insecure as a result of the panic in the Negro community over the National Fugitive Slave Law. His sense of insecurity was heightened because his self-purchase had been accomplished under unusual circumstances. His master had told him that if he could raise $800 he would be allowed to purchase his freedom. Starkey was worth $2,000 on the auction market at that time. It is evident that the master did not believe Starkey would ever be able to raise such a sum. But he did not reckon with the man's determination to get his freedom. Starkey had already saved up $400 and forthwith wrote to New York antislavery papers for a loan for the other $400. A lender came forth. When Starkey presented his master with the money, the white North Carolinian was furious, but he kept to his bargain. However, he warned Starkey to leave the state, saying that if he ever returned, he would be put back in slavery. Due to the fear of slave-hunters that Starkey found in the black community of New York, he was uneasy about remaining there in his ambiguous status and took passage to California.[27]

A combination of events in 1851 made Samuel Burris decide to leave for California. A free Negro and a native of the slave state of Delaware, he was deeply involved in the work of the Underground Railroad there. After moving with his family to the Philadelphia area to take up farming, he remained active in underground work and from time to time returned to Delaware to aid escaping slaves. It was during one of these dangerous return trips that Burris was caught by the authorities. The Delaware court ordered him sold into slavery for seven years. The method of sale was the auction block in Dover. But Burris's long years of work with black and white abolitionists resulted in his own rescue. A Southerner who was known privately to be an abolitionist was solicited by the underground movement to bid for Burris at the auction with funds they supplied to him. In a tense bidding scene, the Southern abolitionist bought Burris. It was only then that Burris learned he had been "purchased" by friends. He quickly hurried off to his home near Philadelphia. While he was again a free man, the efforts of friends and family to raise the funds necessary for this project left Burris without his farm and almost penniless. Finding that he could not make a decent living any longer in the East and with the allure of California still strong, Burris departed with his family for California in the hope of improving his economic condition. He settled in San Francisco. There is no evidence that he was involved in the civil rights activities of the 1850s, but his antislavery concern was again aroused during the Civil War, when he took the leadership in San Francisco in raising funds for the relief of the great numbers of runaway slaves who were flooding into Philadelphia.[28]

The gold mines of California also had a powerful attraction for black men who saw this difficult venture as the chance to buy their freedom more swiftly than they might back home. Unknown numbers of these men were in the hordes that crossed the plains and thronged the routes across Central America. Some left wives and children behind as hostages and departed for the gold fields with the approval of their masters, from whom they hoped to purchase their liberty. Others who were already free hoped to buy freedom for their families. A white Ohio forty-niner noted in his diary, as he was on his way across the plains, "I saw a colored man going to the land of gold prompted by the hope of redeeming his wife and seven children. Success to him. His name is James Taylor." When this Ohioan reached the mines at Ophir (Oroville) he met more blacks in the same position. One of them, a Texan, hoped to buy his wife and children and move to New York or Massachusetts.[29] Jessie Benton Frémont recalled that on her first trip to California to meet her husband, John C. Frémont, she met a free black man en route who was hoping to attain the means of purchasing his family's freedom.[30]

The full stories of the success or failure of many of these struggling black men will probably remain unknown. However, the accounts of two of those who became prominent in California black community activities are known. Reverend Barney Fletcher gained his freedom in Maryland and then went to Sacramento, where he earned the money with which he purchased his wife and children. While in that city, he also organized a black Methodist church.[31] James R. Starkey, for many years one of the most untiring leaders of his people in San Francisco, reached California in 1853, after buying his own freedom in North Carolina.

He worked to buy his son and daughter but did not succeed. The merchant who owned his children went bankrupt in Maryland, and Starkey's children were sold to slave traders. Not until the Civil War was over did Starkey finally track down his children, and that was accomplished through advertisements in the black press.[32]

The California Negro population doubled in the first three years of the gold rush. By 1852 two thousand black men and women (about one percent of the population) were in the state. In spite of the apprehensions of the antislavery press, California had become a free state, though hardly possessed of rights for black people comparable to those to be found in most New England states by this time. But its lure as a land of opportunity persisted in the face of continuing negative coverage in the East. The hopeful black argonaut could brush aside the reports of prejudice, hardship, and death when he heard stories such as that of the black New York leader, William H. Hall. A forty-niner, Hall returned in 1851 in sufficient affluence to be married in a wedding that was reported as having a "splendour" that was "perhaps without a parallel in the history of coloured society in New York." "Coloured society" in New York also came to hear Hall at a public meeting, where he gave an address entitled "Hopes and Prospects of Colored People in California," and this event probably produced more California-bound black migrants from that state.[33] Philadelphia Negroes read in an antislavery paper that two blacks returned to the East early in 1851 with $30,000, accumulated in four months of gold mining.[34]

Tales of business opportunities still abounded, and the hope of high wages also attracted black men to the Far West. Negro cooks, in tremendous demand in California by 1849, were paid $125 a month. Throughout the gold rush decade Negro cooks were much in demand and were noted as being among the most independent of men.[35]

Through 1852 the California fever persisted in many

free Negro communities. In St. Genevieve City, Missouri, Mrs. Alley Brown, a black woman, received a letter early in 1852 from her husband, who was working in the Cosumne diggings in California. He wrote, "This is the best place for black folks on the globe. All a man has to do is to work, and he will make money."[36] Frederick Douglass noted in that year that returning black men were feeding this fever. He said,

> So strong is the excitement that it has become a question who ought to go and who ought not to go. . . . Discretion and reasonable considerations seemed to have been abandoned. Lovers hurried and married their sweethearts and left them. Young husbands left young wives. . . . Some have returned much better off and some much worse.[37]

Some who returned "better off" found the limited economic opportunities for Negroes in the East no longer tolerable. A number of New Bedford blacks who felt this way returned to California in spite of its limited civil rights.[38]

The question of whether or not to go to California became intertwined with another issue that had long absorbed the intellectual energies of the eastern black leadership. This was the debate over whether blacks should migrate to Africa, the West Indies, or South America. While the preponderance of black opinion opposed such migration, at times of great stress or harassment the emigration sentiment showed a considerable rise. But emigration was generally regarded as an emergency measure only. A case in point is the support given by the usually anti-immigrationist leadership to the migration to canada of free Cincinnati Negroes after the vicious antiblack riots there in 1829.[39] The passage of the Fugitive Slave Law of 1850 created a new emergency for blacks in the North and a resurgence of debate about emigration from the United States. Although emigration talk gained new intensity in this period, majority opinion remained unchanged. In 1854 a state-wide meeting of Massachusetts Negroes took up the much-debated issue. This group supported the general opposition to emigration, but it also took the occasion to declare that emigration to California was a different matter and described such emigration as "healthy" and "enterprising." Within six months of this gathering of Massachusetts black leaders, one of the most prominent among them, Jeremiah B. Sanderson, was on his way to California.[40]

The free black migration to California had its amusing touches. The nineteenth-century Negro leader Martin Delaney tells of one black woman, whom he described as a member of "one of the first families" of the New York Negro community, who had no taste for pioneering but was quite ready to join her husband in San Francisco when her spouse told her that it was a large and handsome place. He must have elaborated a bit in order to have her with him as soon as possible in that largely male society. In another case a young black woman found that romantic affection prevented her from going to California. When Jessie Frémont was preparing to set out for California from New York, she wished to take along a young female black servant who had worked many years with the Benton family as a free person. The young woman's black fiancé, however, was intensely opposed to this. He took the unusual step of organizing a deputation to storm the Astor House, where Mrs. Frémont was staying. The group under his leadership thought they were rescuing a free Negro woman from kidnapping. The love-smitten young man won the day.[41]

The human flood that readied itself in Missouri for the historic crossing of the plains and mountains in 1849 and 1850 was typically American. It was black and white and included both free and slave blacks. The hardships that these gold seekers were to face were to be shared equally. Hunger, heat, drought, and disease were experienced by both races. Attacking Indians on the plains or in the mountains did not discriminate. Members of both races were buried along the trails that led to the gold country.

The many black men and women, free and slave, who came by the overland route were members of companies organized by whites. There is no record of any overland company organized solely by and for blacks. It is doubtful that any such record will ever come to light; the money necessary for such a venture would have been very difficult for black men to obtain at that time. These blacks, who must generally remain nameless or known only by their first names, came as members of predominantly white companies. The contemporary accounts noted their presence, but too few of them are mentioned by name. Even the diarists of companies that had blacks were frequently indifferent to them. One must often rely on the occasional commentary of diarists of all-white companies who observed blacks in companies nearby or passing through. The names of slaves who later returned to their home states may be lost forever. But some who gained their freedom in California received notice. Perhaps the best-known Negro who came by the land route is Alvin Coffey, who will be discussed later. Coffey was brought as the slave of a Dr. Bassett from Tennessee and later achieved freedom with his family. He left a record of his experience. He is notable as being the only black member of the prestigious Society of California Pioneers.[42]

Typical of the available commentary about blacks are the following:

> A number of packed pedestrians (nine white and one black), and three ox wagons, passed on. . . .

> The Company was joined on Thursday by five wagons and 21 men which said number grew to 105 men, 15 Negroes and 12 females.

or the Fort Smith notice that read,

> Colonel Bonner's party for California have arrived consisting of 7 whites and 6 blacks.

The blacks noted here were probably slaves. Contemporary observers, nearly always white, seemed to use the designations *Negro, black,* or *colored* interchangeably; they did not distinguish slaves from free men.[43] One observer was more explicit about legal status. He noted:

> Among the wagons that passed us was one train from Georgia, with a carriage or hack containing a man and his wife. That train also had several slaves with them.

More typical is the observation of an overland traveler who simply noted that "Big mule teams from Tennessee used black drivers on the way to California."[44]

Black men in companies organized in the North were uniformly freemen. A group of New Englanders, mostly from Roxbury, Massachusetts, took with them two men they called "colored servants." A black man was a servant for Captain Nathaniel Lyon of Connecticut on the way to California. an Illinois black named Henry Finley was noted as a member of an Ohio company headed by Major John Love of that state. Finley probably encountered this company as it passed through Illinois and offered his services in order to work his way to California. Similarly, Vardaman Buller, a Kentucky free Negro, was hired to drive a team to California for William Gill, a white Kentuckian. Another Kentucky-born free Negro, John, earned his passage to California from El Paso, Texas, by cooking, barbering, and caring for the pack animals for a military unit headed west. He had received his freedom from his master, an officer, at the close of the Mexican War. A New York black went as cook with a company of Germans who had organized their venture in that city. If this group was composed of radical refugees from persecution in Germany, as so many were at this time, this Negro cook was in the most congenial of company. One black man had the misfortune of being associated on the overland trek with a domestically troubled white family. He found himself from time to time in the awkward position of being ordered by the husband to beat the wife. When this group arrived in the mines, the wife complained of this treatment to nearby miners, who then whipped the black man![45]

Rarely does one learn exactly how a free black became associated with a white California-bound company, but the minutes of the proceedings of the Hagerstown (Indiana) Mining Company gives us a glimpse. These notes reveal that at their organizational meeting, in March 1849, the company took on a young unmarried black named Harry Withe. His initiative in the matter appears in these minutes:

> On motion of the Company resolved to accept the proposition and services of Black Harry Withe, to accompany them to California as per agreement hereafter to be entered into.

Harry Withe was then entered on the company lists in April as "Harry Withe, coloured boy" and his duty as cook.[46]

Southern slaveholders who took the overland route very often brought their domestic servants with them. The Loring Pickerings, of later newspaper prominence in California, came from Missouri with two black servants, a male and a female. Dr. Thomas J. White, a St. Louis physician, came overland to Sacramento with three Negro servants who were his slaves in Missouri. Colonel Kinkead, a Missouri planter, sold out his plantation and came overland with his family and several slaves. A Southern company that had organized in Nashville had two slaves, Walker and John, who were the "cash stock" contribution of some members of the company. One Kentuckian brought nine slaves with him on the overland route. It would be difficult to determine whether the slaveowners in the 1849 trek intended to free their bondsmen.[47]

In spite of the paucity of descriptive reference to blacks, one can find occasional insights into their day-to-day experiences in this drama. From time to time, some camaraderie lightened the arduousness of the journey. Peter Decker noted some good-humored bantering on the plains between some Negroes in a Kentucky company and some whites in his own company. One forty-niner recalled an evening when several companies were enjoying Negro songs sung by a white man with a banjo and a black slave from one of the companies. In spite of having walked all day, the Negro began to dance "jim crow" to the cheers of his audience. Members of an Illinois company, which probably set a record for having impromptu "hoedowns" and dances during the evening rest, did not lose their energy for such relaxation even after a back-breaking day of pulling wagons through the Sierra Nevada. In this mountain setting, they were joined in their dances by a number of black men who were probably the slaves of a Missouri company camped nearby. A white forty-niner noted that the black servant in his company continued to say his evening prayers long after his white associates had fallen away from this practice.[48]

Fighting among the travelers on the long journey was fairly common. A fight broke out in one company that included some Germans as well as some Negroes. As the reporters of the incident noted:

> Today about ten miles back we met a wagon containing four of the belligerents, two white men and two negroes who were on their way back. They were bruised, mashed, scratched, gouged, torn and almost literally cut to pieces. On being questioned about it one of them replied, "We had von good fight—very comical, but not very pleasant."[49]

As they increased their distance from the Mississippi River, whether by northern or southern routes, the westbound travelers were forced to guard their livestock and dwindling food supplies from depredation by Indians or Mexicans. Black men shared with white the duties of hunting and nighttime watch duty, as well as care of stock en route. C. C. Cox noted in his diary that he was on duty with "Black Bob" one night on the southern route and that it was Bob who detected an attempt by some Indians to steal the company's horses. While Bob's gun for some reason did not go off, still the horse stealing attempt was frustrated.[50] John Durivage required that his slave do guard duty over their possessions to prevent thievery by local Mexicans on the Gila trail to the gold fields. C. C. Churchill, the Kentuckian who took nine of his slaves on the northern route, sent them with guns to assist in the hunting of the plains antelope. Madison Moorman and his black friend Dick Rapier shared the responsibility of herding the mules in the rear of their wagon train.[51]

The plains took their toll of these adventurers. In 1849 the dread cholera from Europe competed with the gold rush for the attention of the American people. In fact, the gold rush facilitated the spread of the disease. Only the few who plunged west ahead of the crowd had a chance of escaping contact with those who were infected. Late-spring starters had reduced chances of immunity. Four of the nine blacks who came with Churchill, the Kentuckian, died on the plains because of their master's later start.[52] Another tragedy was noted by a diarist simply, "Jones (a black boy) in my mess is very sick . . . ," and a day later, ". . . Jones died." Still another surviving record stated, "A white woman and a colored one died yesterday of the cholera"[53] Slaves had no choice but to expose themselves to the dread disease when ordered by their masters to attend to cholera victims lying along the trail. As George Mifflin Harker wrote:

> An emigrant who falls sick, unless he has some personal friends, receives scarcely any attention. . . . otherwise, he is left to die, gazing on vacancy, after having swallowed a quart or so of medicine, received from the hands of some Negro servant, who hastily throws down the cup and spoon, and rushes away, paying little or no heed to the feeble demands of the sick man.[54]

One of the most terrifying ordeals of the overland route was the trek through the Humboldt Sink, which was the last area to be crossed before ascending the Sierra Nevada. On this lime-dust desert human reserves were taxed to their ultimate. In the first years of the gold rush it was the graveyard for many men and animals. Some of the most vivid recollections that migrants had of this part of the journey were of anonymous black men and women. Forty-niner Amos Batchelder wrote, "We saw a negro teamster on the way whose perspiring face was completely whitewashed with white dust."[55] Many years later, Margaret Frink, who crossed the Sink in the disastrous year of 1850, remembered the destitute-looking crowd and through them all saw

> a Negro woman . . . tramping along through the heat and dust, carrying a cast iron bake stove on her head, with her provisions and a blanket piled on top—all she possessed in the world—bravely pushing on for California.[56]

A compassionate Northerner noted in his diary an encounter with a black slave woman and her owner on the Humboldt Sink:

> For some three miles I waded on before I overtook the last straggler of the day and she was a woman alone and heavily loaded and almost in despair. Cheering her drooping spirits with the hope that the end could not be far ahead, I relieved her of her load and we trudged on with renewed courage. . . . we found . . . only the camp of a low-bred Missourian and his family, owner of the female chattel we had assisted, and without thanks or even a cup of coffee or a morsel of the bacon I had carried, we delivered her over to their clutches.[57]

The terrible ordeal of the Death Valley route was also experienced by a few blacks. A modern historian of this

Western passage counted three black men in a Mississippi-Georgia company that ill-advisedly took this route. From other sources it appears that these blacks were probably slaves and were among the survivors who made it through the valley. The record tells us laconically that they were called "Tom," "Joe," and "Little West."[58]

While the northern routes were the most heavily traveled in the overland journey, the various southern land routes to California were taken by many. They used locations in Texas as departure points and proceeded in most cases, in the direction of the Gila River and then on to southern California. Some companies chose to dip even farther south and do a part of their journey through northern Mexico. Some blacks came to California by these routes, and most of them seem to have been slaves. A great number of slave-owners from the Deep South and Missouri seemed to prefer such routes, which usually went to Los Angeles or San Diego before going on to the mines.

Few of the black men who came by these routes will ever be identified. Judge Benjamin Hays, who came to California by the Gila trail, noted three slaves in the two companies with which he traveled. A Missourian who went to Los Angeles was mentioned as having slaves. One observer on this route said simply that there were two "negroes named Bob and Jane" in his company. Young William Lorton crossed the Mojave River with an Arkansas man who had a slave. While Lorton never mentions the black man's name in his journal, he does report that as they continued on together he slept under the same blankets with the black man.[59]

Added to the usual trials of thirst and hunger on the southern routes were the disadvantages to the black of traveling with whites from slave states. The slave in an Alabama company had the misfortune of being the innocent victim of an altercation between his master and another member of the company. When the master was absent, the other man tried to revenge himself on the slave. Fortunately the black man received some protection from the other men in the company.[60] In another near-tragedy, a free black woman and her very attractive daughter were nearly abandoned on the Gila route by an army major who took exception to the woman's proud spirit. She had probably been hired to perform domestic services for him and the company in order to get to California but then talked "sassy" to the major. Fortunately a white member of a New York company that had chosen the southern route and was traveling nearby took the mother and daughter under his protection.[61]

For blacks, travel by the southern land routes seemed to offer a greater variety of experiences than did the northern routes. Negroes' relations with the Indians or Mexicans encountered on the trail were generally friendly. A white man on the Santa Fe route noted that a black man was preaching to the Indians in their own language at a Baptist mission on the Canadian River. A few days later, while his company was resting near an Indian camp on the prairies, he wrote, "Negroes are very popular and have a great deal of influence with the Indians."[62]

This popularity probably saved lives in an incident that took place along the trail between Chihuahua and Sonora in northern Mexico. The Apaches found the black member of one company most intriguing. He was the first black man they had ever seen and they closely scrutinized his skin in a friendly way. A few days later this same man may have saved his company from combat with another Indian group when he suggested that he, instead of a white man, should carry the white flag. This had the desired result of successful passage through that area.[63] A black man owned by a Mississippian had a more disconcerting experience with the Pima Indians. In a night raid, the Pimas stole him along with some of the horses and mules. One might speculate on how seriously he resisted this form of larceny.[64] The most satisfying experience was undoubtedly that of a Mississippi-born slave in Mexico. The company of which he was part came into a rancho of rather poverty-stricken Mexicans while the landowner was away and only the peons were present. The only chair in sight was offered to the slave and all the white men were left standing. As the diarist of the event observed rather petulantly, "It is notorious that the wooly-headed, thick-lipped African is regarded with more favor and affection than an American by the peons."[65]

It would be hard to believe that as awareness of the gold rush spread through the slave states along the routes to the gold fields, black men did not think of this great movement of peoples as an opportunity to achieve freedom. Even before the gold rush, Texas slaveowners had cause to worry about their slaves fleeing to Mexico. By 1849 hundreds, perhaps thousands, of black men and women had fled south, where they found a friendly haven across the Rio Grande in Mexico.

While records thus far fail to reveal any clearcut escape attempts in connection with the gold rush, it is possible that the Negro in the following incident was harboring such thoughts. David Demarest, on his way to California by the Gila route, noted that leaving Galveston, a black man attached himself to the company with an offer to show the travelers the best grazing places along the way. The company had not gone far when a sheriff rode up, charging them with aiding a runaway slave. The company paid up seventy dollars' worth of goods and money as a bribe to avoid having the member who had made the arrangement put in jail in Texas. What happened to the Negro is unknown.[66] Two slaves who had no intention of going to California were luckier. They were the servants of an army officer whose New Mexico contingent was ordered to California in 1848. In the dead of night, while on the trail, they took a horse and a pony and fled to Mexico.[67]

The most common relationship of black man to white man, in the meandering stream of human beings headed west on the overland routes, was that of servant, laborer, or slave. But there were some interesting exceptions to this relationship. At least three men of African ancestry were guides for overland parties. In 1849, a Virginia company employed a Negro guide to cross the plains.[68] Forty-niner Edmund Green from Michigan recalled that on his way to Fort Hall, after leaving the place of famed mountain man Peg Leg Smith, his party encountered a black man hunting horses who was most familiar with this part of the country and could speak the Indian language. He accepted employment with Green's company to take them as far as Fort Hall.[69] For Ina Coolbrith, who later became a San Francisco poet, it was a matter of safe guidance across the Sierras. James Beckwourth, the black scout, fur trapper, Indian chief, and guide, took the company with which Miss Coolbrith's family traveled safely across the mountains in 1851. She recalled, years later, that she sat with him on his horse on this trek. In 1852 Beckwourth assisted a Virginian and his group who were probing their way through the eastern slope of the Sierra Nevada to the gold fields. The Virginian wrote:

> Here we found old Jim Beckwith, once a mountain trapper, then a miner, now a packer and speculator in provisions, drinks, etc. for the imigrants. . . . we sat around the cabin for sometime looking at the lanlrd [landlord] & the monster pines that overhung his shanty. . . . Here the road forks, . . . but we were persuaded by all means to keep the niger [nigger] trail [Beckwourth Pass].[70]

Dr. Charles E. Boyle and Peter Decker, who were members of the same overland company, reported in separate accounts that they had received valuable information on the Indian peoples they would meet west of Fort Kearney from an unnamed black interpreter who spoke several Indian languages, as well as French. These exchanges took place at Fort Kearney.[71]

M. Durivage, gold rush correspondent for the *New Or-*

leans Picayune, who ordinarily reported the presence of black men to his newspaper only in a derogatory way, thought at one point on the Gila trail that he was dying of thirst. It was his own black servant who brought him water at a crucial moment. In Durivage's words, "A mile ahead was my black servant, Isaac, on horseback rushing toward us at a headlong gallop. Spite his black hide he looked like an angel." Another group took the southern route from Salt Lake City, and as they went deeper into the arid Southwest, they became so thirst-crazed they cut their horses' throats to drink the blood. Among their number was a General Blodgett, who had a black servant. The officer collapsed at one point and, as the diarist of the event recorded it, "General Blodgett then lay down in the valley waiting for his Negro servant to bring him water."[72]

One white man was not so fortunate, despite a black man's intentions. Bayard Taylor heard this story when his ship stopped in San Diego to pick up gold hunters who had just arrived there after completing a hazardous journey by the Mexican route. According to the informant, a sick white man was moving along so slowly on the trail that he was arriving at the company camp a little later each day. Finally, three days passed and he failed to appear in camp at all. But on that third day, a black man traveling by himself came into camp to report to the company that their ailing companion was unable to move. He had begged the black man for water and asked him to bring help from the company. The members of the company did not act. The next morning a group of Mexicans came along and reported that the man was dying. Still his companions made no move to assist him. It was then that the black man

> retraced his steps forty miles and arrived just as the sufferer breathed his last. He lifted him in his arms; in the vain effort to speak, the man expired. The mule, tied to a cactus by his side, was already dead of hunger.

When John Greenleaf Whittier read of this incident some years later, while reviewing Taylor's book on California, he was moved to exclaim:

> A picture commemorating such a scene, and the heroic humanity of the Negro, would better adorn a panel of the Capitol, than any battle piece that was ever painted.[73]

California-bound travelers passing through parts of northern Mexico occasionally received unexpected assistance from black men. Some of these Negroes had arrived there as a consequence of the war with Mexico. These blacks were probably servants or former servants of officers or Santa Fe traders. Some may have been runaways from Texas. One observer saw many persons of Afro-American origin in San Augustin, Mexico. W. Augustus Knapp recalled years later that one such black man was of great help to him with his advice on how to travel.[74]

A black man's help was of importance to Judge Benjamin Hayes when he arrived in Los Angeles after a long and tedious journey by the southern route. He came into town a total stranger, but then, in his own words,

> an old acquaintance introduced himself to me in the shape of Peter Biggs, formerly the slave of my friend Mr. Reuben Middleton of Liberty [Missouri]. Pete was delighted to see me; did not delay to communicate to me many useful items; in fact rendered me services which I deemed valuable.[75]

Dr. Snelling from Missouri, traveling west on the Santa Fe trail with his family, had grown so dependent upon his black servants that he turned over virtually all responsibilities to them. In a highly unusual abdication of overland-journey duties, when his horses stampeded one day, Snelling left the entire matter to his black man Tom.[76]

For several groups that came through the Mojave Desert, the first respite from hardships was the Cucamonga Rancho, situated just to the west of the desert. Here an anonymous black man, apparently the ranch manager, was their benefactor. One of the recipients of his help referred to him not only as a former soldier but as a member of Frémont's expeditions as well. The manager was most considerate in his attentions to the suffering travelers and gave them provisions, while at the same time he restrained them from drinking too much of the wine being made on the ranch. Then, as one of the beneficiaries of this hospitality put it:

> The old Negro sent two of his vaqueros out to fetch beef for [us]. . . . [We] ate what we could, thanked him and started for Los Angeles.[77]

A Negro volunteer with daring spirit probably saved the lives of many gold seekers stranded in the Humboldt Sink. During the late summer of 1850, it became known that hundreds were immobilized, sick, and starving in the Humboldt Sink, while thousands more approaching from the east were destined for the same fate. The natural environment between the Mississippi River and the Sierra Nevada had given out under the unnatural onslaught of tens of thousands of men, horses, and cattle. In this arid region, the meagre water resources were soon exhausted. The native grasses, which the migrants depended upon to feed their horses and cattle, were chewed off to the stubble and had no time to grow back before being grazed again. Intolerably high daytime temperatures further complicated the problems. Word of the impending disaster for the thousands approaching the area spread from coast to coast. In Sacramento a relief movement for those suffering in the Humboldt Sink began in the fall of 1850. When Captain William Waldo, a public-spirited Sacramentoan, issued the call for a volunteer party, only a few responded. There were a number of white volunteers, including several who were employees of Waldo, and a Negro, Ed Lewis, described as "Louis, a black man from Boston," an expert with horses. The men traveled about 250 miles through the mountains and desert to reach the Humboldt Sink. They were appalled at the distress they found. Captain Waldo calculated the emergency needs of the stranded travelers and it was Ed Lewis, "the black man from Boston," who rode the 250 miles "express" to deliver the message to the people of Sacramento. This distress story was well reported in the East. It appeared in the New York, New Bedford (Massachusetts), and New Orleans newspapers. All of these papers cited the *Sacramento Transcript,* where the disaster was reported in full and included the part Ed Lewis played. The New Bedford and New York papers reported all the details. The New Orleans paper left out any mention of "the black man from Boston."[78]

As hundreds of blacks were crossing the broad expanse of the United States toward California in the early years of the gold rush, as many and perhaps more were taking the water route to the same destination. East Coast newspapers carried many advertisements for steamship travel to California. Free black men in the Atlantic-seaboard cities and towns were familiar with water travel, because so many of them worked in the seafaring trades of the Northern states. For those Negroes who had a choice, the water route suggested greater personal security than did the land routes. Although of modest means, these black men and women had sufficient funds or could raise the money for their passage.

The experience of blacks migrating by water is better documented because more than a few were well known before they left or subsequently became prominent in California. Among the first to go by water was a Negro named Jackson, who would later be well known in the Bay area for his culinary accomplishments. He served as a cook for the first company that went to California by way of Nicaragua.[79] Late in November 1849, the *New York Tribune* observed that the first of the future black leadership of California was on its way. The notice read:

> Some merchants of this city have formed an association of colored men for the purpose of mining in California. The company consists of ten men, and is composed of the most intelligent and respectable colored men of our city among whom is Newport F. Henry, . . . confidential porter of Arthur Tappan and Co. J. H. Townsend, late editor of the New York Hyperion, who was educated at Waterville College [Maine] and several other. . . .

This group took the ship *Hampden* for the isthmus of Panama.[80]

More of the future black leadership were on their way to California by the Panama route in the next year. While in New York, Mifflin Wistar Gibbs, a Philadelphian, caught the California fever. He had just returned from a lecture tour with Frederick Douglass when he made his decision. In his recollections, he noted that he managed the trip on the *Golden Gate* from New York to Panama with "some friendly assistance."[81] This comment hints at the possibility that some black men and women of limited means but unlimited daring came to California with the informal assistance of black crewmen or antislavery members of ship management. Thomas Starr King, the antislavery Unitarian minister, once asked his brother, a Boston ship captain, to give employment to a black woman on his California-bound ship.[82] In the same year that Gibbs departed, Daniel Seals and Edward Johnson, both of whom became active in state-wide black activities, left New York on the *Empire City* for California via Panama.[83] And there were others that year. William M. Chipman, a white passenger on the ship *Ohio* leaving New York for Panama, noted several black passengers on board in 1850.[84]

The family of Edward Booth, who was also to become a Negro leader in California, had its own special set of difficulties in joining the Negro migration to the Far West. In November 1851, the four brothers and two sisters, led by

Edward, the eldest, left Baltimore, the city of their birth, where they had always been free persons. Their departure was briefly delayed by the demand of the state authorities that the Booths prove they were free. They finally arrived in New York, where they took passage to Panama. After a difficult journey across the isthmus and a three-week wait for their ship in Panama City, they found that more tickets had been sold than there was ship space. But Edward Booth, who had been a West Indies businessman, discovered that the ship's captain was an old acquaintance of his, and passage was arranged for himself and his sisters. The three remaining Booths found passage on another ship arriving in San Francisco many weeks later. Edward had alerted all blacks who worked on the boats in San Francisco Bay to watch for his family, and they were soon reunited in Sacramento.[85]

Another who came to California by the Panama route in 1851 was Abner H. Francis of Buffalo, New York, a black man with a long career as an antislavery activist. A series of letters that Francis wrote for *Frederick Douglass' Paper* described his impressions of this travel experience. He revealed mixed feelings about the people he observed in Central America—"I would not want to take up my abode among them for all that they possess, although it was gratifying to see colored men in authority."[86] Still, he reported no overt racist insults in the course of his journey.

Not so fortunate was James R. Starkey, the former North Carolina slave, who suffered racist treatment on the Nicaragua route. He took passage on the vessel *Pocahontas* from New York to Nicaragua because he was given assurances of decent accommodations. After leaving port, the captain, a Southerner, moved Starkey and his black companions from their berths, which he gave to white crewmen, and compelled Starkey and his party to sleep in the sailors' berths. Starkey's group also had to wait until all other passengers and the sailors were fed before they could have their meals. After Starkey landed with his party in

Greytown, Nicaragua, at the mouth of the San Juan River, he had another depressing experience:

> This place, a town containing five hundred inhabitants, of which one hundred are white Americans, and the other four hundred are composed of Indians and colored Americans from the American States, suffer themselves to be ruled at the will and pleasure of the few pale faces who come among them, only to benefit their pockets. Out of the eight hotels in this place, five are kept by colored persons from the states; and among them, are some of the best houses in the town. Imagine my surprise, when a few days ago, a colored young man on his way home from California, in company with a number of white companions; they had seen many a hard day together, in the Mountains of California; he was well dressed, and the best looking man, not only in the company but in the house; when the dinner bell rang, he of course, seated himself at the table, having previously bought his tickets at the bar. . . . imagine my surprise, when I saw the landlord (colored) walk up to him and take him by the collar, and say to him in a loud and insulting tone, 'I thought by your appearance, that you had sense enough to know the American character better than to seat yourself at my first table.' For this, he (the landlord) received quite a merited rebuke, not only from the colored young man, but also from the 'American Characters' who were at the table. . . . The young man, and those in company with him, left the house, and went to a hotel kept by a white man and were entertained alike and without distinction.

This experience led Starkey to remark sadly, "He who wears a regimental suit oft is poor, as some recruit."[87]

For one black man the rigors of the trip were accentuated by a racist crew member. On board the *Oregon*, leaving Panama for San Francisco, a black man was sitting alone by the rail enjoying the sea air, when a white fireman, who had just come up from below, attempted to eject him from his seat. The black man refused to give up his place. The fireman then went below and brought up a shovelful of hot ashes and dashed them into the Negro's face, whereupon, to the delight of some of the white onlookers, the black man proceeded to thrash his aggressor soundly. When other firemen came up and attempted to down the black man, a number of whites interceded and told the firemen, "if they offered to do the Negro any more vengeance they would butcher the offender like a bullock."[88]

Many blacks of humbler station, whose lives in California would receive less notice, also came west by the Panama route. Scores, perhaps hundreds, of white Southerners in the early years of the gold rush came to California with their slaves by this route. Most of them left from New Orleans, which became a booming gold rush departure point for the people of the lower Mississippi Valley. The published passenger lists of ships leaving that city in early 1849 for the isthmus reported "servants" on nearly every departure notice. There was at least one ship a week leaving New Orleans for Panama. George Freanor, a correspondent for the *New Orleans Picayune* who was in Panama City in March 1849, wrote, "Not less than 800 or 1,000 persons are now on the Isthmus awaiting transportation, two thirds of whom are southern and western men, some of them with slaves."[89] The number of "servants" on these departure lists varied from one up to the sixteen reported on the *Alabama*, which left New Orleans for the isthmus in October 1849.[90]

Most blacks were accompanying their masters to the mining country. However, many other black men and women were brought west as house servants by white Southern business and professional men who had heard of the high cost of labor in California cities. Southerners of this class also were accustomed to black labor and ill at ease in dealing with white labor. Most of these black domestic workers would eventually become free if their masters decided to remain in the West. Some did not wait for that decision.

The natural hazards of the Panama route were the same for whites and blacks, and many died on the way. For some blacks, however, there was an additional human hazard. As the cash value of the American slave became apparent to the natives, robber bands on the isthmus went into the business of kidnapping slaves to resell in South America.[91]

As the impact of the gold rush burst upon Central America, some side effects developed that are significant for black history. A number of North American blacks decided to go into business in this booming area. They concluded that in Panama and Nicaragua, where the vast majority of people were various shades of brown, a North American Negro could find a congenial environment. By 1850, William G. Hance, who arrived in Panama the year before, was a successful hotel-keeper and restaurateur. There he married a Latin American girl. One New Orleans woman traveler, seeing his wife, was led to believe that Hance was a Spanish Negro. Hance had learned his business as a free Negro waiter in Baltimore. When he first opened his hotel, he named it the "New York Hotel," but later he renamed it the "New Orleans," which may say something about his business acumen. Southerners going through Panama often voiced their resentment of Northern states' dominance in isthmus business.[92] At least one other black hotel-keeper, "Mr. Lyons a colored man from Chicago," was in business in Panama. His hotel was on the Atlantic side of the isthmus, and white Chicagoans tended to stay at his boarding house.[93]

At least one American black was in the transportation business. He had been in the United States Navy for three years and in 1851 was the captain of a launch called *Gorgona.* He hired four natives to row this craft on the Chagres

River. Goldsborough Bruff, who had occasion to use his services when he returned from California, commented on the skill with which "Captain William handled his craft."[94]

On the Atlantic side of Nicaragua, in Greytown, there may have been even more North American blacks in business than in Panama. The captain of a Greytown river boat was a black man from New Orleans. James R. Starkey thought that five of the eight boarding houses and restaurants in Greytown were owned by Negroes from the United States. Daniel Fletcher, a white New Englander, recalled having supper at the edge of Greytown in a restaurant owned by a South Carolina black and his wife, who had purchased their freedom.[95] Perhaps the best-known black restaurant owner of North American origin in Greytown in this period was Barney Ford. Born a slave in South Carolina, Ford had secretly educated himself and in his early twenties successfully escaped to Chicago. When gold was discovered in California, he and his wife decided to try their luck in the West. In 1851 they set out on the Nicaragua route, but Ford fell ill in Greytown. While convalescing, he decided to stay there and go into the hotel and restaurant business. The Fords prospered there until the middle 1850s, when Anglo-American rivalry and internal disorder created by competing Nicaraguan politicians made the couple decide to return to Chicago. They did so nearly five thousand dollars richer.[96]

The flood of Americans passing through Central America as a result of the discovery of gold in California created a troubled situation. Southerners and many Northerners brought with them the racist attitudes of North American life, which came into direct conflict with the anti-slavery currents in Latin American life. Colombia was preparing for the abolition of slavery by 1852; sixteen years earlier the British had abolished slavery in nearby Jamaica. When the effects of the gold rush hit the sleepy and sparsely settled isthmus, black Jamaicans thronged to this job mecca. Many found work loading and unloading ships' passengers' luggage at either end of the isthmus. The Jamaicans also worked on the building of the Panama Railroad until its completion in 1855. Then a number of these men went on to California.

A factor that aggravated race relations on the isthmus was the job competition on the Chagres River. White American boatmen, who were on the scene by 1850, lived on the opposite side of the Chagres from the black boatmen who had been there since the beginning of the gold rush. The Americans used force to gain a monopoly of this work. In one case they ambushed the black boatmen with help from some white California travelers. Eventually, the American boatmen were deterred to some extent by local officials, who began to arrest them when they got out of hand. A white South Carolinian, observing these Americans, had a low opinion of his fellow countrymen. He said they were "men whose only object is to make money at any cost, and are far more dishonest than the natives."[97]

Bayard Taylor of the *New York Tribune* may have been the first to record the racial tensions on the isthmus. He wrote, "Ambrosia (the boatman) told me that many Americans had treated the boatmen badly, and that they would serve no such person well." "We are black," the boatman said, "but muchos caballeros [gentlemen]."[98] Charles Grunsky, a German immigrant to California, in 1850 noted:

> many Americans of the rougher class in large part from the slave states . . . have treated the natives with very little consideration. . . . This treatment of the natives as though they were not better than slaves, I learned in Chagres, provoked much ill-feeling against the Americans.[99]

The bloodiest recorded incident produced by this attitude was called the "Panama Massacre" or the "Watermelon War." A white American named Jack Oliver took a piece of watermelon from a black vendor and walked away without paying. When the vendor ran after him, Oliver contemptuously handed him a coin. However, by this time, the vendor was so enraged that he drew a knife. Oliver, in turn, drew a gun, fired, and wounded an innocent bystander in the mixed crowd that had quickly gathered. This was the spark that ignited the long-simmering hostilities between California-bound Americans and the natives. There were then nearly four thousand Americans in Panama. In the conflicts that ensued all over town, enraged blacks invaded the hotels and the railroad terminal where white Americans had barricaded themselves. Many were killed before the riots ended.[100]

The atmosphere of suspicion engendered by this and other incidents almost cost a white traveler his life. This man had been robbed and left for dead on a trans-isthmus jungle road. A black man found him but left without offering to carry him to where he could receive aid. This white man might have died had not William C. Ralston, later founder of the Bank of California, accidentally discovered him and brought him to a nearby town. Ralston encountered the black man in town and asked him why he had not helped the robbery victim. The black replied that he had wished to but was afraid of being charged with the robbery and attempted murder.[101]

For many, if not most, of the gold-seeking Americans, Panama was a place for impatient waiting. Ship arrival times were never certain and space on ships was often just as uncertain. At all times in these first years of the gold rush there were hundreds awaiting passage for California. How men spent their idle time varied with temperament and background. Some, like Peter Barber, the white Ohioan, attended an all-black concert given by the slaves of a North Carolinian who was taking them to California with him.[102] Others with intellectual curiosity explored the cultural artifacts of this old Spanish city. Black New Yorker Abner Francis, like many of the more peaceful white Americans, walked about the old and new parts of Panama and observed the social and religious characteristics of the native peoples. John W. Dwinelle, who would later represent the cause for equal education for black children in California, observed, "I find that one does not retain his prejudices against the Negro when he comes into contact with him as he is in a state of political freedom and equality."[103]

Most, however, sought out more exciting forms of entertainment. In one case a group of Americans went to a local dance and started a fight in which one man on each side was stabbed to death. J. D. Borthwick noted that when some of his fellow travelers got drunk they wanted to fight, "and more particularly to pitch into the natives and niggers."[104] In 1852 the British consul reported that his work in protecting the Jamaicans from the aggression of the Americans was so arduous and complex that he deserved a raise in salary. He made the very believable claim that his duties had multiplied in the course of his having to

> . . . watch over . . . to act constantly as a mediator and protector of . . . the negroes from Jamaica . . . who are here in such large numbers . . . and whose utter helplessness in the case of any disputes with . . . any citizens of the United States calls for official influence.[105]

A similar situation prevailed in Nicaragua. At the time of the gold rush the port of entry for westward-bound gold seekers was under British control. During this British period Greytown was almost entirely administered by the local citizens, who were people of color. Southerners traveling to California by the Nicaragua route found this most offensive. As one stated it, "they impose a duty of two per cent on all importations. It is not much to be sure but here all this authority is vested in negroes is [*sic*] what makes every American's blood boil." The writer went on to say that there were two British war ships to enforce this authority, and he was impatient for the day when a lot of Kentuckians would come through and set things straight.[106]

This attitude led to violence in 1854. An American river

boat captain killed the black pilot of a native craft during an altercation on the river that bordered Greytown. The officials of Greytown demanded that he be brought to trial, but he was protected by the American consulate. The American minister, Solon Borland, in the course of attempting to protect the American captain, was struck in the face by a broken beer bottle. One thing led to another until the captain of the American sloop of war *Cyane*, which had arrived in the meantime, decided to blow up the entire town. The residents were advised to leave the town to save their lives. From a distance, Barney Ford, mentioned earlier, saw his profitable hotel blown to bits. Most of the property in Greytown was owned by black people.[107]

Whether the gold seekers traveled by water routes, crossing at Nicaragua, Panama, or Mexico, or whether they followed the covered wagons over one of the land routes, blacks and whites alike faced the same hazards. Their eyes were fixed on the same goal of self-improvement in California, through gold itself or in profitable work in gold rush boom towns.

William A. Leidesdorff, a leading Afro-American citizen of pre-gold rush San Francisco. (Courtesy California State Library.)

James P. Beckwourth, Afro-American fur trader, mountain guide, and discoverer of Beckwourth Pass through the Sierra Nevada. (Courtesy California State Library.)

Alvin A. Coffey, black member of the Society of California Pioneers. (Courtesy Society of California Pioneers.)

$100 REWARD—Runaway from MRS. ELIZABETH WARE in the month of October, 1850, from Marysville, a BLACK GIRL, named HAGAR. 5 feet 5 inches high. 24 years of age, dark complexion, round face, broad front teeth. Since leaving she has changed her name to MARY. The above reward will be paid if found in this county, or **$150** in any other county; to be delivered in the hands of the Sheriff of San Francisco. je25 1w

Advertisement from the *San Francisco Herald*, 1852.

Black miners working along with white in Spanish Flat, California in 1852. (Courtesy California State Library.)

Black miner with Chinese and white miners at Auburn Ravine, 1852. (Courtesy the Bancroft Library.)

Black miner in Auburn Ravine, 1852. (Courtesy the Bancroft Library.)

Biddy Mason, an ex-slave who became a successful businesswoman and a leading figure in the black community of Los Angeles. (Courtesy the Bancroft Library.)

George W. Dennis, an ex-slave who became a successful San Francisco businessman. (Courtesy California Historical Society Library.)

Mifflin Wistar Gibbs, California Colored Convention leader, who later became the United States Consul to Madagascar. (Courtesy Provincial Archives, Victoria, B.C.)

Peter Lester became a successful San Francisco businessman and a leader of the black community before he migrated to British Columbia in 1858. (Courtesy Provincial Archives, Victoria, B.C.)

Reverend John J. Moore, California Colored Convention leader.

Reverend Jeremiah B. Sanderson, Colored Convention leader and educator. (Courtesy East Bay Negro Historical Society, Inc., Oakland, Calif.)

Reverend Thomas Randolph, pastor of Marysville Baptist Church. (Courtesy East Bay Negro Historical Society, Inc., Oakland, Calif.)

Phillip A. Bell, editor of the *Pacific Appeal*.

"ARCHY."

TO THE FRIENDS

......OF THE......

CONSTITUTION AND LAWS.

THE COMMITTEE APPOINTED BY THE Colored People having expended a large amount, and incurred heavy obligations in prosecuting and defending the case in the Courts of Sacramento, Stockton and San Francisco, and believing the principles to be vindicated are those which should interest all lovers of right and justice, independent of complexion, respectfully solicit contributions for this object, which will be faithfully appropriated, if left with

m20-3t E. J. JOHNSON, 184 Clay street.

This advertisement appeared in the *California Chronicle*, San Francisco, 1858.

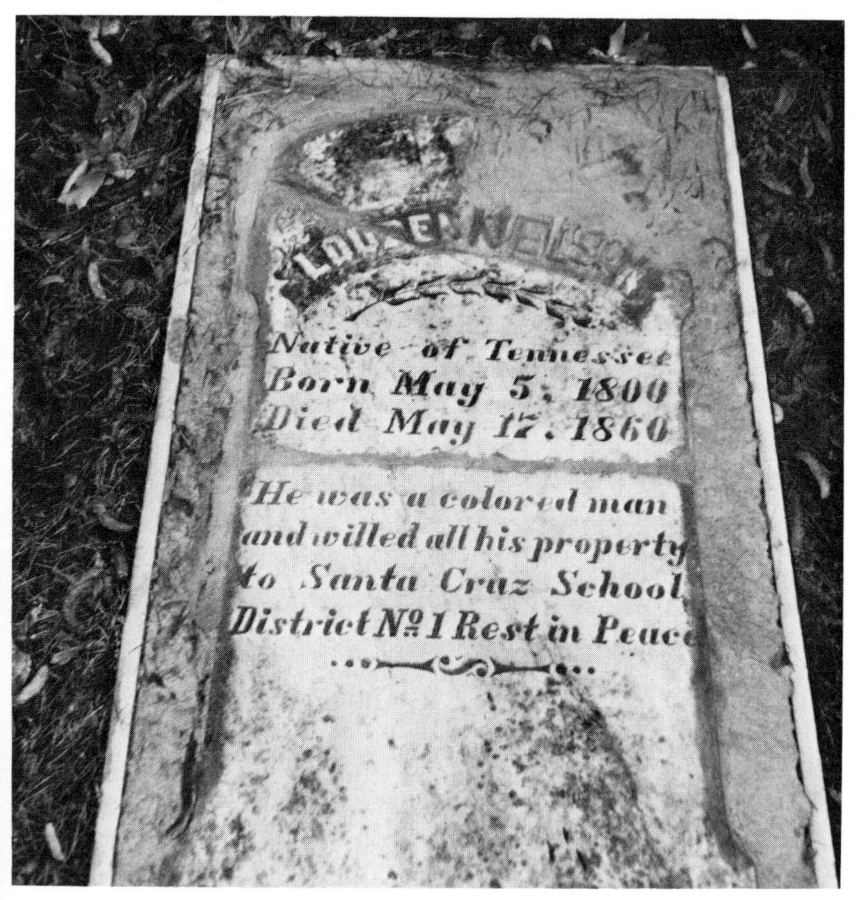

Tombstone of Louden Nelson in Evergreen Cemetery, Santa Cruz, California. (Photo by Patricia T. Lapp.)

3 In the Mines

When the gold rush began in 1848, the black population in California was no more than a few dozen. They were a blend of the earlier, pre-American period, arrivals and those who came with the American conquerors of Mexican California. By the end of 1848, their numbers were augmented by the deserters from New England ships, mostly whalers from New Bedford, Massachusetts, and by the Afro-Latin Americans who came from Mexico, Chile, and Peru. By the end of 1849, the great wave of gold seekers brought blacks from every region of the United States and the West Indies. California played host to the broadest representation of Afro-Americans in the western hemisphere. Black New Englanders met slaves from Missouri, New York blacks met black Jamaicans, and free blacks from Ohio met free Spanish-speaking blacks from south of the border. American blacks were by far the largest group, and more of them were free than slave.

According to the census of 1850, there were 962 persons of color in California, including some Sandwich Islanders (often called *Kanakas*). The majority of those called black in the census, between 600 and 700 living in the gold rush counties, were of North American origin. The others, who included Latin-American blacks, were distributed throughout the state, with some concentrations in San Francisco and Sacramento. Many of the Latin-American blacks, however, soon left California to return to their homes, chiefly in Mexico and Chile.[1]

Well over half of the Afro-Americans in the Mother Lode counties by the beginning of 1850 were free persons. The overwhelming majority, whether free or slave, were classified as miners.[2]

Blacks from the United States who were in the mines by

1850 came from three geographic regions: the free states, chiefly New York and Massachusetts (134); the slave states of the lower and Deep South (91); and the border states of the South, to which Virginia was the greatest contributor (374). More than half of this latter group may well have been free, because the border states had the largest free Negro populations. Also, many of these black men and women, born in border states of the South, had resided in the North prior to their departure for California.

The unceasing flow of people to California had, by 1852, more than doubled the black population of the state, although blacks remained about one percent of the population. There were more than 2,000 Negroes in California by then. While the black communities of San Francisco and Sacramento became somewhat larger, the black population increase was greater in the mining communities. There were over 1,000 blacks in the Mother Lode country, while San Francisco and Sacramento had 444 and 338 black residents respectively. In Los Angeles County there were only 45 blacks. Most of these had come with Mississippi Mormons, their former masters, to found and build the town of San Bernardino.[3]

Gold rush maps of the Mother Lode bear witness to the presence of the Afro-Americans in those frenzied years. One finds, for instance, the place names Negro Hill or Nigger Hill, Negro Bar, and Negro Flat. They represent sites where a black man made a lucky strike or where groups of black men lived and mined. Erwin G. Gudde, historian of California place names, found over thirty locations in the state that used the term *Nigger* or *Negro* and in some cases *Negros* where the Spanish recognized the presence or importance of some black man. In addition to the above, there were sites named Negro Butte, Negro Run, Nigger Bill Bend, Nigger Jack Slough, and Arroyo de los Negros. While the word *Negro* has evaporated from current maps of California,[4] the story of the black gold miners has survived. From splinters of information scattered among obscure sources there emerge tales of good fortune, bad luck, courage, and despair.

Many black miners tried their luck in the gold fields, but only those whose luck was exceptional gained any notice. Perhaps the first of these fortunate gold hunters was a cook named Hector, who deserted the naval squadron ship *Southhampton* in Monterey in 1848. An on-the-spot observer was present when Hector returned to Monterey with $4,000 in gold. One of the richest strikes made by anyone was that of a black man known only as Dick, who mined $100,000 worth of gold in Tuolumne County in 1848, only to lose it by gambling in San Francisco.[5]

The stories of the two Negro Hills tell much of the black experience in gold rush California. The first Negro Hill was located on the American River, not far from where gold was originally discovered on the south fork of the river. The hill was first mined by blacks in 1849. According to one source, these men were a Massachusetts black named Kelsey and a black Methodist minister. Digging in that area continued to prove rewarding, as new finds were being made into the following year. Early in 1850 the San Francisco *Daily Alta California* reported:

> About four miles below Mormon Island on the American River, there have been new diggings discovered which prove to yield exceedingly well. They are called "Nigger Diggings" from the fact that some colored gentlemen first discovered them.

Two years later another strike was made nearby. Its proximity to Negro Hill was felt by miners to insure that a long run of profit would follow.[6]

The original success of the two black men resulted in the growth of a Negro mining community around the hill, as well as on a nearby hill that came to be called Little Negro Hill. In 1852 two Massachusetts blacks opened a store and boardinghouse, around which a concentration of black residences grew up. Since the diggings continued to be sufficiently rewarding, the Negro Hill community continued to survive and was even stable enough to deserve the attentions of a minister. By 1854, a white Methodist clergyman was offering Sunday evening services on a regular basis. A young white New Englander, who attended these services occasionally, commented that the majority of the congregation was black. He wrote to his sister that he would have attended more consistently if he did not have to fight his prejudices every time. By 1855 the Negro Hill community had grown to about 400. Other minority peoples, particularly Chinese and Portuguese miners, became residents of this village. In 1855 Negro Hill was still described as an area with "scores of hardy miners making good wages." However, trouble soon appeared because many of the Negro Hill community were white and prejudiced. That year drunken whites looking for a fight attacked the Negro quarters and killed one black man. They were arrested, tried, and set free by a Coloma court.[7]

The experience of blacks in nearby Massachusetts Flat stands in contrast to that of Negro Hill. This mining community, founded by New Englanders in 1854, was composed largely of Negroes and Portuguese by the following year. Here blacks were never harassed. In the presidential election of 1856, further evidence of the contrast between Negro Hill and Massachusetts Flat is found in the voting returns. The racist Negro Hill community gave Frémont only 22 percent of their vote, while Massachusetts Flat gave this antislavery candidate 75 percent of their vote.[8]

The second Negro Hill story took place in 1851, in the southern mines near Mokelumne Hill, not far from the Mokelumne River. Unlike the Negro Hill of the northern mines, this area had many white miners working there before a black man's lucky strike. The history of this strike is associated with legend that has the ring of truth to it. As the story goes, a black man wandering into the Mokelumne Hill area looking for a claim was told by white miners to keep moving, as every spot he started to prospect was claimed to be some white man's diggings. Finally, some jokester told the black prospector to go to a high point nearby where everyone "knew" there was no gold. It was here, by digging deep enough, that he made an incredibly rich strike. The news of this find spread far and wide. The lucky black (never named in the press) soon had a black partner. As the local paper put it:

> A couple of negroes who had been at work at the cayote diggings of Mokelumne Hill went home in one of the steamers . . . with eighty thousand dollars that they took out of one hole during the past four months.

Thus "Negro" or "Nigger Hill" got its name and immediately became the object of a rush of miners, both black and white.[9]

Because the black miner who gave this Negro Hill its name returned a few years later to the Mokelumne Hill area, and because Andrew Hallidie of cable-car fame, who was prospecting there, happened to meet him, a bit more is known about this man. Hallidie tells us that his name was Livingston and that he

> . . . was a character . . . over six feet, erect and well proportioned, he would attract attention anywhere, had quite a dignified way of talking and used unusually good language. . . .

According to Hallidie, Livingston left for England after his strike, where he had a fine time spending his money, and then decided to return to the scene of his triumph to recoup his fortunes. Livingston asked Hallidie to go into a partnership with him. At first, Hallidie balked, but he soon realized he could not work his claim alone. So he agreed to sell his claim to Livingston and a black associate. The claim was worth eight dollars a day for Livingston and his partner.[10]

From one end of the Mother Lode counties to the other

the lucky finds of black men continued to be reported through the 1850s. Items like the following were noted: From Stockton:

> An impression has got abroad among the miners that this famous old negro has struck upon extraordinary rich diggings about two and half miles from town. . . . Jenkins is known to have been fortunate in all his mining operations.

From Sonora:

> Moses Dinks, a Negro, . . . started from his cabin between Jackass Hill and Tuttletown, . . . he noticed a gleaming object poking its nose skyward. Not wishing to carry twenty-five pounds of gold nor desiring to turn back to his cabin, he buried the chunk of precious metal on the spot.

From Indian Gulch, Sonora:

> A Negro, a few days ago, panned out in a few hours twenty four ounces.

From Mariposa:

> Last week a German boy named Fritz, and a colored man named Duff, . . . found a block of gold bearing quartz, weighing one hundred and ninety three pounds . . . value . . . from $5,000 to $10,000.

On the Feather River:

> Rich diggings were accidentally discovered by a negro on this same river above Ophir.

Again from Sonora:

> . . . a party of colored miners . . . at the southern end of Jamestown, . . . struck upon a very rich lead, prospecting as high as one hundred and twenty dollars to the pan.

And as late as 1859 from Mariposa:

> . . . two colored men named Perkins and Oscar made a rich strike in a small ravine a short distance from Mariposa. . . . they . . . struck a lead or vein of decomposed slate, out of which they took in two days the sum of $1,300.[11]

Actually, the average daily earnings of most successful miners were like those of Mr. Smith, a black miner in Amador County, who worked his claim hydraulically, paid for his water at "two bits" an inch, and made five to six dollars a day.[12]

In the environment of the gold rush it was inevitable that a mythology emerge about blacks and gold. News of black men making lucky strikes took on an aura of almost superstitious inevitability. The mythology was fed by true tales like that of the white prospector whose slave told him that in a dream he had found gold underneath their cabin. The unbelieving miner finally dug under the cabin and came upon a rich find.[13] Borthwick, the English adventurer in the gold fields, thought that Negroes were "proverbially" lucky at gold mining.[14] When the New England Quaker Pancoast heard that a black man had made a lucky strike at Mariposa Flat, he hurried there to take a claim next to him. He must have become a true believer of the myth because while he did well, making twenty-five dollars a day, the black man made one hundred dollars a day just a few feet away from him.[15] However, given the American attitudes toward the Negro in the nineteenth century, most white minds could only conceive of superstitious insights rather than equal ability, tenacity, and luck as an explanation for blacks' exceptional gold strikes.

Black miners, like the whites, from time to time formed associations among themselves for purposes of mutual aid. While there is only one group of this kind recorded, the New York company organized in that city, the evidence suggests there were others in the gold country. They probably came together in the same informal way that so many white groups formed and reformed in the Mother Lode counties. In that uncertain and overwhelmingly white world blacks had a real need for mutual aid. Undoubtedly such organizations existed on the two Negro Hills previously described. The manuscript census clearly suggests that groups such as the eighteen blacks on the middle fork of the American River in 1850 were organized into a company. Eleven of these black miners were from Massachusetts, a state where skills in organizing had long been known by Negroes.[16]

Organized black companies became even more visible when they occasionally associated themselves with whites. Such associations not only served the usual purposes, but for the blacks they sometimes worked as an umbrella of protection against hostile whites. An interesting case of this sort occurred in October 1849, near Hawkins' Bar on the Tuolumne River. The recorder of the event, William Miller from Massachusetts, related that a group of black miners working across the river from him suggested to his group that they pool their resources and dam the river at some selected point for more efficient mining. Miller's group, which seems to have been mostly New Englanders, agreed, and plans were made. A location was settled upon that was scouted by William Foreman, "a coulard gentleman from Boston." Three whites and five blacks associated with Foreman went down the river to the selected location to prepare the way for the rest of the party. The white men who were there previously had no objection to this activity and were willing to join in it. All then went to work to lay the ground for the task ahead. Some time during that same day, "a swaggering looking fellow came along. . . . [I] informed him what our intentions were. . . . He allowed that a white man might come in but a black man could not no how." He then announced that he had a company of twenty-five men who intended to take that very location later in the week. The Miller-Foreman group decided to ignore the threat; they proceeded with their work and went back for the night to their original camp. When they returned the next morning with their full contingent of twenty men, they found twenty-five Southerners armed with rifles, revolvers, and bowie knives. Miller and his white associates tried to suggest that the Southerners were breaking the law but the Southerners dismissed legal niceties with contempt. The entire group concluded that this location might not be worth the trouble and turned to other mining efforts on the Tuolumne River.[17]

Not long after this event, the group lost some of its members to other mining areas, a common occurrence in gold rush history. But those who remained continued as an interracial community. They remained together into at least February of the following year, sharing the Christmas and New Year season together. Their holiday season was enlivened by the culinary art of the black men, especially that of William Henry Garrison, a former New Yorker. Garrison was also proficient with a violin, and it appears that Miller and the other whites in this party had an enjoyable time. Like many other gold rush accounts, Mr. Miller's diary ends abruptly and nothing more is known about this group.[18]

A similar story with a different result occurred about the same time on Mariposa Flat. Near the Mariposa River, where a Philadelphia Quaker and his associates were mining, was a lone black man who was having much greater success than the others. A group of Missourians came along with a proposal to dam the river, and all agreed. When the job was finished, the Missourians announced a lottery in which everybody would take his chance on where his thirty-foot lot would be. The black man and the Quaker and his friend protested, for they were all doing rather well up to that point. However, being outnumbered by the Missourians, they could do nothing at that moment. A short time later, they went a few miles up the creek to complain to a recently elected alcalde (mayor), a six-foot Kentuckian. The Kentuckian took ninety armed miners with him to correct the situation, and the Missourians suddenly found respect for the miner's law. But the ninety miners were so incensed at the Pike County characters that, over the remonstrances of the alcalde, they ordered the Missourians to pack up and leave the area. During the next two weeks of peaceful mining the Quaker made $500 and the black man $3,000.[19]

A striking case of black-white collaboration is that of the company organized by the Scotsman, William Downie, the founder of Downieville. His party had nine men, seven of them black, mostly sailors and most, if not all of them, from the States. Downie had been alternating between mining and storekeeping on the Yuba River in the summer of 1849. For some time he had been thinking of forming a company to prospect the upper reaches of the Yuba River. His opportunity came when several Negro miners who had been working the river nearby dropped in to Downie's store for a drink. The congenial conversation that ensued resulted in a new partnership that made gold rush history.

When the organization of this group was completed, it was composed of Downie, a white lad named Duvarney, and seven Negroes, of whom only Albert Callis and Charley Wilkins are known by name. Downie surmised that Callis was a runaway slave, originally from Virginia. This was not implausible, as some slaves brought to California had effected their freedom by this time.

The nine men proceeded to the upper reaches of the Yuba River, until they came upon the beautiful site of the river forks where the town of Downieville now stands. There they struck gold and decided to remain. Much gold was found here. On Sundays, for religious reaons, the blacks would not do any digging. One of them, Callis, became a permanent resident of Downieville. He eventually turned to his trade of barbering, married, and raised a family.[20]

All miners in the wilds of the Sierra had to deal with the

hazards of nature and the back-breaking toil of the search for gold, but the free black miner had an additional hazard—the racial attitudes of white miners in a setting of frequent lawlessness. The more hooliganlike Americans in the mines were notorious for driving people of color from well-paying claims. In the early lawless years "decent" white men would deplore this practice but only infrequently do something about it. A black man who discovered rich diggings on Long's Bar on the Feather River was soon "crowded from his claim."[21] Daniel Langhorne, who came to California as a slave from Virginia, recalled that when he went gold prospecting to buy his freedom, he did well but had to defend his claim on the Yuba River against a white man. He was fortunate in coming before a fair-minded judge who ruled in his favor.[22] Another black man found the harassment so intolerable that, although he was doing well, he decided to leave for the "Islands."[23] One group of white miners near Volcano, in Amador County, tried to call a miners' meeting to organize the expulsion of black miners nearby who had well-paying claims.

The Volcano story sheds more light on black-white relations in the mines. The journal of young Benjamin Bowen, an Iowan, is most illuminating in this instance. Bowen, his father, and his brother, with two other white men and one black named George W. Mason, became partners in mining near the gold rush town of Fort John near Volcano. This partnership began in 1852 and continued for several years. The easy relationship between Bowen and the others in this group exudes from the pages of this journal. Mason rented out his share of the activities from time to time to other white men or even to other black miners working nearby. In March of 1855, a crisis arose between some members of the local white mining group and the blacks. A group of drunken, prejudiced hotheads among the whites arbitrarily ordered the blacks to leave, as "the niggers had got to be too saucy" and, as young Bowen records it, the whites were "hungry" for the black miner's diggings. At first some members of the black group panicked and prepared to flee. Bowen wrote:

> Jack Kimball, a colored man came to our house this evening with a lot of books which he wished to dispose of as he said he had been ordered to leave the diggings.

The Bowens suggested to Kimball that he not be too hasty in leaving and that something might be worked out. A miners' meeting was called. Blacks came to the Bowens to urge them to attend and the crisis was dissolved through what seems to have been organized disorder. However, Jack Kimball, who with his books seemed to be of the gentler sort, sold out his claim and left the Fort John diggings.[24]

The free Negro miner, especially the northern free black, sought ways of avoiding harassment of the kind described thus far, but many also wished to avoid the degrading etiquette of racism. The crux of the problem can be seen from the words of a white Mississippian who wrote, "Free negroes are insolent when there are any Yankees [about] but when they come across a man from the Southern States they have to toe the mark."[25] The business of trying to mine with a minimum of white harassment led to two general styles of adjustment. One, as we have seen, was to work in combination or partnership with agreeable white miners; the other was to isolate oneself as much as possible, or at least work in an area where there were congenial neighbors.

In general, the best associates for black miners were men like Downie from the British Isles or antislavery Northerners, preferably from New England. However, not all Scotsmen were quite like Downie. Andrew Hallidie, whose brogue must have led the black miner Livingston, mentioned earlier, to believe that Hallidie was free of color prejudice, refused Livingston's offer of a partnership but did agree to sell his claim to the black man when he couldn't find a white partner.[26] It should be noted that for the American Negroes, British accents were associated in their minds with Canada, where so many fugitive slaves fled in the decade of the gold rush. England was also a symbol of emancipation for blacks as a result of the British Emancipation Act of 1833 that ended slavery in the British Empire.

The Englishman Joseph Batty, while prospecting along the Feather River, met a Negro miner from Baltimore who invited him to his mountain cabin. Batty was at first apprehensive of the novel experience of sleeping under the same blankets with a black American, but after three days he reported that he was quite comfortable and enjoying his host's cooking. The black was a freeman who had been a clerk for a Baltimore merchant. Batty marveled at his literacy and knowledge of the Scriptures. He wrote, "I was surprised to find what an intellectual young man he was." Although the black had originally offered Batty a partnership, nothing much came of this mining association. Batty was impressed by the fact that all of the neighboring cabins were occupied by black miners, many of whom also offered him partnerships.[27]

In one community of the Yuba River, known at times as "Negro Bar" and at other times as "Union Bar," several of the members, both black and white, were from New Bedford. There were about thirty whites and ten Negroes in this community, according to William F. Terry, a New Bedford white man who kept a diary. The alcalde of this little community was a white man from New Haven. Several of the black men were from border slave states and undoubtedly found themselves enjoying the easy atmosphere without racial tensions that their New England black brethren had known for some time. A tragedy in the camp in April 1850 suggests how both races shared experiences. A mixed group of six to eight men crossed the river to visit an Indian encampment. The visit turned into a row, and a New Bedord black man, John M. Jones, was killed. The next day two blacks and two whites tried to cross the river to claim Jones's body. The river must have been quite turbulent. The boat capsized and all four men drowned.[28]

Reverend Sherlock Bristol, a white antislavery man, and the black man Isaac Isaacs traveled to the mines together from New York and became mining partners near Downieville in the village of Coyoteville. Isaacs was a powerfully built man who had trained as a boxer in Philadelphia. This fact became known to a nearby white Kentuckian who had achieved some boxing prowess. The Kentuckian kept badgering the reluctant Isaacs to box with him in a public exhibition until Isaacs finally agreed. The results were a disaster and humiliation to the white man; so much so that he drew a knife on Isaacs. Between Reverend Bristol and the white audience the Kentuckian was subdued.[29]

While some Negroes came across the plains with Germans, and many Germans in the United States at this time were democratic refugees from the 1848 revolution in Germany, there were few documented mining associations between Negroes and Germans. There was, of course, the previously noted partnership between the "colored man Duff" and the "German boy named Fritz." Heinrich Leinhard, a German associate of Sutter, recalled that in 1849 he and a mixed group of Germans, Scotsmen, Kanakas (Hawaiians), and a Washington, D.C., black man named Jim were sent out by Sutter to do some gold mining on the American River. Several of the Germans and the black man slept in one tent. It appeared to be a congenial group, but what stood out in Leinhard's memory was an incident between one of the Germans and Jim. This German was bragging a good deal about his fencing prowess and badgered Jim into dueling with him with crudely made poles. Jim protested that he had no experience with this kind of weapon but agreed to play the game out. The result was a defeated German. Leinhard was particularly impressed that the black man did not taunt the embarrassed German.[30]

There seems to have been a wide variety of congenial arrangements in the mines between Negroes and friendly whites, but in most cases the details have been lost. For instance, one miner in the Feather River country simply noted, "I saw a man a short time ago, who told me that he had worked in the same hole with two doctors, a lawyer, two negroes, and an Indian." Whether the blacks were slaves or free men was not stated.[31]

Shared antislavery sentiments explain some friendships between blacks and whites in the Mother Lode. These attitudes were shared in the case of a black Philadelphian, John Smith, who had once been a Massachusetts seaman, and Dr. Lewis C. Gunn and his wife, who were also from Philadelphia. Smith was mining at Murphy's Camp in Calaveras County in 1852; Dr. Gunn was editing the *Sonora Herald* in the neighboring county of Tuolumne. How these two men first met is not known, but their California friendship which began in 1853, suggests common contacts in the antislavery movement in Philadelphia.

Smith was doing very well at Murphy's making about $100 a week and sending money home to his wife. However, he became worried about the money reaching her, because his wife moved after his departure for the mines to a street in Philadelphia where she and their four children were the only black family on the block. Through her antislavery contacts, Mrs. Gunn was able to learn that the mails were getting through and that Mrs. Smith was receiving her husband's earnings. Smith was able to return the favor for Mrs. Gunn when he traveled to Philadelphia in 1855 for a visit with his family. He carried pictures taken in California of the Gunn children to Mrs. Gunn's sister, who in turn gave him thread and needles sorely needed by Mrs. Gunn in California.[32]

While free Negroes made friends with whites in the gold rush counties and sought congenial relationships with those who were unprejudiced, they appear to have shunned proximity with white Southerners. Mute witness to the efforts of the free Negro miner to avoid Southern whites is the manuscript census. In Tuolumne County one finds five black men mining in the midst of a considerable group of Latin-Americans. A random look at Yuba County reveals four New York blacks next to a company of Welshmen. In the same county James Cook from Ohio was surrounded by whites from Ohio, New York, and Massachusetts. In Calaveras County, John A. Lake from New York was with a group of Kanakas. Nearby, George Frank from Massachusetts was with a group of Mexicans. In the same county Ever Brown of New Jersey mined near some white Rhode Islanders. Also in Calaveras County, some free Negroes from slave states chose congenial mixed company. George Ringgold and George Smith of Maryland mined next to a group of Mexicans, and Henry Fox of Kentucky dug for gold alongside two Mexicans and a Frenchman.[33] In Amador County in the mining community of Lancha Plana, a large number of blacks shared a mining camp with about one hundred Chinese miners.[34] James M. Hutchings, an itinerant businessman and journalist who traveled all through the gold country in 1855, noted the close proximity of Negroes and Portuguese in the Negro Hill of the northern mines. He found this ethnic combination in even greater density in nearby Massachusetts Flat.[35]

There is some evidence that blacks were not the only ones who sought proximity to congenial white men as a protective device. White forty-niner Edmond Booth had been traveling to Sonora in the company of several Chinese men and, in the course of the journey on foot, had gotten a bit ahead of them. When they caught up to him, they chided him for his speed and, says Booth, "It was evident that they regarded me as protection to them."[36]

Eastern newspapers published rumors of large numbers of slaves and many slaveholders coming to California. Available evidence suggests, however, that the great majority of those who entered California as slaves came with their masters in groups of three at the most. While the census returns and ship departure notices provide considerable data, the great amount of coming and going in the first years of the gold rush makes absolute figures impossible to determine. However, it is reasonable to estimate that there were at any given time in the early 1850s between 200 and 300 black men and women in the mining country held as slaves. Including those who returned to the slave states, there were probably between 500 and 600 slaves involved in the gold rush. This guess is ventured cautiously, because it is known that census takers in the wilds of the Sierra Nevada were themselves not sure that they had reached all persons. Some slaveowners, worried about the possible loss of their human property, tried to stay out of sight. One Mississippi white with his slave was advised to seek remote mining areas in order not to be seen using slave labor.[37]

Slave expectations must have varied with time and type of master in this unusual journey. Most of those who left their native states with their owners before it was known that California would become a free state must have viewed their journey for gold as of no greater importance than a long trip between cotton plantations, although a bit more interesting. Some were told that hard work at gold mining could result in their freedom. This statement was repeated with greater frequency by masters after they learned California had been declared a free state. They continued to come, although contemporary comment suggests that the larger number of slaves were brought between the first news of the gold rush and the adoption of the constitution in November 1849.[38] Perhaps slaveowners felt safety in their own numbers, as in the case of Stephen Gaston from Arkansas, who left New Orleans for California with a party of ten white men and three slaves in April 1850, nearly half a year after California's free-state constitution had been announced.[39] The most plausible explanation for the continuing immigration of Southerners with slaves to the mining areas is that the slaveowners could easily calculate that the gamble was worth the possible profit. A few years of lucky gold mining with a slave might far exceed in profits one black man's entire working life in Southern agriculture. Others planned to avoid trouble by deciding in advance to give their slaves freedom, usually with conditions. These included both those who went into mining and Southern professional and businessmen who went to the cities or farms with their domestic servants. On balance, it should be said that the vast majority of slaveowners in the South were as cautious in bringing their slave property to California as they turned out to be some years later in the race for Kansas.

Little is known about the black men who came as slaves to the mining country and returned to slave states. More is known about those who achieved freedom in California and remained to become permanent residents of the state. Whether free or slave, the daily lives of blacks in California were probably very similar to that of the average white miner, with the exception of their servile status. Few could have had the experience of "little Harry," held by a group of white Arkansans on the Trinity River, who watched men play poker for the right to his labor. The winner had Harry's labor for one week. In another unusual case, a black lad on board a Sacramento River boat was asked to whom he belonged. He said that he would have to wait until a poker game on board had ended to be able to answer the question. His original master had lost him to a ship's clerk, and he, in turn, had lost him to another player. The game was still going.[40]

Some observers of slave miners left the impression that they were generally contented and uninterested in seeking freedom. Hundreds worked in the mines and returned to slave states, but fidelity to masters was not necessarily always the explanation. Many had left behind friends, lovers, and wives and wished to return to them. One report of a group of returning slaves maintained that they were looking forward to seeing old chums again and telling them of their experiences in gold hunting and of the exotic plants and animals in Central America, through which they had traveled.[41] Some slaves with genuinely kindly masters felt greater personal security in returning with them than in seeking permanent residence in the uncertain and unstable world of gold rush California. Southern contemporary observers were inclined to note such cases. The *New Orleans Picayune* reported the story of a Georgian who had taken his slaves to the gold mines and, after several years of profitable mining, offered them their freedom and a grubstake. According to this account they all refused the offer. Hinton Helper, a North Carolinian who visited California during the gold rush days, told of a fellow North Carolinian who offered freedom to his three slaves, only to find that they preferred to return to North Carolina with him. Conversations with abolitionists in the mines failed to dissuade them.[42]

It is certain that many slaves were kept in bondage by force. A correspondent to a New York newspaper wrote that he heard one slaveowner remark that he would shoot one of his Negroes if he tried to run away. A black man named Sam, who made his break for freedom upon returning from California with his master via New York, noted that he could not think seriously about such a move in California because he was surrounded there by so many Southerners and their supporters.[43] In one case a slave was encouraged by nearby antislavery miners to tell his master that he was a free man in California and ask for a grubstake so that he might go on his own as a miner. The master then publicly announced that he was going to whip the slave for this effrontery, and that if any of his white friends wished to take up cudgels for the black man, he was ready for them. No one stepped forward and the slave was whipped.[44]

The literature of slavery has well described the methods by which slaveowners inculcated in their slaves a sense of dependence. How one owner sustained dependency in his slave in the gold rush environment is illustrated by the technique of a young Kentuckian, George Murrell. He came with a family slave named Rheubin, with whom he went mining on the north fork of the American River. They remained in that area for over a year and were in constant correspondence with his family in Kentucky. Telling features of this correspondence are the frequency with which Murrell sent Rheubin's greetings to his fellow slaves on the Kentucky plantation and, of even more significance, the urgent requests by Murrell that letters and messages be sent to Rheubin by the blacks back home. Rheubin's letter-writing to his friends and "plantation folk" involved his dictation to Murrell, who wrote and mailed them. Noting that there were a number of antislavery men where they were mining, Murrell wrote, "I do not think that their contaminating and poisoning principles has [*sic*] in the least weakened his fidelity and devotedness to me."[45]

Elderly slaves, perhaps with familes back on the plantation, would be most reluctant to strike for freedom. An elderly black man named Daniel, who came from Alabama to the gold fields as a slave, remained in California with a relative of his master's for three years. He later returned to California with his master's son and then went back again to Alabama in 1856 to stay. He brought gold presents for each member of his owner's family.[46] The story of a forty-year-old black man from Georgia was not so cheerful. Elijah Barker was the slave of a white Georgian who brought him to California but returned home, leaving Barker in El Dorado County with some white Georgia miners to earn his own passage back. Evidently Elijah Barker made some lucky gold strikes. The teller of this tale tried to encourage Barker to buy himself and his family and bring them to California. Barker rejected the idea, but he was apparently full of ambivalent feelings. He would break into tears during these discussions and say, "de Lord heard me promise massa Jeems dat I'd come back."[47] Another black miner who had been encouraged to make a break for freedom stated without tears that "Massa, has been good to me and I gwine to be good to Massa. I make all money for um, kase he tells him make me free nigger when I gwine home."[48] Another black man named Elijah returned to North Carolina by himself, while his master remained in California, confident that Elijah would not attempt escape. A lifetime of dependence was a difficult habit for some to break.[49]

Tom Gilman, younger than Elijah Barker and a slave from Tennessee, responded rather differently, but not without some agonizing moments. Young Gilman had gone to California with the commitment to send his first considerable finds of gold back to his master in Tennessee as the price of freedom. This Tom was able to do rather swiftly. But the master then wrote Tom that the price of freedom required a second sum of gold. After that was sent, the master began a correspondence with Tom appealing to some alleged promise Tom had made to take care of his master in his old age. Gilman almost returned on the strength of this unremembered promise, but, according to a historian of Tuolumne County, his friends in Dragoon Gulch, where he was mining quite successfully, persuaded him to change his mind. One is tempted to surmise an additional source of strength for young Gilman in this decision. He was mining in Tuolumne County in 1850, and the census reveals that he was with a group of nine free Negro miners. One of them bore the name Samuel Cornish of New York. The name of Cornish is associated with the most active black abolitionists of New York and Philadelphia. Gilman's thoughts of freedom were undoubtedly kept alive by Cornish and his eight free black associates.[50]

The only black member of the prestigious Society of California Pioneers, Alvin Coffey, came to California in 1849 as a slave. He was twenty-seven years old, the property of Dr. Bassett, a Missourian. Freedom purchase was obviously in Coffey's mind. He dug gold to the value of

$5,000 for Bassett and, in his spare time over a two-year period, earned $700 washing clothes for nearby miners. However, Dr. Bassett decided to return to Missouri and Coffey had to go with him; he had a wife and two daughters held as slaves by Bassett back in Missouri. Evidently Bassett did not have any sympathy for black men who yearned for freedom, and so he sold Alvin Coffey to another Missourian, after taking Coffey's $700 from him. The new master seems to have been a different kind of Missourian. He allowed Coffey to return to California to mine gold for his freedom. This Coffey did, paying $1,500 for himself and, in time, similar amounts to Dr. Bassett for his wife and daughters, who eventually joined him in California. He did all this by placer mining around Redding and Red Bluff.[51]

The cracks did not show in the "unwavering fidelity" of some slaves until they were well on their way home to their slave states. Perhaps for some it required the actual return journey to heighten their awareness of what was happening to them. If the attractions of California were greater than any factors in their home states, the idea of going back became increasingly absurd to them with every returning mile. For several black men the psychological moment came in Panama, where all black men were free. Charley Bates, a Mississippi Negro, made his decision in Panama and found his way back to Stockton, California. Antislavery men in Stockton had to raise $750 to help Bates keep his freedom when one of his master's creditors got a proslavery judge to agree that Bates should be put up for auction to settle the debts of his former master.[52]

Another slave, whose master was a Virginian, also decided to strike for freedom in Panama. While he was in Cruces, a town midway between Panama and Chagres, native Negroes encouraged this black man to make the break. He took their advice and hid out in the garret of one of their homes to wait for the departure of the train from Cruces to Chagres. However, the master and some of his friends decided to get the black man by force. As they went up the stairs to the garret they found themselves looking into the muzzles of a considerable number of Mexican guns. The Virginian and his friends boarded the train without a former Virginia slave. A white man from Maine who observed the entire incident wrote, "We who were not in sympathy enjoyed the entire outcome."[53]

One Arkansas master played a procrastinating game with his slave. When the black man, Williamson Pease, suggested that he stay in the mines to earn enough to buy his freedom, his master countered with the proposal that this money be earned in San Francisco, where he alleged that wages were higher. Once in San Francisco, this master claimed that the city was not a good idea either and the slave was persuaded to go to New Orleans with him. It was not until they reached New Orleans that Pease decided he was being humbugged. He ran away to Canada.[54]

A young Missouri slave named Sam delayed his decision for freedom until he reached New York. He had gone with his master in 1849 from Missouri to the gold mines of California, where they evidently did quite well. Against Sam's wishes, they returned home in 1851, going by way of New York. This proved to be the slaveowner's undoing. In New York the young black was advised that he was legally free the moment he had set foot in California. Sam not only struck for freedom but also had his former master taken to court for $1,000 owed him as his share of his labor in California.[55]

Alvin Coffey is perhaps the best-known black who purchased his own and his family's freedom, but hundreds more accomplished this feat. One elderly black man named Isadore, who had gained his freedom before coming to California, went to work mining for Franklin Morse near Grass Valley in 1850. Morse recalled that the ex-slave "was saving most of the eight dollars per day wages I paid him to buy his wife's liberty."[56]

The conditions for freedom usually took one of two

forms: either a stated period of time during which the slaveowner would have the benefit of the slave's labor, or a specified amount of gold dug for the master. The latter was probably much preferred by blacks because a lucky strike could hasten the day of freedom. However, it is not known whether masters ever gave a choice of method to their slaves. There is a record of only one black who made up his own mind in the matter. He was Jack Marney, who dug one thousand dollars in gold for his master in 1849 and then simply left to join some Northern white miners a good distance away.[57]

Many slaves with hopes of freedom came by water routes to California, especially during the 1850s. William Ellis, a white Ohioan, met some of them boarding a ship that left New York for the gold fields.[58] A much larger group was seen on the *Isthmus* enroute from Panama. On that ship twenty-five slaves from Georgia and South Carolina were going with their masters and with the promise of freedom after two years' digging.[59] Still another group of slaves was promised that they would have half of their Saturday's earnings for a full year toward purchasing their freedom in California.[60] Daniel Langhorne, who came by boat from Panama with his brother and his master, a Dr. Langhorne from Virginia, did not wait to get to California to start earning his freedom money. He practiced barbering on board ship.[61] A black man named Bob came to the gold fields with his master's brother, William Marmaduke, and with the promise of freedom. A letter from Marmaduke to his wife back in Missouri suggests some of the problems freedom-seeking blacks had to face. He wrote:

> Bob is not entirely well as yet, but I have him hired out to cook at 5 dollars per day which in four days more he will have made enough to square all liabilities against him for the winter including doctor bills. I still hold it obligatory upon him to make $1000 for James then he can come and bring the same or stay in

> California—I will give him every chance I can and see that he is righted—and if he can do this and will not—he never shall have his freedom but if sick and cannot, I will bring him home at my own expense.

Marmaduke's final comment in this matter is worth mention. He added:

> I have told Bob this—and he will do his best to accomplish same—unless put astray by some of those mean Yankeys for which the country abounds.[62]

Health and natural hazards undoubtedly ended the dreams of freedom for many blacks in the new and uncertain mining environment. Tragedy struck one Negro named Cupid at Georgetown, just after he achieved his purchase of freedom. He was earning his first monies as a free man at mining when a river bank caved in and killed him.[63]

Some older slaves served out their last years of profitability for their masters in California. A Mississippi slaveowner told his fellow miner, the Reverend Daniel Woods, that he was going to give freedom papers to his elderly slave Allen. However, before he could put his intentions on paper, the master became deathly ill. The old slave, although in anguish over the prospects for his future, could not bring himself to speak about his freedom to his seriously sick master. Allen's travails ended when the sick Mississippian rallied enough to ask Reverend Woods to arrange for Allen's freedom papers. Woods later observed that this same slaveowner, who survived his illness, made no such commitment in regard to freedom papers for a young, powerfully built slave he owned.[64]

It is apparent that many slaveowners gained financially in arranging for a self-purchase condition. The exact amount of monies that flowed to their pockets cannot be computed, but there were estimates by contemporaries. The moderately antislavery editor of the *Grass Valley Telegraph* made inquiry into this matter in 1855 and concluded that in Nevada County alone there were fifty-four Negroes who had purchased their freedom and that the total value of their self-purchase came to $112,750. A historian of this period estimated that $750,000 was spent by California blacks to buy their freedom. This figure includes the cost of family purchase as well.[65]

California wealth gained by Kentucky-born Richard Oglesby paid for the freedom of a Kentucky black man who never saw California. Oglesby, who became governor of Illinois during the Civil War, told an audience that he started to become an antislavery man when he witnessed the brutal whipping of an old black man named Uncle Tim for whom he felt a deep affection. Years later, Oglesby went to California and did well enough to return to Kentucky and purchase that old man's freedom.[66]

Word of the self-emancipation-by-purchase program undertaken by so many blacks in California must have reached slaves back in the South. One wonders how many more hungered for this special opportunity provided by the gold rush but did not dare to ask for it or had asked and been refused.

During the early months of the gold rush, the Eastern press, and especially the antislavery press, reported all sorts of Southern projects to bring large groups of slaves to California. Such stories persisted even as late as 1852, when an ambitious proposal projected a colony as large as 2,000 slaves.[67] This project came on the heels of rumors that southern California might separate and become a new state. Southerners in the East misread the Californian's concern with this issue of separation as indicating an interest in a slave state south of the Tehachapi Mountain. This was far from the truth. Southern Californians were disgruntled with a taxation system that favored miners over agriculturalists, and they expressed this through a convention in 1851 that considered separation. The thought of creating an opening for slavery to come to the southern counties was never expressed.[68] None would resist such a possibility more than that influential group of Anglo-Saxons who years before the American conquest came to California and married into the native dark-skinned Spanish-Mexican aristocracy. They would scarcely encourage a system, based on color prejudice, that would blight the lives of their wives and children.

There were, however, a handful of slaveowners who did come to the mining counties with large numbers of slaves. One might be dubious about the report in 1850 that a Texas Ranger brought thirty-two slaves who were between forty and fifty years old to mine for him along the Sacramento River. It was also said that each slave dug between fifteen and twenty dollars a day and that they were quite contented.[69] Better documented is the venture of a Colonel William F. English, a Georgia planter, who sold out his plantation, outfitted himself in Philadelphia, and arrived in Nevada County in 1851. He set up his community on Kentucky Ridge near Rough and Ready and attempted quartz mining. This did not prove profitable, and Colonel English and his colleagues decided that it was financially more sound to turn their male slaves to placer mining and the women to washing. There does not seem to be any evidence of dissatisfaction by the slaves or reports of attempts to escape. Colonel English had a reputation as a kind master. In 1853 bandits killed the colonel and the colony disintegrated. Its black founders went to Grass Valley and Nevada City, where they continued their lives as free men.[70]

Another Southern colonel, Thomas Thorn, attempted something similar in Mariposa County. Thorn came from Texas with a group of slaves estimated to include as many as thirty. His popularity with his slaves was evidently not as high as that of Colonel English. While in Los Angeles, en route to the gold fields, several of his bondsmen attempted to escape. Some of them succeeded in the course of a near-riot. Two of them were caught and were terribly whipped two days in a row. A Los Angeles policeman named Purdy lost his job and was forced to leave town because he attempted to protect the runaways. Upon arriving in the southern mines, Thorn's group, according to one report, lost even more slaves as a result of the hostility of non-slaveholding miners, who drove them away. Evidently some blacks took advantage of this situation to keep moving, because Thorn's chattel holdings dropped to ten by 1850. A few years later a visitor described Thorn's slaves in terms of "unwavering fidelity," but this seems doubtful, since a neighbor described Mr. and Mrs. Thorn in 1854 as being quite ill with "nobody except the old darkey woman and her two daughters to serve up for the boarders." The Thorns were still living in Quartzburg, Mariposa County, but evidently were no longer mining. A curious last note on the fortunes of Thorn and his slaves is a freedom paper that Thorn made out for a Peter Green, which was executed before a Mariposa justice of the peace in August 1855, four months after the 1852 Fugitive Slave Law had expired.[71]

The experience of General Thomas Jefferson Green suggests that gold miners had little respect for those who arrogantly brought large numbers of slaves to mine. Green, a Mexican War general, came from Texas with about fifteen slaves and started mining along a third of a mile of the left bank of the Yuba River. He and his fellow Texans took up claims in the names of their slaves as well. Incensed miners objected to this violation of local miners' law but were rebuffed by the general. A Yuba miners' meeting was called for 29 July 1849, and a resolution was passed that no slaves or Negroes could make a claim on the Yuba. Plans were made to run the Texans and their slaves out of the area. That night the blacks left for parts unknown and the next morning the white Texans followed them. What happened to the blacks is not known, but many, if not all of them, may have found this event an opportunity to strike for freedom. Within the year Green had abandoned mining to become a state senator from Sacramento and the author of a tax on foreign miners.[72]

Those few Southerners who brought a considerable number of slaves to the gold fields were either ignorant of California's free-state constitution or, knowing of it, decided to take their chances. The vast majority, who felt little risk in bringing human property to California, came with two or three slaves. That some continued to come after California delcared itself a free state may have been due to their intention to grant freedom or to their belief that slavery would yet be supported by law in the state of California (or at least in a separated southern half of it). Why California remained a free state in spite of these hopes will be discussed in chapter 6.

In the early years of the gold rush there was a fragile and spotty democracy that prevailed between free black men and white men in the mines. It occasionally extended to the slave. Frederick Jackson Turner's descriptions of frontier conditions as a wellspring for democracy in America explain this momentary egalitarianism only in part. Men in the mines did face circumstances that muted their concerns about caste or class; but racism on frontiers was rarely totally absent. In the Turner model, frontiersmen were carving out communities that they planned to make into their permanent homes, while the miners of the early years of the gold rush rarely had permanent settlement in mind. White miners did not view their river- and gulch-side neighbors as potential lifetime acquaintances. Their nearly unanimous objective was to return home and resume their former lives, much wealthier than they were before. Men in this frame of mind did not worry too much about the social characteristics of their temporary environment or their self-image in it. Symptomatic of this attitude was the common observation that men who led the most conventional lives in their home states were known in California to gamble, drink, swear, and consort with women outside of the marriage bond. The preacher-turned-card-dealer was the favorite illustration of this phenomenon.

Material gain was, of course, the most important objective of the men of the Mother Lode population, and therein lies the explanation of the racial democracy that had its brief moments in the gold mine country. J. D. Borthwick, an Englishman who spent three years in the mines, came to this conclusion:

> In the mines the Americans seemed to exhibit more tolerance of negro blood than is usual in the states . . . owing partly to the exigencies of the unsettled state of society . . . and to the important fact that a nigger's dollars were as good as any other. . . . Those dollars . . . overcame all pre-existing false notions of dignity.

Borthwick's assumptions were borne out in Marysville's first saloon and gambling house. It advertised itself as welcoming all customers, "with no regard to distinction of color."[73]

In many tent restaurants and boardinghouses throughout the length and breadth of the northern and southern mines, both slave and free Negroes were in great demand as cooks. Cooking was often preferred as a more stable source of income than mining. It was a safer occupation for blacks, since whites would be less likely to harass anyone in this menial occupation. Many slaves were cooks because their masters were not doing well. In the case of George Murrell, his slave Rheubin's work as a cook paid for the board and lodging for both of them when they first arrived in San Francisco. Later, in the mining country, Murrell had Rheubin return to cooking because they were not succeeding at digging gold.[74]

That the Negro cook was much in demand was attested by Leonard Kip, who wrote:

> A Negro cook is one of the most independent men alive. Being a rather scarce article, he can act pretty much as he pleases . . . and he is allowed to enter into certain familiarities, which would ensure him a cowhiding in almost any other part of the globe.[75]

Some blacks set up their own boardinghouses and eateries. One observer thought that wherever there was a black or white miners' community of any size, a black boardinghouse or restaurant was nearly always in evidence.[76] While racial etiquette was somewhat unevenly relaxed in the frontier environment, a black man could be fairly certain of his self-respect in a black-operated restaurant.

The popularity of black restaurants rested on good cooking and cheaper prices. One enterprising black man regularly purchased the oxtails from a camp butcher at Hawkins' Bar on the Tuolumne River and developed a very successful business. The flavor of his meals gave him a local reputation as a first-rate "dabster."[77] The best known of Negro eateries in the gold mines was near Foster's Bar, down the Yuba River from Downieville on the way to Marysville. It was called "Negro Tent." The owner's business was so successful on this well-traveled route that he eventually put up a comfortable cabin. Still the place continued to be called "Negro" or "Nigger Tent." The cabin restaurant was to pass through several hands in the decades that followed, but the name never changed.[78]

An incident involving a successful black-owned boardinghouse on the Yuba River says much about life in the mines as well as something about its black owners. A white miner, who had fallen on hard times, commented on his difficulties to his black hosts while finishing his meal at their establishment. To his astonishment they offered him work at a dollar an hour and board. Without knowing what the work was, he eagerly accepted the offer. When informed that they wanted him as a barber, he was flabbergasted. When they further informed him that he had to clean himself up so that "you can mix with decent colored people and not give them cause to complain that we keep dirty white folks about the house," he fled.[79]

Some black men took in laundry as a side line. This extra

work was most common among Negroes who were trying to purchase freedom for themselves or their families. Many white miners would not take time from mining to wash their own clothes. This made laundering an essential business in the mines and the launderer much in demand. One highly independent black man ran a laundry in Stoutenburgh, near Murphys in Calaveras County. When the white miners came to get their shirts, they were told by this "character" to pick them out of the pile themselves.[80]

Foreshadowing the prominence of Negroes as cooks and stewards in the Bay and river transportation business is the case of the sixty-five-ton steamer *Lawrence*. This ship had been dismantled in Massachusetts by a white New Bedford company of gold seekers in December 1849 and brought to California, where it was reassembled. Launched on the Sacramento River, the *Lawrence* was the first steamer to carry freight and passengers between Sacramento and Marysville on a regular basis. In California the ownership was held by four stockholders, two of whom were black. These two black men were also the cook and steward of the *Lawrence*. The steamer was most profitable, and it ran for several years. Its lucrative career was ended suddenly by a snag on a bar on the upper Yuba.[81]

A rather small group of blacks went into farming. Some were employed by white men who chose to raise cattle instead of mine gold. At least one black in Yolo County was an independent farmer and cattle-raiser. While there was very little industrial activity in the mining counties in the early years, one Southerner is noted as working a gravel pit with slaves.[82]

Here and there in the mining country black men could be found in unusual occupations. A Methodist preacher who wished to preach to a mining community on the south fork of the American River hired a black man to act as his bell-ringer for the event. This Negro performed his task by going to all the saloons and streets of the area. A popular pastime in the early 1850s in California was bull-fighting, a favorite with the Latin-Americans. In Nevada City, in 1851, a black man was seen fighting the bulls. A familiar sight to spectators was the Negro jockey in the Grass Valley horse races.[83]

In the nearly all-male society of the mines, card-playing and drinking, as well as just sitting around the local stores, were major pastimes when men were not at work panning or digging. In spite of the beauties of the mountain environment, miners suffered a great deal of boredom, especially in bad weather. William C. Ellis, who had a store near Bidwell's Bar on the Feather River, wrote home, during a rainy day in November 1851, that a group of men were sitting around the fire in his store singing or talking and in the midst of them "sets a black man smoking his segar."[84] The only thing missing in this scene is a game of cards. In the mines equality reigned when it came to card-playing. When Charles De Long was campaigning for office in Yuba County, he came to a miner's tent where he found a card game in progress with both white and black players.[85] The participation of black men in such games was very much a part of the mining scene.

What may have been the longest-playing interracial poker game in the northern mines took place near Fort John between members of the Bowen company, one of whom was black, and their neighbors, some of whom were white and some black. The games went on from 1852 to at least 1855; at times they were played in the white quarters, perhaps more often in the black quarters. A group of white troublemakers, mentioned earlier, brought these games to an end.[86]

This saloon and card-playing democracy had some of the usual explosive consequences. At Fort John, fighting between black and white gamblers was a common occurrence. In one instance, a white man killed a black named Henry Keaton. Keaton was considered such a troublemaker by members of his own race that they were uninterested in burying him. The white Bowen family took on that responsibility.[87] Alcohol too made its contribution to mayhem. Near Marysville, a white man and a black man had been drinking together, and the drunken white man accused the black of stealing something from him. In the course of the quarrel, the white man broke a gun over the black man's head and the next day killed him in his own cabin.[88] It is not known if blacks and whites shared the services of white prostitutes, but it is certain that both sought out black ones. This at times led to conflicts. In Grass Valley a mulatto woman named Priscilla had a black lover as well as a white one. One night when the white man arrived at the house of prostitution, he found the black already there. In a fit of rage he killed him. The white man went free because there were no white witnesses to the murder.[89]

Another source of conflict between white and black was the temporary weakening of racist etiquette. In the early days of the gold rush, some black men reached the point where they refused anything less than relationships that respected their dignity as men. Alvin Coffey, the ex-slave previously mentioned, recalled that it was in California that he first talked back to a white man.[90] Some had to pay a price for their assertion of manhood. A white forty-niner noted in his log, "A niggro was whipped for fighting his master pretty bad."[91] Another white observer of these early days recalled being present during a quarrel between a white and a black man in a mining-camp store. The black punched the white in the face, and a general fight ensued. White observers who favored the white man interfered and overpowered the black man. They held an impromptu court and sentenced him to one hundred lashes on his bare back. They continued this the next day, but, when the black man fainted, a New Englander interceded and obtained agreement to halt the savage proceedings on the condition that the black man leave the county.[92]

In 1849, the second year of the gold rush, the population of the Sierra Mother Lode counties swelled from hundreds to more than 40,000. By 1852, the number of miners had increased to 100,000. Of these thousands of gold seekers, a large number failed, not unexpectedly, and under the frontier conditions, those who failed began to prey upon those who succeeded. Crime became a prominent feature of mining life. While black men were more often victim than victimizer in these crimes, there were blacks who did engage in criminal ventures. A black man involuntarily helped in the renaming of Dry Diggings (Placerville) to Hangtown, a name it held for several years because of the great number of summary executions that occurred there. This Negro, a cook, who, according to the recorder of the event, was "a nice chap," got drunk and stole $3,000 worth of his employer's gold. He took some of this gold to town to gamble, and there his employer apprehended him. The black man tried to conceal the gold, but it fell through his pocket to the floor. He offered to take his employer to where he had hidden the balance of the gold in return for avoiding punishment. This he did, but the more drunken miners in the crowd were successful in calling for his hanging. Prejudice appears to have been an important ingredient in this action as well as in Hangtown's first notorious hanging. At that time two Frenchmen and a Chileno were charged with robbery and attempted murder. They could not speak English, yet they were denied an interpreter to state their case to another drunken mob, who even threatened to hang their one defender, Edward G. Buffum, the abolitionist's son.[93]

Dame Shirley, whose letters have become a gold rush classic, told a sad tale about her former black cook. Some months after he left her employ, he was charged with having murdered his new employer. The charge was that he had killed for the man's money, and, as Dame Shirley puts it, "He was the last one anybody would have suspected capable of such an act." He was sentenced to be hanged. All efforts to make him confess his guilt failed, and he went calmly to his death.[94]

On the balance sheet of reported crime, blacks were

more often victimized than whites. Press accounts range from the "poor colored man" robbed of $80 by a woman to the black man robbed and murdered for three thousand dollars. A New York black was robbed and murdered for the $150 he was carrying. Black and white men were murdered at times without apparent motive. For instance, one paper briefly noted:

> On Tuesday night, Edward Hoyt was delivered by Constable Smith of Campo Seco to the custody of the sheriff on a charge of murder, committed on the person of a negro known as Calaveras Bill, at Poverty Bar, in this county.

Or in another paper:

> Bodies of two men found near Miner's Ranch this side of Bidwell's Bar. . . . The other body was that of a black man, whose name we did not learn.[95]

During California's first attempted stagecoach holdup between Camptonville and Marysville, a black woman, Mrs. Tilghman, the wife of a Marysville barber, was killed. The robbers, the notorious Tom Bell gang, sought the strongbox carried by the stagecoach, which contained gold valued in various reports at $35,000 to $100,000. Mrs. Tilghman rode on an outside back seat of the stage with several Chinese. The drivers and other passengers successfully fought off the Bell gang and saved the strongbox but not before several were wounded and Mrs. Tilghman killed. An interesting aside to this story is that Joseph Henry Jackson, who wrote the most popularly read account of the Tom Bell gang and this robbery, was evidently unaware that Mrs. Tilghman was a black woman.[96]

One murder with bizarre ingredients took place in Calaveras County. A man who had been introduced around as the brother of Jefferson Davis, then senator from Mississippi, had arrogantly entered the home of a black barber while reportedly drunk. There he proceeded to address the barber's wife in an insulting manner. The presumption here is that this Southerner acted as he might have back in the South, where white men took sexual liberties with black women who were powerless to protest. The black barber then informed the Southerner that if he did not leave the house he would be thrown out. Thereupon the proud Southerner, saying, "No white man ever talked that way to me and lived," produced a pistol and shot the black man to death in his own home. An outraged local white citizenry caught Jefferson Davis's supposed brother. He was held in the Jackson jail and not, as one observer noted, "shot, hanged, nor burnt." A portion of the local citizenry was ready to give him summary justice, but with the collusion of the sheriff, some miners from Georgia spirited him away from his just deserts. A contemporary paper noted that, "owing to informality, no bill was found against the prisoner."[97]

When blacks participated in gang crime, they were rarely, if ever, members of all-black gangs. On the Nevada City road a teamster was robbed by bandits, two blacks and one white. In another case two travelers on the road between Angels Camp and Murphys were accosted by another band of three, two black and one Latin-American, who, however, lost their nerve and let the intended victims escape. In Stockton, a Latin-American and a Negro formed a partnership in stealing goods from loaded wagons and were nearly lynched for their pains. A reported "all-Negro" band that robbed a butcher at Rough and Ready turned out to be three white men who had disguised themselves.[98] Partnership in crime of another sort was noted in the journal of Goldsborough Bruff. With sadness he reported that Andy, a black man who had shown him kindnesses when he was ill, had gone off with several white cohorts and raped an Indian woman. A less successful attempt at rape in Stockton by three Negroes resulted in a public lashing. In some parts of the United States this rape attempt would have resulted in a lynching. The fact that their lives were spared may have been a kind of reverse race prejudice. The woman involved was a Chilean.[99]

The relationship between black men and Indians is not clear, since the evidence is fragmentary. In general it seems that the California Indian related to black men as he would to white men. The Indian saw the Negro in terms of the specific situation. Role, not color, was of first importance. The roles that black men played in their relationships with Indians were simply the functions of their needs in this primitive environment. In this overwhelmingly male environment blacks had the same sexual needs and frustrations as white men and sought satisfaction in the same ways. Indian women were a source of sexual release for white and black men in the mines. Like many whites, some blacks lived with Indian women in a common-law relationship. At times this led to difficulties. A black man named Leroy, who had isolated himself in Northern California and lived with an Indian woman, refused to leave when she asked him to go. As a member of the Wintoon tribe that lived along the Mad River, she called upon two men of her tribe to help her. In the ensuing struggle, the badly wounded Leroy killed the two Indians and made his way back to a white community. The whites took up his cause and a general Indian-white war, called the Wintoon War, resulted.[100] In another case an Indian woman who preferred to live with a black man was killed by her enraged husband.[101]

The search for relationships with Indian women brought grief to other black men. Henry Freeman lost his life in Shasta City this way. He had asked an Indian to get an Indian woman for him and struck the red man when he refused. In turn the Indian stabbed him mortally. Near Jamestown, a huge gathering of Indians who had come together for social and ceremonial purposes attracted a group of blacks. All might have gone well, but one Negro erred in making unsolicited advances to an Indian woman who happened to be the wife of one of the leaders. In the melee that resulted, arrows and bullets flew. Many were hurt and, according to one report, a black man who had nothing to do with provoking the disturbance had a third of his shin bone shot away.[102]

Indians killed and wounded blacks in situations where the blacks were closely identified with white men. As the gold rush got underway, many Indians fought guerrilla warfare against the white invaders, who were separating them from their lifelong habitat. One Negro was wounded by an Indian while on guard duty at a trading post. On the Merced River, five men were killed by Indians; one victim had been the slave of one of the dead white men.[103]

In the uneven struggle between Indians and whites, there were some pursuit-and-vengeance posses organized by the whites that included blacks. Andy, the black friend of Goldsborough Bruff, was a favorite topic of conversation among his white associates for his daring in fighting Indians. From Northern California, where many bloody battles between whites and Indians took place, it was once reported that thirty Indians had been killed, and, in the words of the press:

> This afternoon the party reached town and paraded through the streets . . . each of the party consisting of 16 whites, two Indians and a negro, having a bow and a quiver of arrows, and the muzzle of his gun decorated with a scalp taken from the enemy.[104]

Some of the Indian-Negro contacts were of a more peaceful sort. The law forbade the selling of whiskey to Indians, but this was widely violated. A Negro named James Coran was caught and arrested for this offense. Many Indians had been servants for the dominant races even before the North American conquest of California; here and there they sometimes were seen working as servants for black men. One was seen taking care of his inebriated black employer as they left a mining-town bar in Grass Valley.[105]

Negroes and Mexicans often shared recreation and social activities in the mining counties. In Auburn, the Mexicans established a dance hall which blacks frequented. At times relations between these people of color did not run smoothly. It was in the Auburn dance hall that a Mexican woman had a quarrel with her black dancing partner, who was evidently also her lover, and stabbed him.[106]

Negro-Chinese relations in the gold mining environment were generally congenial. Near Lancha Plana, in Amador County, a black community and a Chinese community worked alongside one another at mining and trading without any recorded friction. Individual blacks as well as black mining groups worked near Chinese throughout the northern and southern mines without any reported tensions. There were, of course, exceptions to this rule. In 1853 near Sonora, there was a bitter battle between ten black men and one hundred Chinese over an unreported issue. In Auburn, a black man, who was described by his black neighbors as a "bad nigger," killed a Chinese man. Ironically, he was not prosecuted because the California testimony laws forbade the use of nonwhite testimony, and no white person was witness to the killing.[107]

The isolation of the mining frontier was especially attractive to interracially married couples. The black husband-white wife marriage occurred as often as the white husband-black wife. In most cases the white wife was from Europe or the British Isles. The American white wife was usually a Southern woman. In the latter cases, the couples probably were similar to those sometimes found in the remote rural regions of the slave states. The same phenomenon has been noted in the western states of the upper Mississippi Valley. The geographical location of these families in the California census suggests that they sought isolation from whites. At times these couples sought the nearness of Chinese mining communities, where they and their children would be least likely to be harassed.[108]

Examples of this kind of interracial marriage were found in El Dorado and Tuolumne counties by 1860. Three mixed-marriage families were living then in close proximity in Salmon Falls, El Dorado County. In Tuolumne County, in Sonora and Jamestown townships, there were several more mixed marriages. In the Moss family, Mrs. Moss was an Irishwoman. The Lapsleys were both from Ohio; the husband was white. In the case of the Hansons of Jamestown, the husband was born in Denmark. Milton Dappin was from Virginia and his black wife was from Louisiana. Dappin worked as a quartz miner, as did most of these mixed-marriage husbands. Dappin probably had congenial working conditions, since the work force he was associated with was overwhelmingly English and Northern-born.[109]

The backgrounds of these interracial marriages in the nineteenth century are usually obscured by the anonymity that the parties involved wished to maintain. But one is illuminated as a result of a litigation after the Civil War. Richard Pearson, a white Louisianan, bought an eighteen-year-old black girl in North Carolina in 1848 and brought her with him to Missouri. Her name was Laura and she was described as "mulatto." A few years later he married a white woman in Missouri, but this was a brief marriage. In 1853, he divorced his wife and left for Utah, taking along his slave, Laura, and his daughter by her. In Utah, Pearson married Laura, and she thereby became a free woman according to Utah law.

The Pearson family then proceeded to California, where they settled in 1855 in Colusa County, an overwhelmingly agricultural county as well as one of the most sparsely settled areas in Northern California. Here he went into farming. By 1865 the family had five children. When he died in 1865, however, his ex-wife sued for his property, claiming that Laura Pearson had been a slave before the Civil War and therefore was not entitled to the estate. The courts ruled in favor of Laura Pearson.[110]

In their leisure time blacks were occasionally the participants or performers in gatherings that called for music or dancing. In Grass Valley, a black woman provided a most unusual musical event for a mining community. She gave public concerts on the piano, for which she charged fifty cents admission.[111] On festive occasions such as Independence Day, which in the mines was always a time for gala celebration, there was feasting and dancing. "Black Dave" (or "Dan") was evidently the only musician in Weaverville in 1851, and his fiddle was much in demand. On the Fourth of July, Weavervillians danced in the streets to Black Dan's music, and on New Year's Eve it was again Dan who provided the music for the festivities.[112] Frederick Windeler noted in his journal that the musical entertainment in his camp, near Indian Bar in Tuolumne County, was provided by a black cook named Joe. One October evening Joe brought a black friend of his into camp, and they

> came with fiddle, accordian and one took two spoons instead of bones, had songs, dances and fun, also pie and brandy.

Joe was also the central figure on the Fourth of July, presiding over "sardines, lobsters, oysters and champagne."[113]

Christmas was a most convivial event for a group of blacks and whites from Massachusetts who were camped along the Tuolumne River in 1849. William Miller and his associate Daniels were invited by their Negro neighbor, William Thompson, for Christmas dinner. Miller, Daniels, and their black partner William Henry Garrison joined Thompson in what Miller described as a "splendid" dinner. Garrison had brought his fiddle along, and they all danced till the late hours. They interrupted this interracial dancing party only once, and that was for the purpose of having a snack in the firelit darkness. The party had a sequel on New Year's Day, when the Garrison-Miller group had a special dinner for the occasion. This was highlighted by an apple pudding that Garrison made and that Miller joyously

employed Chinese workers. There were years when this mine took out over half a million dollars in gold. A Merced newspaper said of Rodgers that "there is no better mining man in the State."[119]

While many Negroes remained in the mining counties as the decade of the fifties drew to a close, a few of them going into agriculture, many others drifted with the white population toward the towns and cities of northern California. There they found hundreds of blacks who had decided during the early days of the gold rush to make their living, and they hoped, their fortunes, in an urban setting.

4 In the Cities

Five years before the gold rush, one of the leading residents of the city-village of San Francisco was the previously mentioned Alexander Leidesdorff. Before the American occupation of California this energetic businessman of Danish-African ancestry achieved prominence as one of San Francisco's most important business leaders as well as one of its central political figures. He remained so during the American occupation of California. His early death deprived history of the phenomenon of a man with African roots taking what would have undoubtedly been a position of great prominence in a major American city.

Leidesdorff died in May 1848, when the gold rush had barely begun. Within months after his death, San Francisco became the point of arrival for hundreds of gold seekers as well as the point of departure for the Mother Lode. This stream of human beings included many men of color from Chile, Peru, and Mexico. It also included scores of black seamen from the United States. Most of them were prospectors, but a small and growing number chose to seek their fortunes in San Francisco, Sacramento, and elsewhere in northern California. The black businessmen who came after Leidesdorff never achieved his stature, but they were known as Negroes and had to face many hardships that never troubled him. Still, large numbers of them did well.

During the first few years of the gold rush, there was little that was permanent or stable in the only two real California cities—San Francisco and Sacramento. People moved from place to place. Both cities suffered a number of serious fires. Sacramento was, in addition, plagued by disastrous floods. Men went back and forth between these two cities and the rivers and mountains of the Mother Lode counties. Organized urban life was a compromise between habits formed in the Eastern states and the temptations of a bustling mining frontier. Food-serving, drinking, and gambling establishments led the field in high visibility and profit. Churches and schools were not organized until later.

Blacks quickly felt the instability of urban life in the West. As early as December 1849, the first attempt at black community organization in San Francisco took place. By that date, a group of thirty-seven Negroes, mostly from New England, had organized a Mutual Benefit and Relief Society and drawn up a constitution. The Society was created to help black newcomers as well as the regular membership. An early public notice of the group suggests that the members wanted to encourage more New England blacks to come to California. This notice appeared in the Boston-based abolitionist *Liberator*. It said invitingly that "We are making from one hundred to three hundred dollars per month" and that "there are colored people in San Francisco."[1]

Like that of white organizations in those early frenzied years, the membership of the Mutual Benefit and Relief Society was unstable. Nothing is now known of its subsequent activities, if there were any. Its members did not seem to remain in San Francisco very long. Few of them gained any mention in the later years of the decade. Undoubtedly most of them, like most other Californians, were swept up by the excitement of gold in the mountains. Negro organizations in both Sacramento and San Francisco were transitory. Reverend Darius Stokes, a black Baltimorean who came early to gold rush California, noted that it was well-nigh impossible to organize a black Methodist church in Sacramento, because, as he lamented, "the few of our brethren who were here, were rushing too madly on in pursuit of mammon."[2]

In these first years of San Francisco's life as a gold rush center, black men were involved in its economic growth, especially in the service occupations. A ship's passenger, arriving at Clark's Point on the Bay, might have been met by a launch owned by a black man offering to take him and his luggage to the shore. On shore he could have encountered another black, who would offer to carry his luggage to his destination in town. When he wished to dine, he could have gone to black Uncle Peter's place on Pacific and Powell streets, where Reverend Williams, a pioneer preacher, took many of his meals. If the traveler wanted a haircut, there were many black barbers to serve him in San Francisco. If he had gone to the famed El Dorado Saloon and gambling house, he would have seen a black porter who was also, according to one observer, serving as cashier. Had the new arrival to San Francisco come on a public holiday, he would have seen a black bell-ringer shouting the news of a bull fight scheduled to enliven the festive occasion.[3]

Blacks were most prominent in San Francisco and Sacramento in the culinary occupations. In 1850 there were at least sixty-two Negro cooks in Sacramento and probably that many or more in San Francisco, although its census returns have been lost. The presence and success of the black cook in San Francisco is beyond doubt. A ship's captain in search of a cook for his crew offered a San Francisco black a position at ten dollars a day. The man laughed and countered by offering the captain a job as cook in *his* restaurant for *twenty* dollars a day.[4]

One of San Francisco's earliest restaurants was the Battery House on Battery Street. It was set up as a side business by two New Yorkers before they went off to the mines. The restaurant, which they anticipated would earn $100 per day, depended on the cooking skills of two black members of their New York company.[5]

In both San Francisco and Sacramento by 1852 the occupation of cook stood at the top of the list of skilled-work classifications for blacks. Of the 464 blacks in San Francisco in 1852, 67 were cooks. Fifty-three of these were American-born and the rest came chiefly from the West Indies. There were 51 black cooks in Sacramento, of whom

43 were from the United States, out of a total of 338 black Sacramentans. In both cities, black stewards and barbers were the next most prominent occupation in the skilled fields. There were 22 black stewards and 18 black barbers in San Francisco in 1852, while Sacramento had 8 stewards and 23 barbers.[6]

Some Negroes arrived in California with little or no money left in their pockets. For some the first means of livelihood in the city was bootblacking. Mifflin W. Gibbs had only ten cents left when he arrived in San Francisco in 1850. He was offered a job as a carpenter, but the employees of his prospective employer told their boss they would strike if a black were hired. Gibbs then turned to bootblacking. In his bootblacking days Gibbs also had part-time employment with the Frémont family.[7] While bootblacking was menial in social status, it was quite remunerative. Working in front of the major hotels and gambling houses, a bootblack could make as much as ten to fifteen dollars a day. In this business, blacks had competition in San Francisco from an unusual quarter. Many Frenchmen were bootblacks in these early years. One might even see at times a Frenchman shining the shoes of a black man. Many of the French who came to the gold rush had been involved in the ill-fated 1848 French revolution and were as much in need of funds as black men. They also seemed less concerned than other whites about doing the same kind of work as blacks. Contemporary reportage reveals that bootblacks in San Francisco were either Negroes or Frenchmen.[8]

A few black men owned their own businesses in San Francisco by 1850. When Gibbs first landed there, he went to a black-owned boardinghouse on Kearny Street, possibly the establishment owned by Sully Cox and Aaron White. The local press described it as a "rendezvous for Negroes." It could also have been the Harper and West Hotel, which was also on Kearny Street. William H. Harper, one of the black owners, had a background of antislavery activities in the East which would have made him an interesting host for Gibbs.[9] Not far from this boardinghouse, a black named John Ross had opened by the mid-1850s, a used-goods business on Pacific Street just below Kearny, variously called Ross's Exchange and Philadelphia House. In 1851, a New Bedford Negro, James P. Dyer, founded one of the first soap factories in San Francisco. In 1856 he sold it to the white Swain family, who were of the antislavery persuasion and probably had known Dyer in New England. He continued to work for the Swains as a soap maker until 1859, when again he opened his own soap factory, calling it by the original's name, the New England Soap Factory.[10]

In the first half of the 1850s, more blacks started businesses in San Francisco. Gibbs entered a partnership in a clothing store with Peter Lester, a fellow Philadelphian and a skilled bootmaker. The two of them later opened the Pioneer Boot and Shoe Emporium, which they ran successfully until they both left San Francisco in 1858. Their success in this business reached the notice of their Eastern antislavery associates, and several abolitionist papers pointed with pride to Gibbs and Lester in their columns. The *Pennsylvania Freeman* editor wrote that they should be an example to "all colored men." Gibbs and Lester had been examples in other ways as well. Both had been officers of an antislavery convention in Philadelphia in the fall of 1848.[11]

Other black men in San Francisco also did well. Henry Cornish opened a second-hand furniture and clothing store on Battery Street. George Washington Dennis, an ex-slave, operated a highly successful livery business in the city. Both of these men were leaders in the black community and were to become activists in the causes of their people in California.[12]

Blacks continued in California an East Coast tradition of working in the maritime occupations. Black men and women worked as waiters, porters, and stewards on the ever-growing water traffic on the Bay and the major rivers that brought ships to and from San Francisco, Sacramento, Stockton, and Marysville. Some of these men became as well-known among whites as they were in the black urban communities. Henry M. Collins had been a river man on the Ohio before he went to California. Soon after his arrival in 1852, he became a steward on the *Comanche.* He later worked on other ships traveling the inland waters. He also applied a knowledge of real-estate investment obtained in Pittsburgh to San Francisco real estate and became one of the wealthiest of the state's black leaders. Virginia-born William H. Yates, who arrived in California in 1851, used his hotel experience to obtain employment as a steward on Bay and river boats. When the very elegant *Chrysopolis* was launched into the Bay luxury traffic, Yates became its steward. Both Collins and Yates, due to the nature of their employment, became key links between the various black communities in northern California.[13]

Some of the banking houses employed Negroes as trusted porters. William Tecumseh Sherman, then a California banker, remembered Henry Sampson, an ex-slave, who worked at his bank as a porter. While on the job, Sampson learned to read and write and thereby improved his income. Nelson Cook, a black New Yorker, worked for the bankers Drexel, Sather, and Church.[14]

Many blacks were employed in a variety of menial occupations. Among such tasks, whitewashing seems to have been fairly well paid and employed a considerable number. At least one black had his own Bay fishing sloop. Another performed the duties of a town crier and was observed calling out to the populace about a lost child.[15]

In July 1853, a group of black leaders opened the San Francisco Atheneum in a two-story house at 273 Washington Street. The first floor was called the Atheneum Saloon and the second floor, the Atheneum Institute. The Atheneum became the means by which the black working class and the black middle class and its ideological leaders came together to plan for the needs of black people. The saloon was managed by Monroe Taylor and James Riker, the latter a New Yorker. According to her biographer, Mary Ellen Pleasants (Mammy Pleasants), a Negro boardinghousekeeper and businesswoman, was one of the financial backers of the saloon. There throughout the 1850s black men came for social gatherings, drinking, and cardplaying. Dances too probably took place there.[16]

The Institute on the second floor was a center for the intellectual life of the black community of San Francisco. Its leadership was a blend of New England, New York, and Philadelphia blacks, all very able men who were devoted to the struggles of the Negro, whether slave or free. Its first president was Jacob Francis, a businessman. The Institute's second most important official was William H. Newby, corresponding secretary. Both had strong personalities and Eastern antislavery backgrounds. They, along with J. H. Townsend, Mifflin W. Gibbs, James R. Starkey, W. H. Harper, and E. R. Johnson, all of whom had been involved in antislavery work in the East, established the Institute. The Philadelphia group wished to recreate with the Atheneum something similar to the black cultural organization they had known in the East called the Philadelphia Library Company.[17]

Within a year they had made considerable progress. Secretary Starkey reported at an anniversary meeting that they were preparing to incorporate and that their library already had eight hundred books. They had a dues-paying membership of eighty-five and had raised the $2,000 needed for their library and reading room. Starkey reported that $1,800 had been contributed by prominent white businessmen in San Francisco. Among them were members of the banking firms of Flint, Peabody, and Company and Palmer, Cook, and Company as well as the book-store owners Le Count and Strong. The *Daily Alta California* reported their call for books, periodicals, "statistical information in print," and "curious specimens of minerals, animals or vegetables."

They set up collection agencies at places of business where Atheneum leaders worked and announced that all items "will be thankfully received at the St. Charles [hotel], on Kearny Street, kept by Mr. Walker, or the City Baths, on Commercial Street, kept by A. B. Dennison, or Gibbs & Lester's boot store under the California Exchange."[18]

It was the Atheneum Institute leadership, especially William Newby and Jonas Townsend, who urged blacks to organize their own newspaper. Townsend's advice came from his experience in editing a Negro newspaper in New York. The *Mirror of the Times*, the result of their zeal, did not appear until 1856, when a wider organization of the black community in the West was achieved.[19]

Unfortunately, no minutes of the Atheneum's meetings survive to give some idea of their debates and deliberations. But it is evident that the Institute's membership was interested in the questions that concerned blacks nationally. In the middle of the 1850s, black abolitionists in the East were giving serious consideration to political action, a policy which William Lloyd Garrison, the white abolitionist, rejected and one toward which Frederick Douglass was moving. As elsewhere, the California leadership was not of one mind on this matter. To sharpen their thinking, the Atheneum Institute sponsored a debate among their membership "on the merits of the controversy between the old antislavery party and the Liberty Party."[20]

Undoubtedly tensions existed between the Atheneum Institute and the Atheneum Saloon. Given the contrast in backgrounds of blacks who used the library on the second floor and those who visited the bar downstairs, some strains must have been felt. Many of the men who passed the bar on their way to the library had associations with the abolitionist movement with its strong temperance sentiments. Furthermore, these men were very sensitive to the public image of the black man and repeatedly commented on the need for blacks to be always on their best behavior. Gambling was also anathema to their temperament, and from time to time the Atheneum Saloon appeared in the local press as subject to police action in this regard. By the end of 1857, the Institute appears to have left the second floor of the Atheneum. New owners of the saloon announced that the second floor would be fitted up "in style for parties and concerts." This suggests that the Institute and Library had moved elsewhere.[21]

San Francisco Negroes also brought one of their Eastern fraternal orders to the Pacific coast. Black Masonry had been a part of black community life in the Eastern free states ever since the American Revolution. Many Negro leaders who had been active members of their black Masonic groups came to California in the gold rush. On 17 June 1854 the first of the Negro Masonic lodges was organized in the city. Before the decade was out other lodges were organized in San Francisco as well as in various other communities of northern California.[22]

In the same year that the first California black Masonic group was organized, the Atheneum Institute gave a proud report of the accomplishments of the Negro community. It claimed that blacks in San Francisco owned two joint-stock companies with a combined capital of $16,000, four boot and shoe stores, four clothing stores, eight express and job wagons, two furniture stores, twelve public houses, two restaurants, two billiard saloons, sixteen barber shops, two bathhouses, one reading room and library with eight hundred volumes, one Masonic lodge, and one brass band. The Institute also reported 100 mechanics, 20 draymen, 100 porters in banking and commission houses, 150 stewards, 300 waiters, and 200 cooks.[23]

This Atheneum Institute Report, published by the prestigious and sometimes friendly *Alta*, was more than a mid-decade inventory of achievements; it was also an appeal. The report concluded with comment about the legal discriminations against blacks that was meant for white people to ponder:

> The laws that are a shield to the white man, defending him and securing his rights, making him a freeman and a sovereign, and giving him an education, a home and nationality, . . . [are] a sword to the colored man cutting him off from the inalienable rights of self-government, and bearing witness, and making him a stranger in the land of his fathers. . . . That such social and political restrictions must have a demoralizing tendency, is perfectly clear, yet the great majority of the colored people in San Francisco are industrious and engaged in those manual and mechanical labors, which have a strong influence to preserve the hope, self-reliance and morality of the laborer.[24]

The small black population of San Francisco grew with the city. During the first half of the gold rush decade the black community clung to the oldest part of the city, near and along the wharves, and expanded slowly from there. On the shoreline, the most prominent landmark was Clark's Point, where, in 1849, Battery Street met Broadway. In the years that followed, Clark's Point was graded away, but the area retained the name for many years. Between the Point and Telegraph Hill a mixed community of color developed. The side of Telegraph Hill that sloped toward Broadway was called "Chili Hill" in 1850. Many whites also lived there, but it was most widely known as the residential area of Negroes and Latin-Americans. Out of the proximity of these people of color grew a shared social life, especially between the seafaring men and the lowest income groups of both peoples. Much of this contact was informal and casual, but some was organized. In 1854, during the pre-Christmas season, Negroes and Mexicans cooperated in organizing a masquerade ball.[25] On a daily basis, life was shared in tents and shacks, saloons, hotels, and gambling houses located on Broadway and spreading west to Kearny and south on Kearny to Pacific and Jackson streets. In old San Francisco these establishments were heavily frequented by Negroes, Mexicans, and Chilenos. In these humble places people of color ate, drank, danced, gambled, and fought with each other. One case of intermarriage between a Mexican woman and a black man was reported in 1852; other such marriages undoubtedly took place.

Segregation laws did not create this community. It was simply a less expensive area in which the poorest of all colors, not excluding whites, tended to concentrate. Another section remarkable for its mixture of peoples, a few miles west of Clark's Point, was Washerwoman's Bay. Here on sunny days came the washermen and laundresses of early San Francisco, many of them black, along with family members of all races, to scrub the week's wash. This pond, which does not exist today, was between Franklin, Octavia, Filbert, and Lombard streets. Some contemporaries found these interracial scenes of the poor a sign of degradation, while others found amusement in them. One journalist was quite taken by the sight of a Chinese man walking along and singing "Carry me back to old Virginny."[26]

Cultural integration did not keep in stride with residential integration in another situation. A black woman, Mary Alexander, who had to work late at night at washing to make a living, had a habit of singing plantation songs while at her labors. Her white neighbor, John Loan, who preferred operatic music, took exception to her late-night singing and brought her to court. The court, impressed with Mary Alexander's references, discharged the case, but Mary was advised to expand her repertoire into the operatic areas.[27]

The relationship between blacks and the ever-growing Chinese minority in the city was apparently friendly. William Newby, one of the city's best known black leaders, wrote to Frederick Douglass that the Chinese were the most mistreated group in the state and that blacks were the only people who did not abuse them.[28] Both shared with the Indian the same civil rights disabilities, in that they could not vote and, more importantly, could not testify in their own or anybody else's defense in the California courts.

By the end of the decade, there were Negroes of sufficient affluence to employ Chinese domestics in their own homes. As can be guessed, they did not live in the areas densely populated by people of color. Two such black families were the Charles Merciers and the James Sullivans who lived in the Fourth Ward, which had Washington Square in its center and was middle-class in character. Mercier was a successful barber from Louisiana, and Sullivan, a Virginian, had real estate valued at three thousand dollars.[29]

From time to time in this decade before the Civil War, black men were recorded as being patients in City Hospital. It is also worth noting that white doctors and dentists advertised themselves in the city's Negro newspaper.[30]

Although little is known about the daily lives of the black minority in San Francisco in those early days, an exceptional event occasionally provides some details. For instance, a fire on Stockton Street in a house that was generally inhabited by Negroes resulted in the death of a white child, which brought out the fact that the child was the daughter of a white prostitute who employed black baby-sitters. In another case the press reported a street scene in which a black woman was struggling with a little girl much lighter in color than herself. Bystanders interferred but were told by the black woman that she was trying to get the child, her daughter, to return to school, from which she was playing truant. They were taken to the stationhouse, where the situation was not settled until the child's Italian father appeared. It is probable that an eleven-year-old white boy never forgot his debt to an anonymous black woman. He had been playing on a parked horse-drawn milk wagon near Stockton Street and had climbed on the horse when, suddenly, it bolted and threw him. He lay on the street with a fractured skull until a black woman picked him up and carried him to the hospital. It was reported that the white driver never made inquiry about the condition of the boy.[31]

San Francisco of the 1850s was notorious for its record of crime. Black men seem to have had their share of places on the rosters of crime. It is doubtful that any blacks were ever members of the criminally notorious "Hounds" or "Sydney Ducks," but there were Negroes who committed assaults on whites or on persons of color, and others who committed larceny. In fact larceny seems to be the most common offense for which blacks were arrested. For this and other crimes in the early days of San Francisco, convicted blacks and whites were put aboard abandoned ships that had been converted into prisons. By the mid-1850s, the city had regular jails and an unsegregated chain gang.[32]

As a result of the rampant crime in San Francisco, the first Vigilance Committee was organized in 1851. This group felt that the police and court system were actually in league with the criminals. In its brief career, the Vigilance Committee had only one case that involved a Negro. The charge was arson, but a most peculiar story emerged under examination. The Negro, Ben Robinson, said that he had committed arson under the direction of his former owner, a Mrs. Robinson, who had brought him to California and freed him. Under further questioning, it appeared that he was still slavishly attached to her, but was also very fearful of the police. The suspicion became very strong that the police, who had a prior history of difficulties with Mrs. Robinson, had frightened Ben Robinson into confession to the arson charge with the promise of leniency if he implicated Mrs. Robinson. The Vigilance Committee threw out the entire case.[33]

Stabbing was a common occurrence in early San Francisco. The press reported with monotonous regularity the frequent "cutting affairs," as journalists chose to describe them. Two stabbing incidents involving blacks are worth mentioning. The *Alta* described one episode:

> The evidence went to show that the old man had been teased and worried into a state bordering on frenzy, by a set of rowdies, . . . and he had drawn a pocket knife and cut the man in the abdomen. Several witnesses testified to the general harmlessness and inoffensive disposition of the old man.[34]

In a second case, a black named Edward Dupugh entered a store that sold liquor and asked for a glass of brandy. He was told that the shop only sold drinks to take out and not to drink on the premises. Dupugh then walked toward the cheese counter near the door, picked up the cheese knife, and stabbed himself deeply. Before he died he told those near him that "he had been brought up a gentleman, did not want to disgrace the people that had brought him up, and warned white people to take care how they insulted colored men."[35]

In ways that were sometimes visible and sometimes not, friendships existed between black and white men in San Francisco. A Negro porter named Nelson, who worked for the banking firm of Drexel, Sather, and Church, was surprised in May 1854 to find that his wife and child had arrived from the East earlier than expected. His employer, Sather, recognizing Nelson's unexpected financial needs, gave him $100 as a gift and lent him $200 more.[36] In the following year an unusual black-white friendship was revealed. Many San Franciscans witnessed a funeral procession in which the pallbearers were some of the most prominent white men in town. The deceased, however, was a black man, William Street, a former slave. The most distraught man in this integrated procession was C. B. Strode, who had been Street's master. In fact, Strode and Street had been companions since childhood and their fathers and grandfathers had had a similar relationship in the slave states. The procession was a long one, and the funeral sermon was delivered by the Episcopalian Bishop Kip.[37]

While life in San Francisco by the middle of the 1850s

imposed all of the proscriptions for blacks with which they had been familiar in the older states of the North, in matters of material gain life was better. By 1854 Frederick Douglass was telling the black world in the East that blacks in San Francisco held property valued at one million dollars. The number of businesses they owned and their prominence in the well-paying culinary trades gives strength to that view. When black leadership in California mobilized its energies in 1855 for the first state-wide campaign for their civil rights, their call for action spoke of their "social and political degradation." The word *economic* was not used.[38]

In the first few years of the gold rush, the black communities of San Francisco and Sacramento grew at nearly the same rate. By 1852, the former had a black population of 444 and the latter 338. By the end of the decade, when the total white population of San Francisco was more than twice that of Sacramento, the black community of San Francisco was nearly three times the size of Sacramento's. The actual figures in 1860 were 1,176 in San Francisco and 468 in Sacramento.[39]

In spite of the slower rate of growth of Sacramento, it appears that its smaller Negro population was the first to build stable community institutions. When Reverend Darius Stokes, the black African Methodist Episcopal minister from Baltimore, complained in 1849–50 that he could not get a church started in Sacramento, he complained too soon. Had he remained there a bit longer, he would have seen the brothers Barney and Charles Fletcher, also from Maryland, successfully put together a small group of pioneer Sacramento blacks who by 1851 were holding regular Negro Methodist Church services.[40]

Sacramento in 1850 was a boom town economically for the small black community of barely 200. In addition to 62 cooks, there were 10 barbers and 9 eating and boarding establishments operated by Negroes. Twenty-two black men were "washermen." Many miners who came to Sacramento periodically for a change of scene brought their clothing to be laundered. The number of visiting miners also explains the relatively large number of boarding and eating houses. Many black miners too came to Sacramento, and many of them decided later to settle there. As the small black community slowly grew, it tended to cluster along Third Street. Residences and businesses of blacks were scattered up and down this street and on other streets close to where Third intersected them. Like the San Francisco black community, this was also the part of town where the poorer peoples of all races settled. The other noticeable minority group was the Chinese.[41]

By the latter half of the decade, Sacramento's small black business community was visible. In these years the visitors from the mines decreased as placer mining declined. However, the number of black boardinghouses, hotels, and bars remained about the same. The Hackett House on Third Street, owned and operated by J. Hackett, a black from Pennsylvania, stood out as one of the most important Negro hotels at the time. A large advertisement for it was carried in the state-wide Negro newspaper, the *Mirror of the Times.* The Hackett House gained popular notice when California's most famous fugitive slave, Archy Lee, was found there in 1858. In the same paper, John Meshaw, a West Indies black, advertised that his boot and shoe shop was connected with the well-known Lester and Gibbs shop of San Francisco.[42] Black hotelkeeper Samuel Gale, owner of the St. Nicholas Hotel, employed three Chinese men.[43] The number of Negroes in the better-paying categories of barber and steward increased strikingly over the number in those occupations a decade earlier.

Of course, a great many blacks in Sacramento held menial jobs. One of the best known of these was an old bootblack named "Mose." A former slave and jockey from Kentucky, he became a town character and seemed to be a favorite among the legislators who were his customers.

There were times when he made as much as ten to fifteen dollars a day.[44]

By 1860 the span of occupational skills among blacks in Sacramento included two doctors, both living in the Second Ward, and an engineer, as well as a bell ringer for special events. The black bell ringer and town crier was not an uncommon sight in early California.[45] An apparent incongruity exists between the 1860 census listing of black prostitutes in San Francisco and Sacramento. Sacramento had eleven, while the much larger city had only one![46] While one may allow for error by the Bay city's enumerator, upon reflection it may not have been too wide of the mark. Both church life and family life were more tightly organized among a larger proportion of San Francisco blacks. Also, in San Francisco the New England black was very much in evidence, along with the Puritanism that he brought with him. Of even greater importance in explaining the larger number of prostitutes in Sacramento was its proximity to mining counties, whose largely male population came to Sacramento for recreation.

The relationships between people of color in Sacramento during these years were uneventful, although friendly. The Chinese in the city did not share any combined activities with the blacks, as the Latin Americans did in San Francisco. Language and other cultural barriers were the probable explanation. Yet there must have been a degree of goodwill between these two groups, because the Chinese allowed their chapel to be used by the Negro Baptists when they were seeking a location in which to start their church.[47] They also shared a common experience in harassment. In July 1858, the press, under the caption "Rowdyism In Sacramento," reported that a bunch of "young men and boys" were persecuting mostly Chinese and Negroes, by breaking the windows of their shops and other places of business and heaping various forms of "malice" upon them. The press called for a more adequate night shift of police to deal with the problem.[48]

Through the many columns of mining and political news that filled the Sacramento newspapers, an occasional item says something about black-white relations in that city. A white man was arrested for assault and battery on a Negro. He was fined only one dollar and costs, because "It appeared that . . . the Negro was grossly abusive." The story is incomplete, of course, but one senses a black man here who had reached his limit of conformity to a racist etiquette. In another press item, a black was arrested for chicken stealing, and he and his white wife Catherine were brought into court.[49]

Two other towns developed sizeable permanent Negro communities: Marysville, the county seat of Yuba County and an important trading center for the northern end of the northern mines; and Stockton, the county seat of San Joaquin County and the main trading center for the southern mines. The black communities of both towns grew slowly but steadily. By 1860 Marysville had 118 and Stockton 88 blacks.[50]

The Marysville Negro community in the gold rush years was clearly the more vigorous one. After incorporation in 1851, the city boomed because of its proximity to the mines and its strategic position at the joining of the Yuba and the Feather rivers. This gave Marysville an important all-water route to Sacramento and San Francisco. The first two blacks to see Marysville were probably the previously mentioned partners on the riverboat *Lawrence* that came to the city in 1849. By 1852 an Ohio-born Negro barber and his hard-working wife were already on the scene. William C. Ellis, an early white businessman in Marysville, described the wife in a letter home:

> Well you have not seen all the folks yet. For ther is the Mulatto girl from Columbus, Ohio (or rather our barber's wife). She comes with our clean clothes home, and "Please Sir, have you any more clothes ready for me to work now."

He could only have been writing about Dorothea McGowan, the wife of Jess McGowan, since none of the other barber families in Marysville came from Ohio. By 1860, the McGowan family was worth twelve thousand dollars in real estate and three thousand in personal estate.[51]

By 1853, there were at least two thriving black-owned barber shops in Marysville. The Virginia-born Gassoway brothers, James R. and John, had their shop on D Street between First and Second streets. Their ads appeared regularly in the Marysville papers, noting that their speciality was "cupping" and "leaching," and also citing the recommendations they had received from local white doctors. D Street was evidently the "barber row"; not only was McGowan's shop there, but in a few years there were more black barbers on or very near that street. Some of these early black barbers bore names like Tilghman and Jackson that continued to be prominent into the next century.[52]

By the last half of the 1850s, one of the most important members of the Negro leadership in California outside of San Francisco, Edward P. Duplex, had a thriving barber shop on D Street. This twenty-nine-year-old Connecticut-born black was the proprietor of the Metropolitan Shaving Saloon and the employer of other black barbers. During the California State Fair held in Marysville in 1858, he advertised that he would have seven barbers in attendance for the event.[53] By 1858, nearly 20 percent of Marysville's Negro residents were in the barbering and hairdressing trades, and as the northern mines continued to prosper, the number of men so employed remained steady into 1860.[54]

Barbering, however, was not the only successful occupation of Marysville blacks. Virginia-born Gabriel Simms opened his small Franklin Hotel on First Street near a cluster of other black-owned businesses. George Stockton may have been the only black pressman in California employed on a white-owned newspaper, the *Marysville Express.* Near the city there were at least a half dozen black farm families.

The value of their lands added to that of the property of the Negroes in the city totaled about $100,000.[55]

A number of Marysville blacks concealed their slave-state origins and substituted free states when giving data for the city's directories. This reflected their feelings of insecurity, generated by the 1850 National Fugitive Slave Law, the 1852 California Fugitive Slave Law, and the Dred Scott Decision of 1857. A prominent Marysville citizen who engaged in this deception was Reverend Thomas E. Randolph, a Negro Baptist minister and barber. He is listed in the 1858 city directory as having been born in Ohio. He apparently felt secure enough by 1860 to list Virginia as his true state of birth. At least three additional Marysville Negroes gave their true slave-state origins in 1860, after having concealed them in 1858.[56]

There are only scanty sources for deeper glimpses into the life of the Marysville Negro community in this period. We know that Marysville, too, had its black town crier. A white contemporary noted in his journal on a Sunday, "Stopped in on our way home to have our boots blacked by Aaron the scientific boot blacker and city crier." As the most visible Negro in Marysville, young Virginia-born Aaron Cobb came in for a good deal of notice. When he worked as the town crier, ringing a bell as he walked along shouting the news of a lost child, it was reported in the *Marysville Appeal.* When he was trying to raffle off his gold watch, the newspaper urged its readers to buy chances. Aaron's name even appeared in the humor columns:

> Why is Aaron Cobb's voice like Charley Legate's head?
> Because it has been BAWLED for many years.[57]

There were Chinese and Latin-Americans living in Marysville in the 1850s, and it is clear that Negroes and Latin-Americans lived close together on First and Second streets near the Yuba River. One west-Indian black was married to a Mexican woman.[58]

Some measure of the character and internal social control of this small northern California black community can be gained from the fact that the census reveals no Negro prostitutes. This is noteworthy since the area between A and First streets was known to have ninety-five houses of prostitution with about 380 prostitutes.[59] Supporting the evidence of a moral strictness among Marysville blacks was an incident involving a badly timed case of drunkenness on the part of a local Negro. The black inebriate decided to show up at a funeral, where he conducted himself in a manner that disturbed the sobriety of the occasion. When the ceremonies had concluded, the offended blacks seized the drunk and gave him a trial just outside of town. The decision was reached to give him thirty-nine lashes. At the conclusion of this punishment, he was allowed to leave town.[60]

Stockton, which had the fourth largest black community in the 1850s, derived its importance from being the upper terminal on the San Joaquin River and a supply source for the southern mines. Ships from San Francisco docked at Stockton's wharves. The city's black community grew a bit more slowly than did Marysville's, but its black population moved ahead by the 1870s. Stockton, however, had two black churches in the 1850s to Marysville's one. The Stockton black community seems to have been less affluent than that of Marysville. The number of barbers was often a rough measure of the income of the black community, and in 1856 Stockton reported only four. In that same year there was only one boardinghouse, and no saloons were recorded. By 1860, when Marysville had sixteen barbers, Stockton had only six. A great many black residents of Stockton were classified as "laborer" and "domestic servant." One important reason for Marysville's lead over Stockton was the fact that the gold rush subsided sooner in the southern mines, which used Stockton as a supply and transportation center. Occupationally, the most interesting blacks were those who resided on the edge or outside of town. Hartwell Bates, born in Mississippi, had an orchard with a value of $500. There were several more farmers in the county and the census shows that three young black men in San Joaquin County were vaqueros (cowboys).[61]

In the 1850s most blacks lived in the original part of town, between the levees. They were especially concentrated in the area bounded by Beaver, Commerce, and Washington streets.[62]

Little is known of the relationship between Stockton blacks and other ethnic elements in the community. Local blacks enjoyed friendly relations with at least one white man who held mildly antislavery views. Captain Charles M. Weber, who founded Stockton and was probably its greatest landowner, was openly friendly to the black community. He supported their church and educational efforts.[63] The scant information about black-white contact in Stockton in this period reveals a closeness of another sort. A rather lurid event in 1858 brought to light the relationship between a white woman and a black man who had once worked for her husband. The young black man, Joe Williams, described in the local press as a man with "a most insulting air of cool, easy assurance," had an affair with his employer's wife. A child was born of this relationship who, with the passage of time, seemed more Williams's child than the husband's. Anxiety-ridden Williams confided in a white neighbor, who told the husband. The husband then shot Williams. The injured Williams was jailed and later killed by "unknown" parties. It is unfortunate that the Stockton press in this decade chose to report little else about the people of the Stockton Negro community.[64]

A measure of the modest development of the Stockton black community in the 1850s in comparison with Marysville is the fact that at the Colored Conventions held in Sacramento in 1855 and 1856, Yuba County sent more delegates than San Joaquin County.[65] But a look at the Stockton City Directory and the census reveals that at least two families living in that city in the 1850s would make their mark in California black history. The Hyer family children later became a talented singing group, and the Wysinger family descendants made the legal challenge in the 1890s that eliminated the last vestiges of school discrimination in nineteenth-century California.[66]

A study of the four cities where blacks were living in urban communities reveals interesting black migration patterns. Since these four cities differ not only in size, but also in character, we may ask if the blacks' residential choice was related to their place of origin. An examination of the data reveals that it was. By 1860, the blacks in a general way chose to make their permanent residence in California communities that roughly approximated their environments in the East. New Englanders and New Yorkers tended to settle in San Francisco and favored, secondly, Sacramento. Of the approximately 700 Negroes from the big Northern states of Massachusetts, New York, and Pennsylvania, over 400 chose to live in the four cities named above. The latter figure may be too low, because many "state of origin entries are illegible or are simply not given in the manuscript census.

In San Francisco, more than half of the Negro population was born in the North, and it is probable that the balance, born in the South, had lived most of their lives in the urban North before settling in San Francisco. In Sacramento, the statistics tip heavily toward slave-state origins. Nearly 200 of the 300 blacks were from slave states. In Marysville, out of over 100, two-thirds were from the South. In Stockton, with its black population of 88, 45 were Southern-born in 1860, with Kentucky, Missouri, and Tennessee the leading birthplaces.

The migration pattern is less clear in the cases of Maryland and Virginia, birthplace of hundreds of California blacks. Many of them lived many years in free states before the gold rush began, which may be reflected by the fact that of approximately 500 Marylanders and Virginians, about half chose to live in the rural areas of California, and the other half chose to live and work in the four cities under discussion.

What is most striking, however, is the choice of residence of Negroes who came from the rural land-locked Southern states of Missouri, Kentucky, and Tennessee. Barely a fourth of more than 600 blacks from those states chose to live in the four biggest cities of northern California. Black Texans appeared to be most consistent in choosing rural residence. Of nearly 50 black Texans in California in 1860, the only ones found in cities were a single Texan in San Francisco and three in Stockton.[67]

Like the white gold rush migrants to California, the blacks were overwhelmingly male. With the gradual emergence of black family life in the cities, the ratio of male to female became more balanced. The 1860 census reported 2,827 black men and 1,259 women. Whereas in the state as a whole black women were 30 percent of the total black population, in the four cities examined in this chapter black women comprised over 34 percent. In some residential areas of Sacramento and San Francisco the numbers of men and women were almost equal.[68]

These black men and women of the early California cities combined the work-ethic philosophy of a later Booker T. Washington with the civil-rights militancy of the contemporary Frederick Douglass. In their daily lives they demonstrated a morality that was a blend of Quaker and Puritan.

5 Southern California

Southern California remained relatively untouched by the gold rush. Even several decades after the gold rush struck northern California, the southern counties remained slow-growing and pastoral. Cattle and vaqueros on horseback dominated the landscape. While Los Angeles and some of the great cattle ranchos nearby were arrival points for many gold seekers who took the southern land routes to California, few people remained south of the Tehachapis to start their new lives.

In 1850, the entire county of Los Angeles reported twelve Negroes. By 1860, after several new counties had been carved out of Los Angeles County, that county alone reported eighty-seven.[1] Many of the eighteenth-century founders of Los Angeles had been of African ancestry, but by the middle of the nineteenth century that ancestry had largely melted away in the census reports. All of these early settlers considered themselves Mexican, without any other qualifications. One of the few surviving reminders of this black ingredient in the founders of Los Angeles was the street Calle de los Negros, which the Americans later called Nigger Alley. In the 1850s, it became a street of saloons and gambling dens.[2]

The only concentration of blacks was to be found in the city of Los Angeles, where they were still so few in number that they hardly constituted a community. In the early 1850s, the best known of them was Peter Biggs, a barber and bootblack, who was considered by his contemporaries to be a town character. Originally a slave in Missouri, Biggs was sold to an officer in the Mexican War who came to California and gave Biggs has freedom in Los Angeles. Here Biggs settled, married a native Mexican woman, and by 1860 had a twelve-year-old daughter named Juana. For a time Biggs had a monopoly of the barbering business. During the 1850s his position in town was enhanced through his friendship with Judge Benjamin Hayes, who had known Biggs when he was still a slave in Missouri. When the Civil War came, Biggs, possibly to ingratiate himself with his Southern customers, achieved a unique reputation as a supporter of Jefferson Davis and the Confederacy.[3]

A small number of blacks of less prominence than Biggs achieved solid standing in the Los Angeles community as men and women with a record of property accumulation. Some of them were veterans of the Mexican War, who had come as servants and slaves of Mexican War officers who settled in southern California. When the white Mexican War veterans decided in 1873 to organize a veterans' society, five Negro veterans still living in Los Angeles at that time became charter members.[4]

A Texas black man and his wife gained a quiet prominence in Los Angeles for their hard work and gradual material accumulations. Robert Owens first earned his own freedom and then, working as a free man, purchased out of slavery his wife, a son, and two daughters. They moved to Los Angeles in 1853, where the elder Owenses became known as Uncle Bob and Aunt Minnie. He worked at odd jobs and his wife took in washing, until he got a government contract to cut wood for local military units. The location of his woodcutting operations outside of town came to be called "Negro Canyon." By 1860 he was in the cattle business and worth $6,500. The embryo of black community life began in 1854 in the Owenses' home, when they invited other blacks in Los Angeles to come to their residence for religious services. Shrewd investments in property eventually made the Owens family quite well-to-do. By the end of the century, two Owens grandsons owned the Owens Block on Broadway near Third Street.[5]

By 1852, another small contingent of blacks had arrived in southern California. This group, of no more than two dozen, came to San Bernardino with those Mormons attempting to establish a second Salt Lake City. Slave-owning Mormons were to be found in the Church of the Latter Day Saints because of the missionary work the church had conducted in the South during the 1830s. When the call went out for Mormons to go to Utah, a goodly number of slaveowners responded and brought black men and women with them. After successfully founding Salt Lake City, the Mormon hierarchy called upon their members to move on, to found a new Mormon city in southern California. The present site of the city of San Bernardino was selected in 1852, and some Mormons originally from the South moved from Utah along with their "servants." In 1858, due to a crisis in the relations between the Mormons and the United States government, the entire San Bernardino Mormon community was called back to Salt Lake City. At this point the Mormon Negroes were evidently given the option of returning to Salt Lake City or remaining in California, where their free status was assured. It seems that most of them preferred to stay in California. By 1860, there were eighteen blacks still in San Bernardino, seven of them children born there. However, this does not account for all who had chosen two years earlier to remain in California. A number of them by 1860 had left San Bernardino and gone to nearby Los Angeles.[6]

As a consequence of the Mormon migration to San Bernardino, southern California witnessed its most important slavery case. The trial took place in Los Angeles and involved a Mississippi Mormon named Robert Smith, two black mothers, Hannah and Biddy, their twelve children and grandchildren, and a Catholic judge, Benjamin Hayes, who had lived in the slave state of Missouri prior to coming to California.

Smith had moved to Utah in 1851. Then, with his family and slaves, he joined the Mormon migration to San Bernardino in 1852. There they all remained for about three years, until Smith decided to move again, this time to

Texas. The route taken by the Smith party led them to a resting place in Santa Monica. It was from here that Smith's slaves somehow conveyed a legal petition to the authorities in Los Angeles. Delilah Beasley, who spoke to the daughter of one of the petitioners many years later, learned that assistance came from a Mrs. Rowen of San Bernardino, who reported to the Los Angeles authorities that the blacks were held as slaves. It is clear that at some point late in 1855, the sheriff took all the slaves into custody, and a petition for freedom was filed before Judge Hayes. The records reveal a vacillation on the part of Hannah, one of the slave mothers, but Biddy's responses apparently convinced the judge that the two women and their children did not wish to go to Texas. This was in spite of Smith's promise to them that their "condition" would be the same as it was in San Bernardino, something between freedom and paternalism. In his written decision to free all the slaves, the judge made a particular point of emphasizing the hypocrisy of Smith telling his slaves that in Texas, of all places, they could expect an unbinding relationship. He went on to remark with feeling that this hypocrisy was particularly vicious in the case of the four children who had been born free in California. And so, because of Biddy's determination and in spite of Hannah's uncertainties, the entire fourteen became free.

What happened to Hannah in the years that followed is unknown, but Biddy, who then took the full name of Biddy Mason, moved from Santa Monica to Los Angeles, where she took up housework and nursing. The determination she showed in gaining her freedom persisted, and Biddy Mason soon owned her own homestead. In the years that followed, she became one of the wealthiest blacks in Los Angeles. She was also remarkable for her efforts on behalf of education for black children. By the end of the 1850s Robert Owens has replaced Peter Biggs as a model for Los Angeles Negroes, and in the next decade Biddy Mason joined him in that role.[7]

Some blacks in southern California gained their freedom

by other methods. James R. Holman of Arkansas brought his slave woman Clanpa into California in 1850 and then discovered that the law forbade slavery. He quickly made an agreement with her, granting freedom for herself and her two children after two more years of labor.[8] But evidently some Southerners kept their slaves bound to them right up to the end of the decade. It was not until 1861 that one black lad decided to run away from Cave Coutts, a Tennesseean who had settled in southern California. The young black man evidently made good his escape. This is known because a certain J. F. Bilderback wrote to Coutts, offering to catch his slave for a reward. Bilderback was not successful, but apparently unaware of the Thirteenth Amendment, in 1866 the would-be slavecatcher again wrote to Coutts, notifying him that he had seen the runaway black and would track him down for a consideration.[9]

For blacks in general Los Angeles in the 1850s was a dangerous place to be. The area was dominated by Americans from Southern states and there was a wide disrespect for the law. In this setting, some blacks had abrasive racist experiences with little or no legal protection. One incident was so outrageous that two separate observers of the event recorded it. The Reverend John Wells Brier recalled that in 1850 his father was a partner in a hotel on the Plaza in Los Angeles that employed a number of black men. One day, as Brier recalled it:

> A number of southern bloods decided to assert their authority upon the negroes employed by our house, one of them was staked down on his back, sorely beaten and left undiscovered, and without food and drink during four days and nights. Our steward, a tall and powerful black man, escaped from his enemies by leaping over a wall eight feet high, while the bullets whizzed about him. A mulatto was brutally flogged and the most trifling [small] negro I ever saw was so tremendously aroused by fear that he distanced pur-

> suit and did not rest till he was safe in Northern California.

The second observer of this outrage said that these "desperadoes" felt that they were on a "lark," and he further observed that no one dared to interfere or protest.[10]

Major Horace Bell, an important political figure in Democratic politics in southern California, told of prejudice blunted by expediency and droll humor. During the state elections in 1853, the major and his cohorts were campaigning in Los Angeles County, when an aide reported trouble at his polling place, where a black man was attempting to vote. This aide, a dyed-in-the-wool Southerner, was ready to commit mayhem on the offender of Southern political etiquette, but Major Bell thought to look into the situation. It turned out that the black man in question could not speak a word of English because Spanish was his native tongue. He considered himself a Mexican and stated to an interpreter that he had always voted before. When it became apparent to Bell that this Afro-Mexican had in mind voting for Bell's candidate, he dealt with his fire-eating aide by giving him an assignment at a polling booth some miles away. After he left, the black man cast his ballot.[11]

Outside of Los Angeles, in southern California there were only a few dozen Negroes living in widely separated locations in the decade between 1850 and 1860. Most of them were laborers, some were cooks, some domestics of Southern families who had brought their household servants with them. Judge Hayes, who traveled great distances in the southern counties in the course of his judicial responsibilities, often noticed black servants in the various homes where he was welcomed for a meal and a night's rest.[12] Robert Owens, previously mentioned, was not the only black in the cattle business by 1860. There was also James Brown, originally from Kentucky, who had a ranch in Temecula township in San Diego County. Brown employed another black man from Georgia as a vaquero. It was undoubtedly Brown's ranch that a traveler passing through Temecula recorded as "Nigger Ranch."[13]

A young Arkansas-born black named Charley Tyler, who was associated with several white farming and stock-raising families in Tulare County, gained a special immortality. His story took place in the period when Indians were beginning to resist further white encroachment in the Owens Valley. Tyler was with the white McGee family when a band of Indians attacked the small group. Tyler fought and killed four Indians in a skirmish that enabled the McGee family to escape. Tyler was probably killed at the butte which bears his name, near Fish Springs in what is now Inyo County.[14]

Southern California was not gold rush country. However, some gold in quartz was found in San Diego County in 1860. When Judge Hayes visited this mining operation while on circuit that year, he observed that there was one black man among the miners, who may have been the discoverer of the mine. He described him as

> the negro Jesse who works like Colonel Benton, "solitary and alone" and to whose industry, indeed we are indebted for first putting this ball in motion.

The man he was describing was forty-year-old Jesse Tower, who was born in North Carolina and about whom little else is known.[15]

The relationship in southern California between blacks and Indians and blacks and Mexicans is not clear. There was the marriage of Petter Biggs to a Mexican woman, and, in addition, Judge Hayes knew a Peter Brannigan who was black and had married an Indian woman.[16] However, implicit in an 1860 court case is the race prejudice of a group of youthful Mexican Californians. Miguel Atencia, described as a Negro, charged in an affidavit that several Mexican boys tripped his horse. When Atencia fell, they pounced on him and beat him.[17]

The growth of the Negro population in southern California continued to be slow in the next two decades. A reflection of this slow population increase is the fact that in 1865, when a state-wide Colored Convention was called, there were no representatives from any of the southern counties. Not until the late 1880s did this area show any significant increase in black population. Then the number of Negro residents increased impressively. This becomes apparent when Los Angeles County is compared with Yuba County in those transitional decades. In 1870 Los Angeles County reported 134 blacks, while Yuba had 152. In 1880 Los Angeles County reported 188 to Yuba's 247. By 1890 the Los Angeles County black population had leaped to 1,817, while Yuba County's blacks dropped to 218. These statistics foreshadow the development in which the number of blacks in southern California would soon outnumber those in the northern part of the state.[18]

6 Slavery and the Fugitive Slave in California

The United States took California from Mexico, a nation that had already made its commitment against Negro slavery. Mexico had abolished slavery twenty-three years before the American conquest in 1846. People of Afro-Mexican ancestry living in California at that time were free men. The new occupiers of this territory had committed themselves to the protection of Mexican civil laws which outlawed slavery. But respect for gold rather than Mexican law was the motivating factor in the rejection of slavery by the makers of the state constitution in 1849.

On 15 March 1848, three months after gold was discovered in Coloma, the pioneer newspaper *Californian* had a long editorial against slavery in California, and its principal reason for this position was that "it is wrong for it [slavery] to exist anywhere."[1] A year and a half later, while the gold rush was in full swing, the territory had its first constitutional convention, and while the delegates forbade slavery in the new state, their sentiments were a long retreat from the newspaper's earlier humanistic statement. In that eighteen-month period many changes had taken place.

In a letter to a San Francisco newspaper published in January 1849, well before the great wave of gold seekers arrived in California, Thomas Hart Benton, senator from Missouri and political hero to Western men, urged Californians interested in quickly joining the Union not to deal with the slavery question. He felt that raising the subject of slavery would only complicate matters related to their admission, because the United States Congress was already locked in debate about slavery in the territories acquired as a result of the war with Mexico. The new Californians ignored his advice and in convention in the fall of 1849 produced an antislavery constitution. However, by 1850, when Congress was presented with California's antislavery constitution as an accomplished fact, much gold bullion had already arrived in the Eastern ports. By this time only a minority of Southern congressmen still wished to deny California statehood, and as part of the Compromise of 1850, California entered the Union as the thirty-first state.

Even before the great wave of gold seekers arrived in the midsummer and fall of 1849, Americans were calling meetings in which they were insisting that slavery be forbidden in California. In most gatherings the sentiment was strong to bar all Negroes from the state. Through January, February, and March 1849, meetings were held in San Francisco and Sacramento, where the overwhelming sentiment was that the future state should forbid slavery.[2] In July of that year, a meeting of miners on the Mokelumne River supported the same sentiments. Their remarks revealed an added ingredient: hostility to the Latin-American miners, many of whom were in the mines before the Americans arrived in 1848.[3] Sentiment in southern California also seemed to be against slavery. An election in San Diego in August produced a very clear antislavery result, although it apparently had some assistance from the passengers of the bark *Oxford*. They had just arrived in San Diego from Boston on their way to San Francisco and were invited to vote. But even without the New Englanders' vote, southern Californians from the United States would have undoubtedly voted against slavery, for in the words of Benjamin D. Wilson (grandfather of General George Patton),

> although most of us [*sic*] southern men, we're positive that we wanted no slavery. We had had enough of a variety of races.[4]

In this latter sentiment Wilson was doomed to be disappointed. In fact, one wonders what he was doing in southern California with such attitudes, since all about him were the pigmentations of the Indian and the Latin-American. At the same time that voting was taking place in southern California, several blacks were reported voting at the polls in San Francisco.[5]

Through September and October 1849, forty-eight delegates met in Monterey to work out a constitution for the new state. On the matter of slavery, they followed the sentiments of the meetings that took place around the state preceding the convention. While lacking any abolitionist fervor, the delegates speedily and unanimously agreed to oppose slavery. One reason for the quick resolution of this question became evident during the much lengthier debate over the proposal to keep free Negroes out of California. This reason rested in the old Jacksonian antimonopoly feeling that was still very strong among white Americans. Delegates Semple and Tefft made this point clear. Said Tefft:

> They [white miners] would be unable . . . to compete with the bands of negroes who would be set to work under the direction of capitalists. It would become a monopoly of the worst character. The profits of the mines would go into the pockets of single individuals.

This kind of "monopoly" had worried white miners even before the state constitutional convention. Months before slaves began to dig gold in California, white American miners had become incensed over Latin-American mining companies employing "large bands of hired men (who are nominally slaves)."

The proposal for a ban on free Negro immigration was based on Eastern stereotypes of the free Negro as a debased individual. This was most apparent in the proposal of one of the delegates that the state ban free Negroes as well as slaveowners who might wish to bring slaves to California for the purpose of making a fortune with them and then freeing them. Apparently a number of delegates who came originally from Southern states had received letters of inquiry from acquaintances in the South about the feasibility of bringing slaves into the state. This was reported to the convention with a sense of alarm.

The basic assumption for this fear was the widely held belief that free blacks were undesirable. Delegate Robert Semple, of Bear Flag Revolt fame, expressed the feelings of most of those who held this view when he said that he was not concerned with those few free blacks who were already in California but rather with the great number who might be brought to the state by slave masters and freed after a period of mining. This he described as "one of the greatest curses that could be entailed upon California." He claimed that such free blacks would be "a burthen on the community." Delegate W. E. Shannon countered Semple's sentiment, claiming that few slaveholders would be so foolhardy as to bring slaves to the state. He also expressed his feelings about free Negroes when he said that in his home state of New York,

> many men of color there are most respectable citizens; that they are men of wealth, intelligence and business capacity; men of acknowledged ability.

The driving force for the anti-Negro immigration clause was a Kentuckian named M. M. McCarver. He was frequently called "General" because he had been a militia officer in Oregon before he came to California. He took his defeat rather hard, and as one friendly journalist put it,

> it had been his darling object, his hobby, and Napoleon could not have mourned Waterloo more than did the General the annihilation of his free negro preventative.

Near the end of the convention he exploded over a minor debate and walked out of the hall. Another delegate asked that McCarver be excused since he was still feeling badly about the fate of his anti-Negro project.[6]

The convention went on record on 19 September to instruct the first meeting of the state legislature to pass a law that banned free Negroes as well as slaves.[7] Two weeks later the delegates began to have second thoughts about instructing the state legislature. The new sentiment was for the convention to take no action on black immigration and to let the forthcoming state legislature make its own decisions on the matter. The most important reason for omitting the anti-immigration clause was the knowledge of the difficulty that it might create in gaining Congressional approval of the new state constitution.[8]

One month after the state convention adjourned, having easily agreed on a free-state constitution, in December 1849, the first state assembly passed a bill outlawing the immigration of free Negroes into California. The assembly action was urged by the state's first governor, Peter H. Burnett, who had a long history of hostility to the free Negro. The assembly effort at banning the entry of free Negroes ran into trouble in the state senate. On the bill's second reading in the senate, Senator David C. Broderick successfully moved to postpone the bill indefinitely, which effectively killed it.[9] Thus ended the first attempt to ban the immigration of free Negroes into California.

The decision of the constitutional convention to ban slavery coupled with the inability of the legislature to pass an anti-immigration law for blacks created serious legal loopholes. Had an anti-immigration law passed, it would have included the ban on slaves as well as free Negroes. Since this did not happen, not only did free Negroes continue to arrive in small numbers to join those who were already there, but slaveowners continued to bring slaves to California. There was nothing in the law before 1852 that told them whether they had to free their slaves upon arrival, nor did the law tell them how long they could safely hold on to their human property. For a variety of reasons, the slaveowners did not seem concerned. For one, they felt, with reason, that the composition of the state legislature and executive was friendly to their interests. Some had planned to free their slaves in California after they made their fortunes. Others felt sure that their slaves were too dependent or fearful to try to escape. On this last point, a goodly number of slaveowners were to be quite surprised. And yet they should not have been, because there were warnings as early as January 1849. In that month the *New Orleans Picayune* copied from the *New York Tribune* the widely publicized interview with John Parrott, San Francisco businessman and former United States government official, in which he stated, "The inhabitants are strongly opposed to it [slavery] and no man taking slaves with him would be able to keep them long."[10] Some Southerners reading this article may have heeded its advice, but others may have felt like young Robert Givens, who wrote to his father in Kentucky in 1852 in response to a query about the safety of bringing their slave Patrick:

> Under the present law it is impossible to hold a slave any longer than the expiration of the present year. I don't consider there is any risk in bringing Patrick alone, under the law as no one will put themselves to the trouble of investigating the matter.[11]

As will be seen, young Givens did not allow for the interest that politically seasoned free Negroes would show in their slave brothers.

In the meantime, the lack of law enforcement made it possible for slavery to exist in many parts of the state. Exactly how many blacks were kept in a slave status will never be precisely known. As a free state, of course, the California census made no provision for such a category. But other kinds of records tell us that slavery was practiced. The earliest evidence was revealed as a result of a letter written by the Congregationalist minister Timothy Dwight Hunt, who came to California in 1849. This letter, printed in the *Newark Daily Advertiser* and widely reprinted, lamented the fact that slavery was being practiced. It described a transaction in San Francisco in which a black woman and her child were sold by a man from Oregon to a Rhode Islander for $1,900. The Rhode Islander, it was claimed, had difficulty in getting servants in California.[12] The need for domestic servants appears to have been the most common reason for the purchase of slaves. When the Bascom family arrived in San Jose from Kentucky in 1849, Dr. Bascom paid $800 for a black cook. In spite of the antislavery law, the cook remained with the family for four years.[13] A certain J. R. Harper felt so secure about chattel property in California in 1850 that he placed an advertisement in the *Sacramento Transcript* to the effect that he was selling

> A valuable Negro Girl aged eighteen, bound by indentures for two years. Said girl is of amiable disposition, a good washer, ironer, and cook.[14]

The reference to the indenturement suggests that the young woman had been promised her freedom after two years' labor for Harper and that her potential purchaser would probably have to agree to that eventuality.

A routine court record in Sacramento reveals that a certain Christian Kollar, on 22 October 1849, claimed as private property a black man branded with an *A* on his hip and an *M* on his shoulder. In this court action, Kollar was making his ownership of the black man a matter of record in California. Even more ironically, in 1852, three years after the antislavery constitution was adopted, one slaveowner felt so confident of the protection of slavery in California that he placed an advertisement in the *San Francisco Herald* calling for the apprehension of a runaway black girl he had held as a slave in Marysville.[15] Perhaps her flight was aided by the Marysville black community.

In the early years of the gold rush, the most abundant proof that slavery was practiced in California was the hiring-out system, a common practice in the slave states which produced income from slaves when they were not profitable on the plantation. Contemporary comment is replete with observations of slaves being put out to hire. In California slaves were hired out for two reasons: first, the slaveowner and his slave were not panning enough gold to support both of them and it was more advantageous for the master to mine alone and hire out his slave as a cook, waiter, domestic servant, or laborer; second, neither was earning enough for even one person and the slave was put out to work to support both of them. The former case occurred more frequently. The income from hiring out varied from $150 to $300 a month. One hiring contract stipulated a payment of $900 for six months. An Alabaman who brought three slaves with him to California and hired them out for $300 a month in 1849 wrote home that he had no difficulty "retaining" them. A Tennesseean wrote home in the same year that he had brought a slave with him to California with the express purpose of hiring him out as a cook for $150 a month.[16]

The existence of a slave relationship surfaced in Sacramento in an unexpected way. Within twenty-four hours after Congregational minister Reverend Robert Deal performed the marriage ceremony for a black woman named Margaret and a black man named Lawrence in May 1850, their honeymoon was rudely interrupted. During the marriage night of the newlyweds, William Marr broke into their bedroom with gun in hand and forced Margaret, his alleged slave, to return with him to his household. He claimed that she preferred to be with him, but later offered to let her return to her husband upon payment of $1,000.[17]

As late as November 1853, a Mr. Olivio of Stockton paid $700 to a man for his slave, with whom he was preparing to return to the South. The value of the slave had been placed at $1,000, and the balance of $300 was actually paid *by the slave* to his former master! It is clear that this black man was looking forward to gaining freedom in California. Three years later, when the Negro was expecting his freedom, Olivio reneged and a court case ensued. Olivio's tactic then was to demand payment for room and board at the rate of eight dollars a week. This was after three years of labor worth thousands of dollars. Olivio's actions were so blatantly inhumane that an elderly Kentucky-born lawyer took the case to plead for the freedom of the black.[18] The outcome of the case is unknown.

In the years between 1849 and 1852 it became apparent that while the antislavery features of the constitution were not being enforced, neither was there any police system to keep blacks in slavery. As slaves became aware of their opportunities under these circumstances, they proceeded to try to take advantage of them. This resulted in an increasing number of successful flights from servitude, as well as a few fugitive slave cases. An observer of this development wrote:

> Some remain with their masters to work for them under indentures, but the large majority find it as easy to dig gold for themselves as for others and leave for "parts unknown" soon after arrival.[19]

This sympathetic observer was perhaps too sanguine in seeing a "large majority" flee their owners, but many flights did take place.

When fugitives from slavery came before the courts, there was frequently the problem of a proper mix between the laws of the United States and the laws of Mexico. While American law at the national level condoned slavery, the Mexican law unequivocally opposed it. In these court cases, the judges were faced with the problem of which set of laws should prevail. One of the first cases to test this question occurred in Sacramento in 1849 before a Southern-born judge and was reported nationally. A white man sued a black man, said to be a slave, for a sum of money, with the threat that he would sue the black's master if payment were not forthcoming. The judge ruled that Mexican law was in effect and that the black man was not a slave; therefore the proceedings were against the black man and not the alleged master.[20] The nature of this case prevents one from being sure whom the judge was protecting, but of importance is the fact that the antislavery aspect of Mexican law was honored. Thus a legal precedent was set in Sacramento.

In the same city, not many months later, Mexican law was again tested in a case that received national notice. Lindall Hayes was a white man who was determined to take a Negro named Charles back to slavery. Charles was equally determined not to go. The turmoil that resulted brought these two men twice before Sacramento judges. On the first occasion, Hayes sought a judgment from Judge Thomas establishing that Charles was his slave. However, Judge Thomas pointed to Mexican law and adjudged Charles a free man. What brought these two contestants into court again was the fact that Hayes refused to accept Judge Thomas's decision and on the streets of Sacramento proceeded to try to beat Charles into submission. Hayes was unsuccessful until another white man struck Charles, and by that time police officers had come along and took all parties back to court. This time the men faced Justice Sackett. The charge against Charles was resisting an officer. When Sackett heard the details, he freed Charles again, stating that the second arrest was illegal, as Charles had a right to resist a return to slavery. Of additional interest here is the legal talent that Charles had on his side. It included Joseph W. Winans and Joseph C. Zabriskie, both of whom would be seen again offering their legal talents to black men.[21]

Black men continued to strike for freedom. Early in 1850, another fugitive slave case came to court, but the black man was not as fortunate as Charles. The incident opened with a remarkable street scene in the San Jose city square. Observers witnessed a fight in which the black man first had the white on the ground, and then with the aid of a third party the white man had the black man down and was beating him so mercilessly that the gathered crowd cried, "Shame!" When brought before the court, the white man made a series of revealing remarks:

> That negro is my slave. I brought him from home with me. He has been among the *free* negroes of the town, getting drunk and doing as he pleased. I made up my mind to leave this town this evening, and determined to take him along with me. I met him in the street and told him he must go. This he refused to do. I then leaned down to take up a stick to chastise him, when he seized me and flung me down. I then broke a stick over his head which I had a right to do. He is my property and I intend to have him, and to give him a good two hundred lashes in the bargain.

The judge in this case, completely in sympathy with the slaveowner, placed the Negro in jail and had him whipped as well. Several San Jose lawyers rushed to the legal defense of this black man, but by the time they had the papers they needed the Negro had been spirited back to slavery.[22]

In the mining counties, slaves were making attempts at freedom with some recorded failures and some successes. Richard Ness, an Englishman mining near Owsley's Bar in Yuba County, worked near a slave who had been brought out by some Texans. Ness wrote in his journal that when the slave attempted to escape from his master, the Texans intercepted him and gave him two hundred lashes.[23] Near Sonora, an elderly black man and his wife attempted an escape that failed, and the man was whipped. This came to the notice of a free Negro from Ohio, who then engineered a successful escape for the old couple.[24]

In San Francisco, street life was occasionally punctuated by the sights and sounds of slaves attempting escape and masters seeking to recapture them. On a morning in January 1851, bystanders near the steamer *Columbus* saw a slave named Sam being forced aboard against his will. Friends swiftly went to work on his behalf, and later in the day, just before sailing time, a constable arrived with a writ of habeas corpus to free him. But Sam could not be found anywhere on the ship. One can surmise that he had friends aboard ship as well as on land. In July that year, a wounded black man was seen being hurried down the street to Long Wharf, but he was not as lucky as Sam. Several armed men escorted him.[25]

Sometimes the action took place on shipboard. Abolitionist whites often boarded vessels just before sailing when they had reason to believe that slaves being returned to bondage were aboard. They would tell these blacks that the laws of California made them free. One North Carolinian who lost two slaves this way was heard by his neighbors, long after he had returned home, still swearing at those whites who "interfered."[26]

When Peter Lester, the Philadelphia black abolitionist, came to California in 1850, he found to his sorrow that slavery was still a fact of life in this free state. He had his first contact with slaves when he settled in San Francisco. There he saw them working as domestic servants or hired-out slaves. Remaining true to his lifelong commitments, Lester chose to do something about it. He began the practice of inviting such blacks into his home, where he would lecture them about their rights and end the evening by teaching them antislavery songs. In his own words, "When they left we had them strong in the spirit of freedom. They were leaving [slavery] every day."[27] A German contemporary observer, commenting on men like Lester, said:

> The wealthy California Negroes have become especially talented in such stealing. The negroes exhibit a great deal of energy and intelligence in saving their brothers.[28]

One day in October 1851, this "energy" was evident in a case of mistaken identity. The San Francisco black barber, Robert Ellis, and a black associate observed a black man being rushed aboard a ship, and, assuming he was a man being sent back to slavery, they attempted to rescue him. In court it turned out that this assumption was not the case and all parties were dismissed.[29] But this incident reveals the rising level of free black involvement in the cities.

A most important fugitive-slave case took place in Judge Morrison's court in San Francisco in March 1851. Known as the Frank case, it was important not only for its outcome but also because it seemed to set a precedent. The courtroom was full of lawyers from the city seeking guidelines for this type of case. But of equal importance was the highly visible presence of the San Francisco black community, now some 400 strong. On 31 March, the first day of the case, the *Alta California* reported:

> There was quite an excitement in this city yesterday, among the brethren of the colored persuasion, caused by the fact that a negro boy had been taken by his master and confined.

This was probably the first occasion on which the city's black organizational talent came together in a common and familiar cause.

As the case unfolded the following facts were revealed: A Missouri slaveowner named Calloway brought eighteen-year-old Frank to California in 1850 to work in the mines. In January 1851, the young black decided to take his freedom and evidently found his way from the Sierra Nevada to San Francisco. Frank enjoyed his freedom for two months, until Calloway came to the city, found the young man, and confined him in a building on the Long Wharf. While Frank was held prisoner on the wharf, an affidavit was prepared and delivered to Judge Morrison in which Frank claimed he was being detained against his will in preparation for his return to Missouri as a slave. How the affidavit was obtained was a mystery as far as the local press was concerned. Fortunately J. B. Pierce, a white abolitionist, reported the case to Eastern antislavery papers, revealing how Frank found his defenders. Pierce reported that "friends" brought the case before Judge Morrison. Apparently in his two months of living as a free man in San Francisco Frank had made important contacts in the Negro community. These black men now rallied white support in Frank's behalf. Attorney Samuel W. Holladay was retained as Frank's defense lawyer. (Some years later Holladay, like other lawyers who defended blacks, became a member of the newly founded Republican party.)

Judge Morrison handed down a decision in the Frank case which stunned the proslavery community. He said the National Fugitive Slave Law of 1850 had no bearing on the case, because Frank took his freedom in California and did not cross state lines in doing so. He added that Calloway provided no evidence to the court proving Frank to be his slave. Calloway's lawyers attempted to establish that Frank was a slave by using the black's own words. Evidently Frank had said somewhere in the proceedings that he had been a slave in Missouri. Judge Morrison's reply to this must have been hemlock to proslavery onlookers, who supported the denial of black testimony in the courts. Morrison coolly rejected Frank's remarks about his slave status with the reminder that the California State Legislature had just the year before made Negro testimony illegal! When the judge's decision was completed, the *Herald* wrote, "Mr. Frank went his way rejoicing amid unbounded applause of his colored brethren."[30]

Slaveowners and their politically powerful supporters now began to see a real threat to their ownership of slaves in this Western state. In January 1852, Assemblyman Henry A. Crabb appeared on the scene as a champion for slaveowners. Crabb, a Southern aristocrat who was to lose his life a few years later in a proslavery military adventure in Mexico, introduced a Fugitive Slave Bill designed to make running away from masters illegal if it took place *within* California's boundaries. The bill would have given white men arbitrary powers in returning black persons they claimed as slaves in the Southern states. Assemblyman Ellis tried unsuccessfully to amend the bill, suspecting that it might be a backdoor way of introducing slavery in California. When the unchanged bill reached the senate, David Broderick was among those who were disturbed by it. Broderick feared that the arbitrariness of the law would make it possible for the kidnapper to perform his cruel work on legally free blacks. The proslavery forces, however, were too strong in Sacramento in 1852, and in April of that year the California Fugitive Slave Law was passed by the senate in a fourteen-to-nine vote. It had a twelve-month tenure to its effectiveness, was renewed twice, and then was allowed to lapse in April 1855 in a temporarily changed political environment.[31]

The fears of Broderick were not unrealistic. A year later a Missourian named Brown attempted to have Lucy, a black woman who was living in Auburn, arrested on the charge that she was a fugitive slave from Missouri. When the deputy sheriff apprehended Lucy, she called for her trustworthy white lawyer, P. W. Thomas, with whom she had been shrewd enough to leave her freedom papers. Brown's father back in Missouri had given the black woman her freedom papers in 1851. Local Auburn opinion held that the younger Brown knew this but had counted on the papers being lost or out of reach.[32]

Another case that resulted in freedom for a black person occurred in 1854 in Gold Springs, Tuolumne County. A black man named Stephen S. Hill had come with his owner Samuel Tucker from Arkansas in 1849. At some point in the early 1850s, according to Hill, Tucker gave him his freedom papers before returning to Arkansas. This is quite credible, for Hill had manifested none of the behavior pattern of a runaway. He remained in Tuolumne County, where he became a produce farmer and accumulated land estimated at $4,000 in value.

On a day in August 1854, a group of men led by a Mr. Rozier, who claimed to be the agent of Hill's former master, seized Hill at his home in Gold Springs and carried him to Sonora, claiming he was a fugitive slave. In Sonora, Judge Quint allowed time for Hill's white friends to hire a lawyer and to make a search of his cabin to locate the paper that would prove his right to freedom. But the freedom paper was never found. Local people believed that those who had seized Hill had taken care to remove all papers from his cabin. In jail in Sonora, Hill was now clearly on his way back to slavery in Arkansas. While Hill was detained in jail, Rozier returned to Hill's cabin, where he found that all of the black man's crops had been harvested and his stock spirited away. This had been done quietly by Hill's white friends and sympathizers on Hill's behalf. One of them even picked a fight with Rozier in an unsuccessful effort to get him thrown in jail. When Rozier returned to Sonora, he took Stephen Hill with him to Stockton and from there put him in chains aboard the ship *Urilda* to be taken to San Francisco. At this point, the developments became almost theatrical. At the St. Charles Hotel in Stockton, where Rozier was staying, some friendly "strangers" from Gold Springs plied him with drink and conviviality at the bar. During those amiable hours the *Urilda* lost one unwilling passenger. On 25 September, the *San Joaquin Republican* wrote, "This Stephen Hill finally won his war for personal independence." Perhaps the "Gold Spring Boys" who had harvested Hill's crops and had taken care of his cattle provided Stephen with a grub stake with which to start life again elsewhere.[33]

A curious case, involving a Sacramento fugitive slave, occurred after the California Fugitive Slave Law was passed but preceding its test before the state's supreme court in 1852. It began with an Alabama-born hunchbacked Negro hiding out in Sacramento under the protection of friends. But the black was soon discovered by his alleged owner. Benjamin Lathrop, a Northern man, had lived for many years in Alabama and had recently opened a hotel in Sacramento. Lathrop had the black arrested and brought to Justice of the Peace Fry, who judged that the runaway was

Lathrop's slave and eligible for immediate return to Alabama. Lathrop first planned to send the black man back to the South but evidently had second thoughts. Instead he placed an ad in the local paper announcing that he was willing to sell the Negro for $100, which he declared to be a $200 loss. The advertisement contained slurs and taunts at "abolitionist brethren" and challenged them to pay for the slave instead of "stealing" him.

A local merchant, Caleb Fay, saw the advertisement and instructed his lawyer, Joseph W. Winans, to purchase the slave for him so that Fay could give him his freedom. Winans agreed on condition that he share the costs with Fay. They went to Lathrop's hotel, where they were led to a dark locked room where the slave had been interned. In a touching scene, the hunchbacked black man thanked his deliverers and went on to his freedom. Some years later Fay saw the Negro working as a bootblack on the streets of Sacramento. He told Fay that he had saved $2,000 toward buying his mother and sisters out of slavery. In 1852, shortly after Lathrop had received the $100, his hotel burned down and he left for Redwood City, California, where he became an important political figure.[34]

It was inevitable that the constitutionality of Crabb's Fugitive Slave Act would be tested. What gave poignancy to the test case was the fact that the black men involved understood themselves to be legally free men. Robert and Carter Perkins and Sandy Jones had been brought separately from Mississippi to California to mine gold. Jones was a man in his sixties, with a wife and grown children still in Mississippi. In the mines the three men worked at different times for C. S. Perkins, their owner, as well as for his Mississippi associates. Early in 1851 they were all placed in charge of Dr. John Hill, with whom they stayed and worked until 15 November 1851. On that day, Dr. Hill told them, in effect, that their "time" was up and that they could leave his employ as free men. From 15 November on they worked together as free men, accumulating property and gold near Ophir.

In the middle of the night of 31 May 1852, they were seized in their beds by the sheriff of Placer County and five other white men, including Perkins. They were charged with being fugitive slaves, put into their own farm wagon, and rushed off by a circuitous route to Sacramento. There they were taken before Justice of the Peace Fry, whose sympathy with slaveowners was now well established as a result of the Lathrop case.[35]

At this point concerned blacks and whites in Sacramento moved into action. Cornelius Cole, an attorney with an antislavery record in the East, recalled that he first knew of this arrest through Mark Hopkins, who asked him to handle the defense of Jones and the two Perkins. Hopkins, in turn, had been alerted by one of his Negro servants, who asked if he would look into the matter. The black community of Sacramento engaged Cole as well as Joseph Zabriskie and Joseph Winans, who had previously aided blacks in slave cases.[36] They drew up a habeas corpus, and the three alleged fugitives were taken to Judge Aldrich's court, where their attorneys pleaded their case. In an oral opinion, the judge declared the three to be fugitive slaves. With this decision in his hands, C. S. Perkins, accompanied by proslavery friends, proceeded to take the three black men to San Francisco and from there planned to ship them back to Mississippi.

At this point the white lawyers and the Sacramento blacks, now aided by the San Francisco black community, decided to fight Judge Aldrich's decision. The concerned blacks were determined to liberate the three men. The white lawyers, unwilling to risk publicly declaring themselves abolitionists, maintained that they were out to prove the California Fugitive Slave Law unconstitutional. Meetings were held, funds were raised, and more legal talent was employed. The immediate result was a dramatic rescue that took place on board the ship *California*, docked in San Francisco. Police officers with an arrest warrant, probably arranged by Cornelius Cole, who had followed the defendants to San Francisco, took the three men from the ship and jailed them until their case could be heard by the state supreme court.[37]

The California Fugitive Slave Law had been in effect barely a month when the Perkins case erupted. Between 1849 and the passage of this law in 1852, freedom attempts by courageous blacks had been highly individual in character. Black men or women striking for freedom depended on their own luck, assistance from an occasional anonymous white or black citizen, and the good fortune of having their case possibly heard before a sympathetic judge. Starting with the Perkins case, for the first time in California, freedom attempts were no longer strictly an individual matter but were openly supported by both black and white segments of the community.

The Perkins case in 1852 brought urban black involvement in fugitive-slave cases to a new high. The case was to go before the state supreme court on 1 July, the first such case to go before that body. The month of June was therefore one of intense activity for black community leaders, who sought to obtain funds and sympathetic white lawyers. While there were lawyers to be found, there was no evidence of their providing legal services without fees, as was so often the case among abolitionist lawyers of Boston and elsewhere in the East.[38] This view is supported by a revealing letter to Cornelius Cole, while he was on the Perkins case, from James Pratt, a friend to the Perkins cause, who wrote:

> The truth is Brown who has as much influence here as any man in the city with the judges of the court and the rest of the people is not willing to take hold of the dark side of these cases without a handsome fee being paid in advance. . . .

(Harvey Brown later became associated with the case.)

> If the parties suceed in raising money and I don't see why they may not the fees of both yourself and he might as well be paid in advance as afterward and much better. . . .

> In fact, Mr. Cole, I think that the colored men by paying a little each might raise at least the sum of five thousand dollars which would pay pretty well you know for the trouble. . . . Do what you can to make them raise a handsome fund for the purpose intended.

After Pratt concluded his financial calculations, he turned to more humanistic thoughts and noted,

> Now that man who brought me your letter is really an intelligent man and I shouldn't wonder if he was a good man. I begin to think that some of these negroes ought to have been white men—some of our white men negroes.[39]

Still Pratt never thought the black he referred to was "white" enough for him even once to mention his name. However, despite these matters of money, the cause got underway. White men in the ministry, whose motives were less materialistic, were also involved in this case. Through the words of Reverend S. D. Simonds, we see how one Methodist was involved; we also see some of the problems of the black community. Writing to Cole of the activities in Sacramento, he said:

> The Colored people here have been applied to by a committee of a meeting held in Sacramento for aid. They write here that they have fee'd lawyers and paid court expenses to the amount of 4 or 500 dollars and are now straitened for funds. I make no doubt that all necessary help can be had here. I write you to desire you to make a statement to me of what amount and for what purpose money will be wanted. Let us guard the interests of benevolence . . . as well as the interests of Liberty. God and the Right! Push the case to the last point.[40]

William H. Newby, an editor of the first California Negro newspaper, considered Reverend Simonds a man who "has done more for the colored people than any other man in the State."[41]

When the Perkins case came to the state supreme court on 1 July, the defense for the slaves included Harvey Brown and his law firm as well as Cornelius Cole. The defense argued that Robert and Carter Perkins and Sandy Jones were legally free by the terms of the California constitution and that they had been in California so long with their master that he could not be classified as a sojourner. They contended that the state Fugitive Slave Law of 1852 was an ex-post facto law designed to protect slaveowners long after the time intended by the state's constitution. The court decided that no law could possibly impair the rights to slave property guaranteed by the federal constitution, since to do otherwise would violate the rights of the slave states. This was a clear victory for the proslavery elements in California, and Carter and Robert Perkins and Sandy Jones were ordered back to slavery in Mississippi.[42] Before long they were seen aboard the steamer *Cortez* on its way to Panama. However, W. C. Ellis, a Marysville antislavery man, wrote in October to Eastern friends, stating with certainty that the men had made a successful escape while in Panama.[43]

The Perkins case was marked by some additional elements. Colonel Zabriskie was harassed to the point where he felt it necessary to publish a statement of explanation for his interest in the Perkins case. Cornelius Cole, who was even more involved than Zabriskie, was so alarmed by physical threats that he felt it impaired the effectiveness of one of his court appearances.[44] Violence and the threat of violence against the white critics of the Fugitive Slave Law continued as long as the law lasted. In April 1854, when the Fugitive Slave Law received its last and much-debated renewal, Senator Colby of Sacramento, a critic of the law, was clubbed in the state capitol by Senator Leake of Calaveras County, who was one of its ardent supporters.[45]

During the three years that the 1852 California Fugitive Slave Law was in effect, numerous anonymous black men and women were carried back to slavery. In the absence of precise records, the exact number of blacks who were returned unwillingly to slavery will never be known. Besides the fugitive-slave cases that were covered by the press, an occasional noisy or colorful departure of a struggling slave would be deemed newsworthy. Seven blacks who were hurried through Sacramento back to slavery in 1852 would never have been heard of, had not W. C. Ellis of Marysville noted the incident in a letter to friends.

The law was allowed to expire in April 1855,[46] and it was during this crucial month that a case occurred in San Jose. Early in that month, a young black named George Mitchell, who had been brought to California in 1849, was arrested by his alleged owner. Three San Jose lawyers took up his case and achieved enough delays to keep the case undecided until after 14 April, when the law expired, and until they could get the case transferred to the friendly court of Judge C. P. Hester. Judge Hester easily concluded the case by agreeing with counsel for defense that the California Fugitive Slave Law was no longer operative, and he set Mitchell free. A friendly crowd in the court received the decision with obvious satisfaction.[47]

The Mitchell case and the expiration of the California Fugitive Slave Law marked the end of a series of prominent and significant fugitive-slave cases. With a number of moderately antislavery men among its leadership, the rising American Party, better known as the Know-Nothings, augured some improvement in the political climate from the point of view of antislavery men. This slightly improved atmosphere may have contributed to the organization of the first state-wide Colored Convention in 1855, which signaled the growing maturity of the black communities of California as well as their increasing activity in civil-rights matters.[48] From this point on, the rescuing of slaves was mostly a matter of reaching blacks who remained in servile relationships in various isolated parts of the state and telling them that they need not do so. Some of this kind of work continued through and even beyond the Civil War period.

With the California Fugitive Slave Law dead and buried and the atmosphere in the state seemingly improved, unexpectedly a fugitive-slave trial erupted that was to become the state's last and most famous case. Fortunately it took place when the Negro community was best equipped to deal with it.

This was the Archy Lee case. An eighteen-year-old black, Lee had been brought across the plains from Mississippi in the fall of 1857 by Charles Stovall, the son of his owner. Stovall settled in Sacramento and hired Archy out for wages. Stovall taught school for several months, a fact which later proved destructive to the image he tried to give of himself as a sojourner passing through the state with his family slave. When, in time, Stovall began to worry about Archy's fidelity, he attempted to send him back to Mississippi. But his efforts failed. Archy hid in the Hotel Hackett, an establishment owned by free Negroes. Stovall searched him out and had him arrested. Legal talent was immediately available for Lee, and the first of a series of dramatic court battles began.

On 7 January 1858, in Sacramento County, Archy Lee appeared in Judge Robert Robinson's court with attorneys John H. McKune and Edwin Bryant Crocker by his side. Crocker had been an antislavery man in Indiana and was the brother of Charles Crocker, who later founded the Southern Pacific Railroad. The next day, when Judge Robinson took up the case at greater length, the courtroom held many black observers. Legal maneuvering proceeded for several weeks, until the case came before the judge again on 23 January. This time Archy had the well-known antislavery lawyer, Joseph W. Winans, at his side. More arguments were heard and judgment was delayed until 26 January, when the judge rendered his decision. He declared Archy a free man, but the young black had hardly heard those words when he was immediately arrested again. Stovall's lawyers, anticipating this decision, were ready with a new warrant and had arranged, through a friendly state supreme court justice, David Terry, to have the entire case brought before that body.[49]

This meant more weeks of waiting in jail for Archy. Then, on 11 February, the state supreme court handed down its strange decision. The court declared that the law was valid that said that persons who came to California with the intention to live in the state could not own slaves. But since his master was an inexperienced young man and not in good health, and since this was the first case of its kind, the court acceded that Archy should be given to Stovall to return to slavery! Most of the legal profession and the California press roared in derision. It was a decision that was to live on for many years as a judicial absurdity. Archy was readied for departure from Sacramento to San Francisco, where he was to be placed on board a vessel and returned to Mississippi.[50]

In the meantime, the Bay area black community was thoroughly roused and determined to fight the decision. By 1858, they had had three State Colored Conventions. Their experience, as well as their numbers and material resources, had increased, and they knew what support they could depend on in the white community.

Stovall and his friends must have been fully aware of the determination of California Negroes to free Archy Lee. Every precaution possible was taken to keep Archy out of sight until he could be secreted aboard the ship *Orizaba* on 5 March. But the resources of the black vigilance committees were too much for Stovall. The visible resources were the blacks who patrolled the wharves and docks of San Francisco all during the preceding days; the invisible allies informed the lawyers that Stovall had hidden Archy in a boat anchored off Angel Island. As the *Orizaba*, bound for Panama, sailed away from the Embarcadero toward the middle of San Francisco Bay, a rendezvous took place between the larger ship and the smaller one that came out from anchor at Angel Island. Stovall and friends lifted Archy aboard and were immediately confronted by the law. Archy was "arrested" for safe-keeping and Stovall was served with a legal writ for holding a slave illegally. The *Orizaba* sailed on without Archy or his master.[51]

The legal struggle began anew in San Francisco. The very afternoon that Archy was rescued from the *Orizaba*, a meeting was called by San Francisco's black leadership to raise funds for the forthcoming battle. Appeals went out to black communities throughout the state. Advertisements were also placed in the white press. Some of the Negro leadership put themselves in debt in order to raise money. And a new and more powerful team of white lawyers was engaged to fight for Archy's freedom. Heading them was the well-known Republican attorney, Edward D. Baker, one of California's most powerful orators. Baker, whose parents were Quakers and whose friend from his Illinois days was Abraham Lincoln, was a man who had no fear of taking on an unpopular case. He had once said, "And if I ever forget, if I ever deny, that highest duty of my profession, may God palsy this arm and hush my voice forever."[52]

Days of legal skirmishing took place, with much courtroom drama in which blacks were active participants. Local blacks and black people from out of town attended the trial. Riots in the streets seemed imminent to some observers but never actually took place. On 17 March, before Judge Freelon's district court, Colonel Baker made a dramatic presentation in which he showed his contempt for the supreme court's decision on Archy. He said:

> Judge Burnett [of the supreme court] said he would set aside the constitution and the law, because Stovall was ignorant of our law. God Almighty sets a premium on knowledge; the Supreme Court offers a reward for ignorance. If a learned, wise and great man had brought Archy into the State the Judges of the Supreme Court would have shaken the Constitution in his face indignantly; but for Stovall they set that document aside.[53]

He put in question the validity of their decision, claiming that what they had ruled was no decision at all and well worth ignoring. He concluded by appealing to Judge Freelon to put himself on the side of freedom.[54]

The conclusion of this day's work was to provide another period of suspense for Archy and his supporters. At the end of his presentation Baker asked the judge for an outright discharge of Archy Lee. Judge Freelon then turned to the lawyer for Stovall to ask if he objected. To the astonishment of all in the courtroom, attorney James J. Hardy said that he did not. Judge Freelon then declared Archy a free man. His words were hardly uttered when a United States marshal hovering nearby placed Archy Lee under arrest again.[55]

The Stovall forces had sensed the defeat they were about to face in Judge Freelon's court and had prepared one last desperate strategy. They brought the case before the United States Commissioner, a Southerner named William Penn Johnston. Their charge was that Archy was in violation of the 1850 National Fugitive Slave Law. As a federal official, the commissioner could rule in that kind of case, and since he was a Southerner, the Stovall forces felt that they had a sympathetic ear.

Archy had maintained his composure through many weeks of strain, but this time he was heard to cry out that he would never go back to slavery and preferred to die first. The scenes in front of the courthouse on Kearny Street were tumultuous as Archy was led away. Many fist fights between whites as well as between blacks and whites were barely averted. One black man struck a white man and was then overwhelmed by other whites. An angry Negro preacher from Marysville was arrested for expressing his sentiments.[56]

Several hearings were held before Commissioner Johnston. In one of these, Colonel Baker made one of his most impassioned pleas for freedom and one of his most devastating critiques of the Stovall case. As his most telling legal point, he brought out Stovall's opening of a school in Sacramento as an activity hardly suitable to a sojourner. Baker spoke to the general principle of freedom when he dealt with the request by Stovall's lawyer for comity between the states of the United States—meaning that California should recognize Mississippi's slave laws. To this Baker said:

> If I were a judge, and called on to decide on comity, I would have some regard to other things than courts or governments, or empires. I would show some comity to the great principles of freedom of human liberty.

He then established that Archy was not a fugitive across state lines but had made his strike for freedom *within* California.[57] This last point, he argued, placed the case beyond the concern of a federal official. Baker's argument formed the rationale for Commissioner Johnston's decision on 14 April. On that day he declared Archy a free man.[58]

The joy that followed in the black San Francisco community can well be imagined. Archy was carried off like a hero, and that night there were many victory celebrations. During the days that followed, Archy, according to one chronicler of this period, made his home at the boardinghouse of Mary Ellen "Mammy" Pleasants. A few weeks later, when several hundred California Negroes decided to go to British Columbia for reasons that will be explained elsewhere, Archy went with them to put greater distance between himself and the caprices of American law.[59]

During the tense days between the decision in Judge Freelon's court and the decision of Commissioner Johnston, and as a result of the turbulence following Archy's re-arrest, the leadership of the San Francisco Negro community had felt it necessary to publish a statement about their objectives:

> EDITOR EVENING BULLETIN:—We respectfully ask permission to publish in your columns the following Card to the Public, which has been caused by the times:

"At a public meeting of the colored citizens of San Francisco, held in Zion Church, on 25th March, the undersigned were appointed a committee to publish a card setting forth the views of the colored people of this city, and their true position, in relation to the slavery under which we live.

"There has been a disposition manifested by a portion of the press in this city, to misrepresent us, by characterizing us as a rebellious and turbulent class of persons, who disregard the laws of our country, when we come in contact with them, or when they happen to oppose our peculiar views. Now we wish to inform our friends and the public generally, that we are a law-loving, and law-abiding class of persons, who have always quietly submitted to the unjust enactments that have been imposed upon us, in this our common country, from time to time. We have been the subjects of innumerable wrongs without any just cause, yet we have borne up under them with scarcely a murmur, and can appeal with pride to our character and standing throughout this entire State, and point to our industry, integrity and moral worth.

"It has been publicly asserted that we had counseled and determined to rescue the boy Archy from the custody of the officers who had him in charge and that we had no confidence in the legal tribunals of this State—or in the United States Commissioner, before whom he is to be tried.

"All of this, we pronounce an unqualified falsehood, gotten up by our enemies for the purpose of making political capital against us in the community. As a class, we are liberty-loving people, who are deeply interested in whatever pertains to the welfare of mankind. In the case of Archy, we feel that we are maintaining the laws of the State of California, and ask for his liberation upon just and legal grounds, believing that he is rightly entitled to his freedom, which we are interested in securing according to law, and which we will leave no proper means untried to accomplish. We are well satisfied that the reflecting portion of the people are disposed to act justly by us in this case, and award us all that we merit—that of being a quiet and orderly class of people."[60]

Involuntary servitude of any kind was offensive and immoral to blacks. This was strikingly illustrated in a case that did not involve a black victim. In fact, the "victim" was an Indian child named Shasta. When the black community of San Francisco suspected that a black man had been the informer responsible for returning the Indian girl to servitude, a community meeting was called in a San Francisco Negro church to investigate the charge. The inconsistencies of reportage prevent us from knowing the outcome of this informal trial. Had the man been proven guilty of the charge, he would undoubtedly have been declared an outcast, the usual practice in punishing immoral behavior in the black community. Of added interest in this case is the fact that the Indian girl was allegedly in servitude to Dr. Oliver M. Wozencraft, who had expressed decidedly proslavery views as a delegate to the 1849 Constitutional Convention.[61]

Almost exactly one year after the Archy Lee affair concluded, another similar case seemed about to occur in San Francisco. It involved a frail young black man named William Mathews, aided by a re-aroused black activist community. Dr. McCormick and his wife brought three slaves with them when they came to California in 1858. In January 1859, the doctor, who was an army officer, made plans to return to his native Maryland. Word spread in the San Francisco neighborhood where the McCormicks lived on Clay Street near the Plaza. It was an area that included many black businesses and boardinghouses. News of the McCormick family's departure reached blacks, who gained the impression that the young slave Mathews was about to be returned to slavery against his will. They therefore proceeded to rescue the young man.

Dr. McCormick first learned of the situation when he received a report that a group of seven or eight black men had carried off his young slave to parts unknown. The doctor immediately assumed that an abduction had taken place and informed the police to that effect. Abduction did not quite describe what had happened, because the action occurred during daylight, and three of the Negroes involved were so easily identified that their names appeared on the abduction charge. When the three men were arrested, young Mathews was with them, and the facts proved to be quite different from the Archy Lee case. Apparently Mathews had gone willingly with his "abductors." Although he was not unhappy with the doctor, he was reluctant to return to a slave state, even though many members of his family were there. As a result of this statement of facts, the three alleged abductors were freed. Mathews, however, did not go off with the three black men but walked up to the doctor and stood awkwardly and silently in front of him. One senses here the agonized ambivalence of this young black man, who was torn between the taste of freedom he had found with his new black friends in San Francisco and the security he had with the doctor, toward whom he had little if any hostility. Had he been a more robust young man, like Archy Lee, who weathered a journey across the plains and mountains, his decision might have been different. But when the *Sonora* carried the McCormick family through the Golden Gate, William Mathews was with them.

This account is significant for the sustained interest it reveals on the part of some San Francisco blacks in fighting slavery in this uncertain period. The three men who undertook to aid Mathews in gaining his freedom were William F. Freeman, from either Connecticut or New York, and Charles Moreno and William R. Mathews from Massachusetts. The census of 1860 indicates that the older Mathews was the owner of the Golden Gate boardinghouse, which catered exclusively to black seamen. One of these seamen was William Freeman. Moreno cannot be found in this census, although it may have been his wife who was involved in an attempt to harbor the Indian girl Shasta. When young Mathews was first "abducted," more than a half dozen black men were involved. If one were to reconstruct the case, it would appear that Mathews gave the alarm to the seamen in his boardinghouse.[62]

Later in 1859, the alertness of two freedom conscious seamen saved a young black man from being sold into slavery. Griffin Dodson, a black San Franciscan, described as a "respectable waterman," indentured his thirteen-year-old son Henry to another black named Sanford A. Taylor, who was in the barbering trade. Taylor took Henry to the lumber boom town of Crescent City near the Oregon border. There Taylor did not prosper as well as he had anticipated and unfeelingly abandoned Henry and departed for British Columbia. The thirteen-year-old black lad wandered about for a time and wound up in Orleans Bar. There he fell into the hands of the white Missourian Wrights, father and son, who, after some weeks, took him to San Francisco. During all this time Griffin Dodson had heard nothing about his son and became increasingly apprehensive.

In San Francisco the Wrights confined Henry so that he could not contact anyone. They then took passage on the steamer *Uncle Sam* and had Henry held below. They clearly intended to sell him into slavery in the traditional manner of free-Negro kidnappers. The lad's salvation came in the form of a black man named Lewis and the ship's baker, a white man. Upon learning the fate intended for Henry Dodson, they took him into custody, with what must have been the cooperation of the ship's captain, and when the *Uncle Sam* docked in Panama the Wrights had to go on without Henry. Young Dodson then returned with the ship to San Francisco and to his family.[63]

Archy Lee's was the last significant legal case of the gold rush decade. But it produced the greatest rallying of blacks and their white allies around a fugitive-slave case ever seen in California. It was inevitable that the fugitive-slave fight in California would be a major preoccupation of the increasingly militant black community.[64] In the early years of the decade, the very fluidity of legal interpretation was an invitation to activity. As the decade went on, and the numbers of those with wealth and political skill increased, the imperative of commitment kept the struggle going. This commitment was fortified by the large number of black veterans of civil-rights struggles in the free states in the East who joined the westward movement and settled in the cities of California. These men were simply picking up where they had left off in New England and elsewhere.

7 Churches and Schools

The churches and schools of the California black communities grew slowly in the decade of the 1850s. The predominantly male and transient character of the entire California population was the prime factor in this slow growth. Men tend not to establish stable institutions where they do not plan to remain permanently.

The first religious services that black men attended in California were conducted by white men. One of the first white ministers in the gold fields, Reverend Daniel Woods, described his open-air congregation sitting on a river bank and composed of all nationalities and colors. As early as 1849, some blacks were married by the Congregationalist Reverend Timothy Dwight Hunt. After the black Methodist Reverend Darius Stokes left Sacramento in 1849 or 1850, white Methodist clergymen preached to the small Sacramento black group from time to time until they had their own minister. When Abner H. Francis, the black New Yorker, arrived in San Francisco in 1851, he went to Presbyterian services. He noted, with satisfaction, as he sat himself where he chose to, that the service had "none of that spirit of caste too often practiced at home."[1]

It was not long before blacks sought to organize their own independent churches in California. The tradition of independence had begun during the era of the American Revolution and the early national period of American history. In those years the Philadelphia black Methodists, who had been given second-class status in the white Methodist churches, decided to endure it no longer and organized a separate Methodist church. Thus was the African Methodist Episcopal (A.M.E.) Church born. The Philadelphia-oriented black Methodists added the name Bethel to their denomination. By the 1820s, the New York black Methodists had also separated from the white Methodists, calling their church African Methodist Episcopal Church Zion to distinguish themselves from the Philadelphia group. The New York group was soon followed by the New England black Methodists. The desire for independence at times led to the formation of small and lesser-known groups. The resentment against racist etiquette in this period also produced separate Baptist and Presbyterian black churches.[2]

Thus by the time blacks came to California, the tradition of independence in religious matters was already firmly established. Black Protestant Christianity had become the one and only truly black-controlled institution of American life in the North, and from it sprang much of the Negro leadership of the nineteenth century.

From the fragmentary materials on the first years of the 1850s it is fairly certain that the first separate religious organization of blacks in California took place in Sacramento. Between 1850 and 1852, an A.M.E. group existed under the guidance of the Fletcher brothers, Barney and George, who had been born in slavery. While Reverend Barney Fletcher was called "Reverend" at that time, he was apparently not fully ordained until later. In the meantime, the group recorded its continued interest in obtaining an ordained minister during those years. This congregation was frequently preached to by ministers of the local white Methodist church, but of special interest is the frequency with which the white Methodist records reveal the black group's request for a black elder. Yet, by July 1851, this small congregation had collected $1,500 for religious purposes and they owned a debt-free church. A founding member recalled that the Reverend Isaac Owen, the Sacramento white Methodist minister, was very devoted to this black congregation and helped carry the lumber for the construction of their church on Seventh Street between G and H streets.[3]

Another black Methodist church, the first black church

in San Francisco, was founded in 1852. It was organized by the Reverend John Jamison Moore, who had been born a slave. This A.M.E. Zion church was established on Stockton Street between Broadway and Vallejo. By 1856 it was in a brick building worth $4,000, had a sabbath school with fifty pupils, and possessed a library of 250 books. In 1854 Reverend Barney Fletcher came down from Sacramento to help organize another A.M.E. church that was to be called St. Cyprian. Located on Jackson Street between Stockton and Powell, it soon became the larger of the two. Operating on a daily basis in the church basement of St. Cyprian was an elementary school for black children. Before the year was out, Reverend T. M. D. Ward had arrived to take over St. Cyprian, with Reverend Darius Stokes as his assistant. By 1856 Reverend Ward was the highest-ranking black Methodist clergyman, and it was he who organized the California conference of the A.M.E. churches.[4]

By 1857 there was a third A.M.E. church in San Francisco, called Little Pilgrim Church. Its preacher was Reverend Jeremiah B. Sanderson, who was to achieve considerable renown as an educator of Negro children and as a fighter for the black community's share of public school tax funds. He had arrived in California in 1854, the same year as Reverend Ward, both of them coming from New Bedford, Massachusetts. Sanderson's church was located up the hill, to the west of the other churches, on Scott Street, between Pacific and Broadway.[5]

In 1856, St. Cyprian Church returned to the ministry of Reverend Barney Fletcher and Reverend Ward took up state-wide work. But the congregation apparently moved to Reverend Sanderson's church by 1859, although the basement of St. Cyprian's continued to be used as an elementary school for children, probably because it was closer to their homes. Church membership may well have declined in 1858, due to the departure of several hundred California blacks for Victoria, British Columbia, and the newly discovered gold regions of the Fraser River. After St. Cyprian's congregation moved to the Scott Street church, the building was offered for sale. Peter Anderson, one of the Colored Convention leaders, noted with distress that in the interim period some blacks in the community were using the former church premises as a place of entertainment and were presenting minstrel shows.

Black churches were not exempt from the work of arsonists who periodically plagued all of San Francisco. In March 1854, an attempt was made by unknown vandals to burn down St. Cyprian Church. The fire was fortunately discovered and extinguished in time.[6]

As elsewhere in the nation, in California the Baptist denomination was the other major church for blacks. It was usually the church of the less affluent and prestigious, especially those who were Southern-born and raised. The first Negro Baptist church in San Francisco, called the Third Baptist Church, was organized in 1852, the same year as the first A.M.E. church. It was located some distance away from the A.M.E. churches, on Dupont (now Grant) Street near Union. It started with thirteen members and held to a few dozen until 1857. Up to that time the church had no regular pastor and was presided over by one of its members, Joseph Davenport, who had been a licentiate in the black Baptist church in New Orleans. From time to time, the black ministers of the A.M.E. churches would present sermons to these Baptists.[7]

Early in 1857, Reverend Charles Satchell came from Cincinnati to the Third Baptist Church, and after that the Negro Baptists in San Francisco began a decided growth. Reverend Satchell presented his church to the black community with a bit of dramatic effect in order to increase its visibility. On a Sunday morning in February 1857, he held a public baptism at the foot of Stockton Street by the Bay waters for a few new members. Several thousand persons, most of them whites, witnessed the event. It was reported that among the whites there were dock loafers and vagabonds who tried to exceed each other in vulgar remarks. Objects were thrown at the participants standing in the water. But this was no deterrent to church growth, and in the first year of Reverend Satchell's ministry, the Third Baptist Church doubled its membership, bringing it to eighty-one. But they were not free of financial difficulties. In December 1857, they still lacked funds to build a desired new church.[8]

Reverend Satchell, like his A.M.E. counterparts, was evidently not shy about his antislavery sentiments, in spite of the fact that his church was part of an overwhelmingly white association. In the 1857 report of the San Francisco Baptist Association, the Third Baptist Church's contribution to the *Minutes* included their support for the Association's struggle against intemperance, gambling, and "all other immoralities, including, as a matter of Christian consideration, AMERICAN SLAVERY." This antislavery statement shows the clear hand of Reverend Satchell. He had been a man of courage in more dangerous situations than California. As a Baptist preacher in Louisiana, he had become the object of suspicion when antislavery sentiments crept into his preaching. He eventually had to leave Louisiana for his physical safety.[9]

In 1858, the Third Baptist Church suffered a membership loss because of the Fraser River gold rush and the subsequent departure of many blacks to British Columbia. For the first time in that decade, for the years 1858 and 1859 the Third Baptists gave no membership report to the California Baptist Association. By 1860, they had lost Reverend Satchell and were down to thirty-one members.[10]

During the Civil War years, and with the return of many Negroes who had migrated to Victoria, the A.M.E. and the Third Baptist churches experienced a new growth in membership. By 1862 the Third Baptists reported a membership of seventy-four, and by 1863 the A.M.E. churches in San Francisco had a membership of nearly one hundred.[11]

It was not until 1856 that a Negro Baptist congregation, called the Siloam Baptist Church, was formed in Sacramento. The first meetings were held in a Chinese chapel with a group of twenty-one persons. The Reverend Charles Satchell came up from San Francisco from time to time to aid them in their services. By 1859 the congregation had enjoyed some modest growth and could boast of a pastor of their own, the Reverend J. W. Flowers. To finance the purchase of a permanent church building, through 1859 and 1860 this small group sponsored fund-raising events that culminated in a much-publicized Christmas fair in 1860. The building they purchased with these funds cost $800 and was located on Fifth Street between N and O streets. Earlier it had been a Jewish synagogue.[12]

While the most prominent Methodist and Baptist churches were found in the major black population centers of San Francisco and Sacramento, there were smaller but tenacious congregations scattered throughout northern California. The most important ones existed in Stockton and Marysville.

Stockton of the 1850s had both an A.M.E. and a black Baptist church. The A.M.E. church, called Ebenezer, was founded in 1852, with Reverend Virgil Campbell serving as its minister for most of the decade. The church was located on Commerce Street near LaFayette. The size of its congregation in the fifties is not clear, but one report noted twenty-nine members in 1863. In 1859 they built a new church on ground given to the Stockton A.M.E. by Captain Charles Weber, the German-born founder of the town. The Baptists established their Second Baptist Church on Washington Street, between Commerce and Beaver, in 1854. While they were small, having only sixteen members in 1857, they seemed to weather the British Columbia exodus a bit better than the other Negro Baptist churches. In 1858 and 1859 they were one of just two Negro Baptist churches to report to the California General Baptist Convention.[13]

Marysville during most of the 1850s had only a single Baptist church. Despite its small size, the church seemed to hum with activities, which were well reported in the friendly *Marysville Herald.* In 1853 the black Baptists of Marysville, with the aid of white friends, obtained a building lot on which to erect their Mount Olivet Church. Until 1857 the work of this congregation is obscure, but in that year a sharp burst of activity took place. This is undoubtedly related to the arrival in Marysville of Reverend Thomas Randolph, a Virginia-born Baptist, who until 1856 had been living in San Francisco. Through the summer and fall of 1857, the church women's committees conducted "Ladies' Festivals" as fund-raising events in order to build a church on the land they owned. Marysville whites were invited to attend and to spend their money on the bakery goods and knitwear that were offered. In October of 1857, a public baptism of some members took place in the Feather River; this was witnessed by a large crowd of Marysville residents. The *Marysville Herald* applauded the work of the Mount Olivet congregation and urged its readers to support them. By January 1858, the congregation's construction efforts had out-paced the rainy season and the building was completed. On the corner of Sixth and High streets, the Marysville Negro Baptists now had a church with a basement for a schoolroom. If the Baptist convention reports are accurate, this building project was accomplished by only fifteen men and women. By 1859 or 1860, when Marysville had about two hundred Negro residents, a small A.M.E. church was founded.[14]

From time to time, religious gatherings by blacks were noted in various parts of northern California and in the gold fields, but they seem to have been of a transitory character. For instance, an A.M.E. church is noted in 1855 in Placerville, but its history is not clear. The next mention of it is in 1863, when it had only six members. The one small congregation in the gold country that survived the population mobility of the mining counties and was not in a significant urban center was the A.M.E. church in Grass Valley, Nevada County. As early as 1854, this group of ten persons held a festival to raise funds for a church. In a friendly environment, partly created by the local white Methodist and Congregational churches, they succeeded in building their church. Some years later they erected a small schoolhouse in back of the church.[15]

Until nearly the end of the decade, there seemed to be no black church activity in the counties of the southern mines. A fire in Sonora in 1860 revealed the fact that buildings "scorched" by the conflagration included the "colored church," which was located in a racially mixed community that included many Mexicans. This was an area of dubious fame called the Tigre District. The denomination of this church was not recorded. The only other evidences of church activity among Negroes in the southern mines were the elusive stories about a black woman who was preaching to mixed audiences in Calaveras and El Dorado counties in 1857 and 1858. She was described as "respectable" in her profession, and she stated that her objective was to raise funds for a church in Mokelumne Hill in Calaveras County.[16]

There is no evidence of any significant effort by the major white denominations to seek Negro members in California during the 1850s. In those years the white Protestants were frantically involved in reaching their own roving and gold seeking white coreligionists, whom they felt to be in great danger of damnation in the California environment. White ministers who had settled congregations and who themselves held antislavery views would content themselves with giving aid to blacks who wished to have their own churches. By this time most white ministers were well aware of the wish by blacks to worship separately. Open-air mission churches, such as that of Reverend William Taylor which attempted to bring religious services to seamen in San Francisco, were available to Negroes, and at times they did attend these services. The Protestant

Episcopal Church (Episcopalian) made some feeble efforts to interest blacks, but it was not until 1866 that anything tangible was accomplished. At that time they ordained as deacon Peter Williams Cassey, a black who was then teaching in a San Jose school for black children. Whether the Episcopal church had anything to do with this school is not clear.[17]

While some Latin-Americans with African ancestry undoubtedly attended Catholic churches in California, they were not identified as blacks. A few American blacks from Louisiana were reported as Catholics, but there is no evidence that the Catholic Church sought to reach Negroes in this period.[18] As the Catholic Church became more Irish in its leadership, proselytizing blacks would become even less likely, since Irish-Negro relations were hostile in the nineteenth century.

Education for all children in the California of the 1850s was meagre. Public schools were the victim of an uninterested legislature, Democratic-dominated, with a very strong Southern flavor which held that education was a private affair and not a public responsibility. Governor Burnett's first message to the legislature in 1849 did not even mention education.[19] In 1851, the state legislature allowed municipalities to set up schools at their own expense, and in 1852 the state began to provide some funds. But no provision was made for minority children. School districts were left the responsibility of making their own decision about support for schools for children of color. In these years the idea of integrated schools was considered unthinkable by most Americans. By 1860, California Negroes were asking for more financial aid for their schools. They were also, with the support of a few whites, calling for integrated schools and pointing to New England, where such schools were operating successfully. In the same year that these voices for integration were raised, the legislature passed a law forbidding integrated schools on pain of forfeiture of funds.[20]

In the early fifties, there were very few black children anywhere in California. In 1852 there may have been about two dozen school-age children in San Francisco and about a dozen in Sacramento. But after the wives of black men began to join them and families increased, the need for primary schools for their children grew. Due to the high degree of concern for literacy among the California black leadership, the movement for schools soon got under way. The Negro churches were the first sponsors of schools for black children.

The first school for black children in California opened in San Francisco on 22 May 1854. It was located in the St. Cyprian A.M.E. Church on Jackson Street, where the street began to rise sharply toward the west. It was on a corner where a small side street called Virginia Place met Jackson, between Stockton and Powell.[21] For ten years, from 1854 to 1864, this church basement room, which was very uncomfortable in bad weather, provided virtually the only opportunity for formal learning for San Francisco Negro children. This was true in spite of the fact that the number of black school-age children in the city had more than tripled in that ten-year period.[22]

When this school opened, its first teacher was Reverend J. J. Moore. He had twenty-three students whose attendance was regular, although the total initial enrollment was between fifty and sixty-five. Nearly a year later, the school was reported to be growing and doing well under the "indefatigable" leadership of Reverend Moore. At the same time, the San Francisco grand jury noted the need for another "colored" school, but nothing was done about it. At about this time Mayor Stephen P. Webb of San Francisco, commenting on education in a public message, noted the inadequacy of a white school in a Baptist church but had no comment about the black school.[23] The St. Cyprian's school was a "mixed," or ungraded, school since all grades were taught in the one classroom. The school included both sexes and a considerable variety of ages. These "mixes" were not uncommon in the early stages of many rural white school systems in the United States. San Francisco black children did not receive graded education until 1875, when they were permitted entry into the already-graded white schools.

Prejudice in education was observable in another respect. When a teachers' convention was called in 1855, Reverend Moore attended it and participated in its deliberation as the only black teacher present. The result was an absurd charade that appeared in letters to the anti-Negro *San Francisco Herald.* A Sacramento delegate started the exchange by charging that Moore "voted" at this gathering, which to his way of thinking marred the proceedings and nullified its deliberations. He also alleged that San Francisco City Assessor Stillman *saw* the black teacher vote, as he, Moore, and the San Francisco teachers sat in one group. Stillman then replied, saying that he had told all the city's teachers that Moore's presence at the gathering absolved them from having to remain at the conference. But, added Stillman, he did not see Moore rise to any of the calls for votes. There is no evidence that any of the teachers departed. The embarrassed president of the convention tried to silence this tempest in a teapot by saying that he too never saw Moore do any voting. What Reverend Moore thought we do not know, but William Newby reported the incident to Fred Douglass, saying in conclusion, "truth is that the convention did not have the moral courage to array itself against pro-slavery opinion."[24]

In 1855 the state legislature delivered a blow to the hopes of California Negroes that some of their taxes might be returned for schools for their children. In that year it passed a law that based state school appropriations on a count of white children only. Paul K. Hubbs, the state superintendent of education at that time, made a public statement that Negro children were naturally inferior to white children.

Within the next two years, San Francisco was to lead the way in California by being the first to provide some funds for black children, and in June of 1857 Reverend Moore, who was now receiving a salary from city funds, was officially appointed by the city board of education as principal of the Negro Children's School. At that time the city's school superintendent noted that there were 114 black children of school age, slightly more than 1 percent of the total school-age population.[25]

In May 1858, just before several hundred California Negroes were to leave for British Columbia, a newspaper reporter visiting the St. Cyprian School noted that it had forty students, some of them as old as twenty-one years. These adults were probably ex-slaves whose first opportunity to overcome their illiteracy came in California. The reporter received a favorable impression: "The classes in reading and arithmetic show considerable training and progress and singing was excellent." Within a few weeks of this report, Reverend Moore and many of these young people and their parents were on their way to Canada. When the next sessions of this school took place, its new teacher and principal was Reverend Jeremiah B. Sanderson.[26]

Just prior to the Canadian exodus, a racist incident occurred in the San Francisco school system involving a young, very light-complexioned black girl of superior intelligence. Sarah Lester was about fifteen years old, the daughter of Peter Lester of the boot firm of Lester and Gibbs. She was so light-skinned that some conjectured that her mother may have been a white woman. For three years Sarah had attended the otherwise all-white primary school that served the essentially white area where the Lesters lived. Then she took the examinations for the only high school in the city at that time. Her examination scores were second highest in general studies and highest in music and art. Sarah was accepted and had been attending classes for some weeks when the trouble began.[27]

It came in the form of an anonymous letter to the proslavery *San Francisco Herald* in January of 1858, calling upon the board of education to "do its duty" and remove Miss Lester to the school for Negroes.[28] In the weeks that followed the furor mounted and the newspapers kept the issue alive. The press seemed divided between those who wanted her expelled immediately, to avoid the precedent of "race-mixing," and those who felt that since she had done so well she should be allowed to complete her studies, with the reservation that the "error" should not be repeated.[29] At the same time, Superintendent of Education Henry B. Janes had received applications from other black families whose children were just as light as Sarah Lester. The superintendent then asked the board of education for a policy statement.

An emotionally torn board of education took up the question through February and March. It went through a variety of motions and delays that reflected the acceptance of an exclusionary policy. However, the debates also expressed the wish by some, perhaps most, board members to make an exception of Miss Lester and allow her to finish the term. The board discussion suggests that some members detested the whole racist business but feared the climate of opinion in the state. This was the year in which the state legislature would try to pass very harsh anti-immigration laws against blacks. The *San Francisco Herald* continued to badger the board unmercifully on the Lester case. The rest of the city press gave lip service to the principle of exclusion, while some papers said an exception should be made for Sarah Lester. White people from Sarah's old Spring Valley School neighborhood petitioned the board to allow her to remain, and some of her white fellow students even threatened to leave the high school if she were forced to go.[30]

But this was to no avail. The agonized board passed a much-debated resolution affirming a policy that black students be placed solely in the one black school in operation. This was not quite the end of the matter. By the second week in March, the distraught superintendent could not get himself to expel Miss Lester. Several of the city's newspapers lost little time in railing at the gentleman, and as the *Chronicle*, which had a distaste for indecent haste, put it:

> A stranger on reading these sheets would think that Negro and white children were mixed up promiscuously in the schools.

With mixed caveats the *Chronicle* went on to say,

> None are more strongly opposed to anything like amalgamation of opposite races than we are but we do not [*sic*] think that in this single case . . . a little relaxation of natural prejudices would not be productive of injury to anyone.[31]

In the course of the debate over Miss Lester, a number of distortions of fact and absurdities of logic appeared in the press. In a lengthy discussion of the case, the *Herald* pointed to Boston, erroneously contending that segregated schools were the rule in that New England city.[32] Actually, Boston three years earlier had integrated its schools, the last city in Massachusetts to do so.[33] The *Daily Evening Bulletin* had its own brand of logic:

> We hold it to be wise and true policy to maintain the social distinctions between the white and inferior races in our State, in all their strength and integrity. . . . Nothing could possibly have so powerful an effect in destroying these prejudices as educating the two races together; for if children are taught together and allowed to play promiscuously, the whites will lose their natural repulsion to blacks, and grow up with a feeling of equality and fraternization.[34]

The Lesters solved the problem for the board of education by withdrawing their daughter from the high school. Lester and his partner Gibbs shortly went to Victoria, where they became prominent members of that Canadian community. But their daughter's experience would not soon be forgotten. In a letter to a friend in Philadelphia, written a few months after the event, Mrs. Lester said, "I can scarcely bear to talk about schools."[35]

Shortly after the Lesters' departure, a number of black families requested, in May 1858, that the board of education set up a separate black high school. In October of that year, Superintendent Janes responded:

> I have solicited reliable statistics upon which to base a recommendation to the Board. . . . This class of citizens [is] taxed in common with others for the support of the schools, and is doubtless entitled to a full participation in their benefits.

Nothing came of these efforts.[36]

Over the next few years, the number of black youth of high-school age increased throughout the state. While they were too advanced to continue in the ungraded black primary schools, they were barred from the existing high schools. As a result, during the Civil War years, a movement mounted within the black communities of the state to establish a private high school for Negro youth. A meeting was held in Sacramento in January 1861, where plans were made to raise ten thousand dollars with which to establish such a school in either San Francisco or Sacramento. In this effort the blacks encountered many difficulties and eventually failed. Not until the 1870s did the public school doors open appreciably for black youth ready for high school.[37]

St. Cyprian's elementary school continued to have its problems in 1860. It was rumored that several members of the San Francisco board of education felt the attendance of the Negro school did not warrant the appropriation provided by the city. In the Bay city there were officially 100 black students in the segregated public school; the average daily attendance was 39. However, Reverend Sanderson, the black instructor of the school, gave an even harsher picture of education for black children. According to him, the city had over 200 eligible black children, while the average attendance was 32. At a meeting of black citizens, a committee was set up, composed of familiar names: Collins, Anderson, Fletcher, Sanderson, and Ruggles. This committee later reported a plan of action, and made an appeal to all black parents to come to the rescue of the school by seeing to it that their children not only enrolled but also attended. They reminded parents that the school and the appropriation for it were not easily achieved; it would be tragic to suffer the loss of the appropriation.

The committee went further and proposed a plan in which committees of parents would be established to monitor regular attendance and encourage other parents to come more frequently to the school. The report of the committee revealed that some parents had sent their children to private schools about which little was known. These parents were asked to return their children to the public school. Suggestions had been made in the past that the school hold exercises and an exhibition at the end of the term to instill pride in the school, and these were presented as something that should be institutionalized.

The reluctance of Negro children to attend school was understandable. The basement classroom at St. Cyprian's had an abandoned feeling about it. It lacked maps and blackboards and other essential ingredients of an educational environment. The noises of the street and practicing musicians on the floor above were constant distractions. Little could be done about the noise, but an appeal was made for funds to provide some minimal essentials through voluntary cash contributions. The committee also called upon black parents to pack the classroom so full with their children for the rest of the term that the board of education would not only continue their appropriation, but would even consider their need for an extra teacher. These emergency meetings took place in 1860, but real change and improvement of facilities would wait for another four years.[38]

In 1864, in the favorable political environment temporarily created by the Civil War, the ten years of education in the basement of the old St. Cyprian's Church came to an end. In that year a new school opened for the city's Negro children on Broadway near Powell, a few blocks north of their old school. But this victory was not to be enjoyed immediately. Before this site was purchased by the board of education there were to be months of delay. Reverend Jeremiah B. Sanderson, who would be the school's first principal, wrote some years later about this problem.

> Who would sell a lot for a colored school? Property holders usually object to a school upon or contiguous to their property or homes. They dislike the crowds and the noise of children. Added to this was the old prejudice against the Negro. They said, "What! A nigger school in our neighborhood! No! No!" There was no lack of lots for sale, but when it came out that the lot was wanted for a colored school, either it was "No lot for sale" or an exhorbitant [*sic*] price was demanded.[39]

After this problem was solved, San Francisco School Superintendent Tait wrote in his report:

> The colored children richly deserve their present comfortable and neat school house, after having endured unmurmuringly, for many years, their former squalid, dark and unhealthy quarters.[40]

But the superintendent was not quite accurate about the murmurs from the black community. In 1862 the community had submitted this petition:

> To the Honorable the Board of Education of the City and County of San Francisco: Gentlemen—The undersigned, residents of the city and county of San Francisco, parents, guardians and friends of children in the Public School for Colored Children, respectfully represent to your honorable body that the condition of the

school appropriated to the children is such that we deem it our duty to call your attention thereto. There are about fifty pupils in attendance, at the present time, of both sexes. The room in which they are taught is unsuitable for the following reasons: It is a basement and below the grade of the street. It is badly ventilated—the air from the west and north sides comes laden with the effluvia of cellars, sinks and vaults contiguous, and is foul and unhealthful.

The hall above the school-room is occupied by a military company. The loud sounds arising from their exercises, at times, greatly disturb those of the schoolroom. The plastering is broken and falling from the ceiling, so that the water from above runs through the floor upon the desks and floor of the schoolroom beneath.

The yard appropriated as a playground and for the necessities of the girls, has only an area of about 12 × 20 feet. The boys are compelled to go into the street, where they play over the neighboring parts of the city—the smaller exposed to dangers from passing horses and vehicles. All [are] continually tempted by the excitements to overstay the half hour of recess or play truant. At a time when your honorable board is doing so much to improve the public schools; for the health and advancement of pupils; the character, convenience and efficiency of teachers, we respectfully ask you to consider and provide for the pressing wants of the colored children.

There are now upwards of 300 colored children in this city. To accommodate them we have but one school, kept in a room only large enough to accommodate sixty.

We need another, better and larger place; a building convenient, healthful and capable of holding, at the least, one hundred and fifty pupils. We need a school of a higher grade. We need additional teachers. We are here with you: our children are in your midst. We are increasing in numbers, intelligence and wealth, in spite of powerful adverse influences.

We are willing—have ever been willing—to bear our share of the public burdens, and when the time shall come, we shall be ready to stand in the place assigned to us, to help defend the laws and uphold the government of our country.

Our children—as yours—are passing on to manhood and womanhood; they will be virtuous or vicious, respectable or disreputable, educated or ignorant. We feel the same deep and absorbing anxiety touching the future of our children, that you feel for yours. While you are making such wise and liberal provision for the school of the youth, deeming your labors and money so expended good economy, because children are the true jewels of the state—educated they are its riches, its strength, its hope and glory; the basis of its perpetuity—permit us to suggest what, no doubt, you have felt deeply in your own hearts, that the same arguments apply to colored children. Respectfully submitted J. B. SANDERSON, BARNEY FLETCHER, H. F. SAMPSON, ISAAC REED, JOHN KINNEY, CHARLES SMITH, P. ANDERSON, J. MADISON BELL, SAML. E. BURRIS, A. B. SMITH, R. T. HOUSTON.[41]

The Sacramento black community followed San Francisco by two years in establishing its first elementary school for black children. In 1854 a black woman from New Bedford, Massachusetts, Elizabeth Thorn, opened a private school with fourteen students in her own home. After about a year, Miss Thorn married and had to give up teaching. Help came in the form of Reverend Jeremiah B. Sanderson who, with his reputation preceding him as a worker for black education in Massachusetts, came up from San Francisco to continue Sacramento's first black school. At this time there were about thirty black children eligible for the school, and Sanderson set about relocating the students in space offered by the A.M.E. church. In an attempt to get some financing for the black school, he appealed to the Sacramento City Council to include it as a regular part of the city's school system.[42]

Sanderson's efforts to persuade the city to give financial support to his school were not as productive as he had hoped. In late 1855 the city council voted approval, which was shortly vetoed by Mayor English, of an ordinance to include the black school as a "separate" school. As a man who had successfully fought for school integration in New England, Sanderson had been disappointed at the "separate" stipulation. Furthermore, the council's approval would have been a hollow one, because there were no available funds to finance the black school. As Sanderson wrote to the *Liberator,* before he knew of Mayor English's veto:

> The School Question still remains in status quo [*sic*] and is likely to be for the present. We have got an ordinance . . . through much tribulation for a separate school. Here we are in the condition to take the half loaf; we have "Hobson's Choice"!

Mayor English vetoed the gesture of the city council, saying:

> While I freely admit the necessity of educating the youthful portion of our population . . . , I cannot overlook the fact that the appropriation of any portion of the taxes levied upon them to the education of colored children, would be particularly obnoxious to those of our citizens who have immigrated from Southern States. These, I believe, constitute a major part of our population.[43]

Members of the new board of school commissioners elected in 1856 had a favorable attitude toward education for black children, and twenty-five dollars a month was appropriated for the "colored school." The school was taught by Reverend Sanderson until he returned to San Francisco in about 1857. In the meantime, the school had to raise funds to supplement the meagre sum given them by the city. Parents of the school children conducted fairs to raise funds. These fairs were given publicity and support by the largest paper in Sacramento, the *Union.*[44]

By 1859, the school was on O Street between Ninth and Tenth, and a white teacher was in charge. This woman, Mrs. B. F. Folger, had taken over the teaching duties of Reverend Sanderson. She must have been a devoted teacher, for she worked for the small amounts that the black community could muster to supplement the city's contribution, which amounted to half the salary paid to teachers in white schools. By 1860 there was an average attendance of twenty-three pupils. Thirty to thirty-five were enrolled, nearly double the enrollment of four years earlier, but many of them could only attend school when they were unemployed. Like the San Francisco Negro school, this one was also a "mixed" school.[45]

During the first year of the Civil War decade, the *Sacramento Union,* the most important Republican newspaper in the state, gave more than ordinary attention to this small black school. Mixed School No. 2, as the Negro school was called, was visited several times that year by the *Union* reporter and its classroom exercises observed. This O Street schoolroom was described as housed in a dilapidated frame building which had to be closed during bad weather. Mrs. Folger was given much praise, not only for her pedagogical successes with the pupils under these conditions, but also for her courage as a white woman teaching in a black school. The reporter said that if ever a school deserved to be called "mixed," it was this one, because some of the students were as white as any in the white schools. He also noted that most of the students were girls and that three of them, in April 1860, won silver medal achievement awards given by the Sacramento board of education. The three girls bore the family names of

Dorsey, Yantis, and Caldwell; their fathers were respectively a barber, an expressman, and a hotel steward.[46] It was not until the spring of 1863 that black children in Sacramento were given a new school building. It was erected on Fifth and O streets but was never occupied by the children. An arsonist destroyed the building and all of its contents. It was not rebuilt untill 1866.[47]

In the mining counties, school-age children were not numerous and educational facilities struggled feebly. Whenever there were black young people to be found in these remote areas, some effort would be made to gain literacy for them. One of the earliest evidences of such efforts comes from Grass Valley, where a number of ex-slaves were part of the small Negro community and a school for children was established in 1854. A census taken of the children revealed that three of them, to all appearances white, actually had black parents. When they learned of this, a group of Grass Valley whites demanded that the children be expelled. But School Commissioner E. A. Tompkins balked at this cruel demand, and the irate racists carried their complaint to State Superintendent Colonel Paul K. Hubbs. They claimed that Tompkins was violating a law that said that no state funds would be given to any district that allowed nonwhite children into its classrooms. Tompkins in turn asked Hubbs for confirmation of such a rule. Superintendent Hubbs then replied in the affirmative, saying in part that the law was "intended to elevate the self-respect of children and not to degrade them"! According to one source, Commissioner Tompkins, with the support of Grass Valley citizenry, defied Hubbs, but this is not clear.[48]

A letter from a Southerner, signed "Virginian," was printed in the *Marysville Herald* in 1855, attacking Mayor English of Sacramento for denying public support of black schools. It was an eloquent appeal for the rights of free blacks to an education. This anonymous Southerner pointed out the unfairness of taxing blacks while denying their children the benefits of their parents' money. However, in 1855, there were probably fewer than five Negro children ready for school in Marysville. Two years later, though, there were about twenty, and their parents began to work for a school. The basement of the Mount Olivet Baptist Church was examined as a possible schoolroom location but was found to be in poor condition. Next they approached the city council and received a $500 appropriation to remodel the basement into an acceptable schoolroom. By 1858, a school of about twenty children was in operation with a Mrs. Sherman as the teacher. In this same year, white school children moved out of the basement of the Methodist church into a new public school building.[49]

Little is known about the education of black children in the smaller communities in the state. In Columbia, in Tuolumne County, a battle of letters in the *Courier* revealed the fact that a young black girl was attending the public school and that a (fired) former county superintendent, in his pique, was trying to embarrass the district by pointing to her presence and then asking for her expulsion. His letters, signed "Romeo," were answered by "Juliette," who took issue with him. After this flurry of correspondence, the *Courier* failed to give any news of the outcome of the controversy. Another glimpse into the recesses of this kind of experience is found in a letter that a schoolteacher wrote to his wife back East. He was teaching near Salmon Falls, in El Dorado County, in a community dominated by Southerners, especially Missourians. They had expelled "a mullatto boy" from his class. This cowed Northerner noted to his wife in the privacy of his letter that he "kept up a great thinking that he [the boy] was as white as either of these trustees."[50] This remark takes on special meaning, because the 1860 census reveals that in Salmon Falls there were several racially mixed marriages.[51]

It becomes evident that in these more remote communities, some of the black parents with very light-skinned children tried to get an education for them by having them attempt to "pass over." Unknown thousands of Americans with African ancestry have achieved partial or total passing over in the hundreds of years of the African presence in American life. Some of them undoubtedly succeeded in the California of the 1850s, and some of their descendants today may have no inkling of the African ingredients in their ancestry.

In the next decade, one school district after another began to provide support for segregated black schools and, by the 1870s, even for some integrated schools. However, in many rural locations state public support and integration were such a long time in coming that black parents began to look to the San Francisco Bay area better black schools for education for their children. In 1862, the *Pacific Appeal,* a new Negro weekly, printed a letter from a Yreka black parent asking for information about schools for black children. By this time the black school in San Francisco that Reverend Sanderson served, as teacher starting in 1859 and as principal too through the war years, had achieved a fine reputation among blacks throughout the state. This reputation, however, did not spare Sanderson the effects of institutionalized racism. When his black assistant, a young woman, had to leave her position, only a white woman could be found as a replacement. Racial etiquette would not permit a white woman in any subordinate position to a black. A white principal was found. Reverend Sanderson lost his status as principal and was transferred to another San Francisco Negro school. In 1868 Sanderson accepted an offer to teach at the school for Negro children in Stockton, which by this time had been absorbed by the Stockton public school system. It was in Stockton that Sanderson gained his greatest reputation as a black teacher. Black parents from as far away as Los Angeles sent their children to him. While Sanderson's salary was sixty dollars a month, white teachers at his level received seventy-five dollars a month.[52]

In 1866 the California legislature passed a law that

required the trustees of any school district to provide a separate school where there were at least ten children of African, Mongolian, or Indian descent. The law also stated that where education for these children was not provided, they should be permitted to attend the white children's school unless the parent of any white child objected. The 1870 legislature modified this law by eliminating "Mongolian" children from its benefits. In 1872, due to another state supreme court decision, school districts had to admit African and Indian children to the white schools if separate schools were not provided.[53] As a result of these laws and decisions, desegregation gradually became the rule, with some exceptions in balky outlying districts.

In San Francisco, however, there were separate Negro schools which all Negro children were expected to attend. In 1872 the black community of San Francisco decided to challenge this. The parents of twelve-year-old Mary Frances Ward claimed that the all-white Broadway Grammar School was much closer to their home than the closest separate Negro school at Vallejo and Taylor streets. The Ward family proceeded to apply for their daughter's admission to the Broadway school. On the basis of the 1870 state education law, the principal of the Broadway Grammar School, Noah F. Flood, denied admission to Mary Frances Ward. Thereupon, with the support of the black community, the Ward family took the case to court.[54]

The timing of this court case was not accidental. Blacks in California now had the vote, as a consequence of the ratification of the Fifteenth Amendment in 1870. Within a year of acquiring this new source of strength, Negroes called a state-wide convention in Stockton with education as its single concern. The convention leadership decided that the time had come to take the problem of segregated schools to the state legislature in the form of a petition campaign. They were successful as far as getting Senator Seldon J. Finney of San Mateo to introduce a bill to desegregate the schools, but the bill was defeated on the floor of the state senate. With this defeat, but still interested in continuing the struggle for desegregation, the black leadership cast about for a case to take to the courts, and coincidentally the Mary Frances Ward case had just surfaced. The men and women from the Stockton convention on black education sought out the legal assistance of John W. Dwinelle, one of the finest liberal lawyers in the state.[55]

Dwinelle fought this case for two years before the supreme court, a court which delayed decision interminably because of the strength of racist feeling in the state. Dwinelle's case was based on the Thirteenth and Fourteenth Amendments and the Civil Rights Act of 1866. He contended that separate schools create "an odious distinction of caste." The court denied this contention but admitted with reservations that race prejudice might be alleviated in an unsegregated school situation. It hedged, however, on how much it felt obligated to do something about this. The court did state with some strength that where there were no separate schools provided for black children they *must* be allowed to enter the white schools. But they denied Miss Ward the right to go to the white school near her home, because San Francisco did have a separate school for Negro children.[56]

Within a year, however, Miss Ward was in an integrated school in San Francisco. The board of education decided in 1875 that the separate black school was too expensive to support, and it integrated the city's educational facilities, outflanking local negrophobes with the argument that this was an economic operation during the depression of the seventies. The *Appeal*, a San Francisco-based Negro newspaper, wrote, "Both white and colored citizens should rejoice that this last relic of slavery has at last disappeared from our great Metropolitan City of the Pacific Coast."[57]

The last legal battle came in 1890, when most California schools were already integrated. In Visalia, where Confederate sympathies were quite strong during the Civil War, a young member of the black Wysinger family was denied entry to high school by the local board of education. The family sued, and in a historic case *Wysinger vs. Crookshank* blotted out the last remnant of legal segregation in California.[58]

The Wysinger case was another reminder that many black parents in the state were interested in having their children educated beyond the elementary level. Thirty-two years earlier, the unsuccessful efforts of the Peter Lester family to obtain a high-school education for their daughter had captured public attention. From then on, black parents in San Francisco repeatedly requested the board of education to provide a high school for black children, with no effect. However, a movement to establish a private Negro high school arose. Its efforts resulted in the organization of the Phoenix Institute under the principalship of Reverend Peter Cassey, a Negro Episcopalian. The Institute was established in San Jose after the Civil War and struggled for several years with financial difficulties. As black students gradually gained entrance into the public high schools, the ever-uncertain support of the Phoenix Institute drained away and its short career terminated.[59]

What was probably the last school to be established for Negro children in California before the Civil War was the one in Red Bluff in Tehama County. By the middle of the Civil War it had two women teachers, one white and one black. The school came about as a result of the efforts of two black families, both named Logan, who came from the slave states of Kentucky and Arkansas. A touch of fame came to this school because its white teacher was Sara Brown, the daughter of John Brown. This was the John Brown who had been on the front pages of every newspaper in the United States the year before as a result of the Harper's Ferry incident. The black teacher was one of the Logan daughters.[60]

A crumbling tombstone in an old cemetery in Santa Cruz memorializes the love one black man had for education.

The tombstone was erected by whites in Santa Cruz to honor a North Carolina-born ex-slave named Louden Nelson, who came with his master to the gold fields. Nelson died in Santa Cruz in 1860. His stone reads:

> He was a colored man
> and willed all his property
> to Santa Cruz School
> District No. 1 Rest in Peace

Nine years after Nelson died, a black resident of Santa Cruz wrote to the *Elevator* expressing his frustrations with education in that city.

> There are not many colored people here. . . . what few are here cannot obtain any education for their children. There are not enough to demand a school from the trustees under our partial and proscriptive school laws, and they will not admit colored children in the public school.[61]

8 The Background of the Colored Convention Movement

The first black forty-niners were in search of the same object as their white counterparts—Gold. The desire for riches was the primary motivation of this wave of humanity that spilled on California's shores and poured across its mountains. Most of the argonauts planned to return home as soon as they had dug out of the earth the wealth they sought. But as the months passed, the word spread back East of the attractiveness of California as a place to settle permanently. Less than two years after the first waves of gold seekers had arrived, a new kind of black was coming to California. He was usually a man who had known freedom most of his life. He planned to find employment and then send for his family to join him. He went into business, if he had the capital and the skills; if not, he sought out any employment that would give him a start. He generally entered occupations in which he already had some experience. This kind of man became the mainstay of organized Afro-American community life.

As institutional life began to take form in the new state, blacks started to re-create those organizations with which they had been affiliated back home. Churches and educational institutions came first, then Masonic lodges. But the new black arrivals felt the need for something else. They had not been in California long before they found the same legal infringements they had known in the free states of the East, with some exceptions in New England. From the beginning California blacks were disfranchised; by 1851 their testimony in the courts was disallowed and the first schools were denied to their children. These conditions brought forth still another organization in the new Negro communities of California—the colored convention.

This was a continuation of a movement going back to 1817. At times it took the form of a national Negro convention and at other times conventions in particular states. In 1817, Philadelphia black leaders issued a national call to oppose the organization of the American Colonization Society, which proposed to send blacks to Liberia. A broader-based meeting of blacks in 1830 dealt with domestic issues, in particular the destitution of their brethren in Cincinnati who were the victims of white mobs in that city. The organization gave financial support to the move of Cincinnati blacks to Canada as an emergency measure but still opposed emigration in principle.[1]

From 1830 on, black conventions occurred with greater frequency throughout the Eastern free states and even in states as far west as Ohio, Michigan, and Illinois. More than half of the conventions took place before 1850. Schools for black children, the right to vote, and equal rights before the courts were the main issues at these meetings. The colored conventions proved an effective training ground for black leadership in the pre–Civil War years. The convention leaders were generally well educated and they had all the skills of articulation. Frederick Douglass is the best known of those associated with this movement. Such men, under conditions of equality, might have attained the highest levels of leadership.[2] Fortunately for the new black communities in the West, some of these leaders came to gold rush California. It was they who organized three statewide conventions in California in the 1850s, a record number of colored conventions for any state in that decade, with the exception of Ohio.

For most people, life during the first years of the gold rush was a frenzied business of finding a place to live and gaining an income. It was even more so for blacks, who at best had very modest grubstakes. In spite of the immediacy of these concerns, shared by all new Californians, the black Easterners attempted to keep in contact with their former communities. In addition to engaging in cross-continental personal correspondence, many subscribed to their favorite Eastern newspapers. The newspaper choices of blacks, particularly of the leadership group, say much about their political orientation.

By the winter of 1849, the first San Francisco-bound copy of Frederick Douglass's weekly, the *North Star*, was on its way west from Rochester, New York. James P. Dyer, a New Bedford black, an early San Francisco soap manufacturer and a future convention leader, subscribed to Douglass's paper as soon as he arrived in California.[3] When James Rylander Starkey, only two years earlier a slave, arrived in San Francisco in 1852, one of the first things he did was to subscribe to Douglass's paper, now renamed *Frederick Douglass' Paper.*[4] While still a slave and already adult he had managed to achieve literacy. This future convention leader had an unusual passion for freedom. He was at one time prepared to go to the much-condemned Liberia in order to be his own man.[5] By 1854, it was quite clear that the independent weekly of Fred Douglass was the favorite paper of California's black leadership. They seemed to prefer a black abolitionist paper edited by a black man. Such future convention leaders as H. M. Collins, George Washington Dennis, John Lewis, William M. Yates, Fielding Smithea, Abner and Jacob Francis, Peter Lester, and Mifflin W. Gibbs were all subscribers. Henry M. Collins, a black man with experience as a steward on an Ohio River steamboat and as a successful real estate investor in Pittsburg (who probably owned more real estate in San Francisco than any other black), was the strongest promoter of *Frederick Douglass' Paper.* Collins alone sold between forty and fifty subscriptions to the paper in 1854. He was a delegate to all three of the California Colored Conventions of the 1850s.[6] Three prominent California white subscribers to this independent black abolitionist paper in 1854 were Mark Hopkins and the two Crocker brothers.[7]

The preference for Douglass's paper by the California

black leadership reveals their position in the ideological spectrum of abolitionism. The middle of the 1850s was marked by intense debate within the ranks of white and black antislavery forces, over such questions as political action versus its total rejection, espoused by the Garrisonian wing of abolitionism. The Garrisonians were also challenged on their advocacy of the use of nonviolence to end slavery. The fact that Douglass had begun to consider the use of the electoral system in the fifties was upsetting to Garrison, his former mentor. A more subtle factor in their split was Douglass's earlier show of independence by the publishing of his own newspaper, which would inevitably compete with Garrison's *Liberator.*[8] If there were any black subscribers to the *Liberator* in California, they must have been very few in number. Black Californians, even those from New England, where Garrison's influence with blacks was greatest, were clearly in Douglass's camp. Not a single Garrisonian abolitionist group existed in California, nor was there a white abolitionist society of any kind. Whites with antislavery sympathies worked as individuals, without organizational labels.

Blacks in California not only subscribed to *Frederick Douglass' Paper*, but a number also wrote articles for it. Throughout the entire decade of the fifties, correspondence appeared in this Negro paper from James R. Starkey, William H. Newby, Abner H. Francis, and Edward P. Duplex.[9] Jeremiah B. Sanderson and Julius Lester wrote for other antislavery papers. Reverend Sanderson had come from New Bedford, a city close to Garrison's home in Boston, where the white abolitionist's influence was powerful and the affection blacks had for him was strong. But in 1854, when Sanderson left New Bedford, factionalism was wracking New England antislavery groups. Sanderson's best friend in Massachusetts, William C. Nell, was devoted to Garrison. Occasionally Sanderson's letters from California to Nell were printed in the *Liberator*.

When Nell organized a movement to buy a homestead for the financially precarious Garrison family in 1857, it was to Sanderson that he wrote to carry the fund appeal to black Californians.[10] Perhaps the feeling of California Negro leaders towards Garrison is best illustrated by the sentiments of William Newby, another convention leader. In a letter to *Frederick Douglass' Paper* in 1855, Newby remarked that he "occasionally" saw the *Liberator* and that the name of Garrison still made him feel a sense of reverence.[11] Similarly, Sanderson held Douglass in high regard, as Douglass did Sanderson.

While Peter Lester subscribed to the Douglass paper, he wrote at least one letter to the *Pennsylvania Freeman,* an antislavery paper out of Philadelphia. Lester and his wife were from Philadelphia, and the *Freeman* was his contact with old friends in his home town. The only black subscriber to the *Freeman* from California who can be identified was Jonas Townsend, the New York Negro forty-niner.[12] The other large antislavery paper in the East was the New York *National Anti-Slavery Standard.* In California, its only subscribers, with the exception of J. Smallwood, a black barber of Georgetown,[13] were a few antislavery whites.[14]

California blacks with strong political interests did more than subscribe to these papers to show their continued interest in the national scene. In 1852, in a Pennsylvania fund-raising event to aid the defendants in a fugitive-slave case, the more concerned and affluent California blacks contributed $250, while blacks in New York sent only $130.[15] The widely publicized case took place in Christiania, Pennsylvania, a small town bordering on a slave state, where a large group of blacks as well as a few whites were charged with aiding fugitives from slavery. At this same time, many California blacks were also involved in raising funds for California's Perkins fugitive-slave case.

There were other ways in which these transplanted black Easterners showed their continued attachment to the work of the antislavery movement. It had become a tradition of the abolitionists in the United States to give a festive observance of the British Emancipation Act of 1833, which had given freedom to the blacks of the British West Indies. This was done through celebrations on the first of August, which were usually presented in a park where a picnic atmosphere prevailed. San Francisco blacks held their first such celebration in 1854. The date coincided with the arrival in the city of one of the best New England black orators. This was Jeremiah B. Sanderson, whose reputation as a speaker and antislavery activist, especially in and around New Bedford, where he was born, had already preceded him to California. He had barely set foot on San Francisco's shores when he was enlisted to make the major presentation for the August first event. The handsome veteran of Eastern black conventions gave an eloquent speech outlining the history of the antislavery parties of England and America.[16]

While most of the black leaders with antislavery records in their Eastern backgrounds were well-read and articulate, some of them had better-than-average formal education. California Colored Convention leader Jonas Townsend had gone to college in Waterville, Maine. Four other convention leaders, Daniel Seals, Frederick Barbadoes, C. M. Wilson, and Fielding Smithea, had attended the progressive and courageously interracial college in Ohio called Oberlin.[17]

Organized Negro activism in the state appears to have begun in 1852, three years before the first California Colored Convention, for it was then that the first blacks came together to fight for fugitive slaves in the Perkins case. Fugitive-slave cases occupied the energies of blacks from time to time throughout the decade, but the one campaign that held their constant attention in the 1850s was the struggle for the right of equal testimony in the courts of California. This was an issue about which politically conscious as well as nonpolitical blacks felt keenly. Protection of life and property was involved. Between 1850 and

1852, blacks had doubled in number in California and their material possessions in property and businesses had improved at a rate far exceeding that of blacks in the Eastern states.

In April 1850, the state legislature passed a law that denied nonwhite testimony in any cases where whites were involved. It provided that

> No black or mulatto person or Indian shall be permitted to give evidence in favor of or against any white person. Every person who shall have one eighth part or more of Negro blood shall be deemed a mulatto, and every person who shall have one half Indian blood shall be deemed an Indian.

The following year the testimony feature of the same act was amended to read "Negroes or persons having one half or more Negro blood" could not testify in cases "to which a white person is a party."[18] This modification in practical terms had no meaning for blacks. Thus whites might murder or rob blacks, Indians, and Chinese and escape justice as long as there were no white witnesses who would agree to testify on behalf of the injured parties. A dozen people of color might be witness to the outrage, but their testimony would be inadmissible under these laws. The fruits of this legislation were not long in ripening.

The decade of the fifties is punctuated with cases in which people of color were violated in one way or another without any recourse to the law. In many ways the Chinese and Indians were even more victimized than blacks. The outrages against them were so great that those whites who were incensed by this racist testimony law often gave priority in their concerns to the Chinese and Indians before noting that blacks were also abused. But blacks suffered as well. A very important case occurred in the Lester and Gibbs boot and shoe store in 1851. In a vicious kind of game, two white men entered the store. One of them tried on a pair of boots, which he decided he liked, and asked that they be held for him. The two then left. A bit later, the other so-called customer returned alone and said that he would like to try on the pair that his friend had held aside. This done, he proceeded to walk out and laughingly said that this was all right with his comrade. Shortly after that, both returned and the first "customer" asked for "his" boots, knowing full well where they were. This caper then concluded with the first "customer" caning Lester, who dared not return the blows, and then departing in pretended fury. Gibbs had to stand by helplessly, for the hoodlums were armed and there were no other witnesses to this event. Here was a case that affected property as well as person, and the injured parties were two of the most articulate and organization-wise members of San Francisco's Negro community.[19]

Blacks not in business were also affected by this discriminatory law. A particularly unsavory case occurred in Sacramento, involving a young black woman victimized by a white man who had moved in and was living with her. He robbed her of her money and took some of her possessions. There was little doubt that he was guilty, but because the black woman was the only witness against him, the case was discharged.[20] Throughout the decade this undemocratic testimony law plagued blacks. One San Francisco black found his legal helplessness so intolerable after his house was robbed by whites that he emigrated to Australia in 1854. There he spoke out for the Chinese, who were facing discriminatory legislation.[21]

The still somewhat unsettled state of court practice in young California made possible wide and varied interpretations of the law, at times to the point of absurdity. One black man in San Francisco had to face the charge of grand larceny on the complaint of having enticed away the black wife of another black man. For some reason the court judged that the law did not allow for this kind of criminal action and reduced the charge to one of stealing her clothes. There was no evidence that she was out of them when the "stealing" took place.[22] In San Jose, an attractive black woman caught in a grand larceny was brought before Judge Redman, who found the situation awkward because, as the historian of the case strongly hints, he had an "interest" in this woman. What made things especially difficult was the fact that she confessed. But the racist testimony law came paradoxically to her rescue. The judge ruled that her confession could not be accepted because she was technically a slave, and he acquitted her![23]

Black and part-Indian Latin-Americans were also caught in the net of this discriminatory law. Their cases were thrown out of court or their testimony challenged. A Portuguese named Augustus Negreto who lived in Santa Clara was assaulted by a white named George W. Vincent. Negreto brought Vincent to court in San Jose. Because Vincent's lawyer charged that Negreto had "negro blood," the case was dismissed. Many of these men had had full civil rights before the Americans came to California. The irony of this was noted in the *Pacific,* a San Francisco religious paper, in an article entitled "Beauties of Our Witness Laws," in which it stated:

> M. Dominguez, one of the signers of the Constitution of this state, is prohibited by the present law from giving testimony in our courts, being half Indian.[24]

This would have applied also to the prominent Pico family, who had some African ancestry.

The opening gun of the fight for testimony revision was fired in March 1852, when San Francisco black leaders, including Mifflin W. Gibbs, Jonas Townsend, and William Newby, organized a petition campaign to call upon the state legislature to repeal those parts of the testimony law that denied them the right of testimony on an equal basis with whites. The petition read:

> To the Honorable the Legislature of the State of California:
>
> Your memorialists beg leave to represent, that by the

> Third Division of the Ninety-ninth Chapter of the Statutes of this State, entitled "An Act concerning Crimes and Punishments," passed April 16th, 1850, black and mulatto persons are rendered incompetent as witnesses to give evidence against white persons;
>
> That this provision of the Statute in effect denies to all such colored persons, the protection of law in the enjoyment of the rights of property and personal security; and the vicious and unprincipled take advantage of this disability and prey upon those rights with impunity.
>
> In the name of republicanism and humanity, we pray your Honorable body to repeal the aforesaid provision of the Statute, and restore to the colored people the right of protection which that provision withholds from them. And your memorialists, as in duty bound, will ever pray.
>
> San Francisco, March 10, 1852.[25]

Whether the movement of the San Francisco Negro leadership was meant to be state-wide or limited to the city is not clear. Gibbs's recollections leave the impression that it was an effort confined to San Francisco, but his writing was done about half a century after the event.[26] However, the obscure journal of a white Sacramento lawyer, G. E. Montgomery, reveals that almost simultaneously with the work of the San Francisco group, blacks in the second largest city of the state also became active on the matter of testimony discrimination. On 10 January 1852, he wrote:

> The colored men of Sacramento County called upon me some days ago to draw up a petition to the legislature of California, requesting the repeal of the law which disqualify them as witnesses against white persons in civil and criminal actions.

He went on to note that he drew up such a petition for them and presented it at a formal meeting of Sacramento Negroes in the dining room of a black hotel, where he was most enthusiastically received. The man who presided over these proceedings was Daniel Simpson, a washerman from New England. The plan was to gather Negro signatures to the petition, which Montgomery would then present to members of the legislature with whom he was acquainted. Reflecting the gold rush Californian's mixture of occasional social consciousness with self-interest, Montgomery noted in his journal, "This, I think secures me the colored business of Sacramento."[27]

The story of what happened to the efforts of the Sacramento Negroes has been lost, but the work of the San Francisco black community is known. They gathered more than four hundred signatures, apparently those of most of the blacks living in San Francisco. The *Liberator* noted that many of the black signers were from Massachusetts. San Francisco assemblyman Alfred A. Ellis, a former New Yorker and a Whig, agreed to present the petition to the state assembly, an act which took political courage in those days. In March 1852, this petition was presented to the state assembly, but as chance would have it, Ellis was not the presenter. He had persuaded another assemblyman, Patrick Canney, a Democrat from Placer County, to present it for him. The scene that followed was a shabby one. Henry Crabb, the slave-catcher's friend, assumed an insulted posture at the very thought of Negroes daring to be so bold. Others said that such a petition should not even be received. The only assemblyman who pleaded for a polite and civil treatment of the petition was Augustus Hinchman of Santa Barbara, a preconquest Californian who had married into a native family. Not even Canney supported the petition. One assemblyman called out sarcastically that the petition should be handed back to Ellis to return to his "negro constituents," a reference to the fact that blacks could not vote in California. A vote was taken on the issue of receiving the petition; only one was cast for its reception, and that was from Hinchman.[28]

In the following year, the undaunted blacks tried again

to present their petition to the state legislature. It is not known if this was a new petition or the same rejected one of the year before. It might have been a new one, because there is a hint that some San Francisco whites had added their names. But the scene in the assembly was much the same, and only a few of the faces were different. This time it was Thomas C. Meredith, a Democrat from Tuolumne, who presented the petition for the blacks. Again voices were raised to refuse even to accept the petition. Meredith's fellow assemblyman from Tuolumne, John C. Hoff, also a Democrat, was the one to speak for acceptance of the petition for discussion, but when matters came to a vote, the assembly rejected it unanimously! Hoff and Meredith evidently had capitulated in order to protect their political futures.

In the same year, Chinese testimony was given a death blow by the state supreme court. Chinese were the only witnesses to a murder by a white man. The latter was convicted by this testimony at first and then freed by the supreme court.[29]

There were no new petition efforts in 1854 or 1855. William Newby wrote to *Frederick Douglass' Paper* in March of 1855 that the "shameless" treatment the petitions had received at the legislators' hands discouraged them for the time being.[30] But the debate about testimony continued. A considerable body of white public opinion supported the introduction of the testimony of people of color. However, their line of argument was typical of the intellectual limitations of the nineteenth century. The San Francisco *Daily Alta California* referred to by black leader William Newby as the "paper par excellence," sometimes reflected the strains of racism among the supporters of nonwhite testimony. In March 1854, an editorial appeared in the *Alta* with the following comment:

> We are not conscious of any undue love for the unfortunate races who are thus to be cursed by the law,

> but justice to ourselves as well as to them, demands that they should be permitted to testify like persons of other colors. Their evidence should not carry, as a general rule, so much weight with a Court or Jury as that of a white man; but it does not follow that their evidence should be excluded entirely. . . . The evidence furnished by a dog, by a leaf, by a drop of blood may lead to the conviction of a murderer, but this law would prevent a man of dark skin from having the weight of a brute or an inanimate object. . . . Although the majority of the Negroes, Chinese, Malays, and Indians are not reliable witnesses, yet, there are exceptions.

The *Alta* went on to point out that the existence of the ban on nonwhite testimony was a constant invitation to the criminal to commit his crimes with impunity as long as whites were not nearby. In its attempt to prove that there were some very reliable blacks whose testimony could certainly be respected, the *Alta* singled out Reverend Darius Stokes for mention, saying that he was a "colored preacher, who makes a respectable sermon, and is probably as upright as the majority of Americans." It added, "Among the Chinese there are many men of intelligence and acknowledged probity."[31]

The Congregationalist and Northern Methodist press also put in their gentle remonstrances for the right of testimony for people of color. Their columns told of outrages on them by hoodlums, who took advantage of the inability of Negroes, Chinese, and Indians to testify. Their appeals to Christian conscience at times were most circuitous in their efforts at persuasion. When the state passed a Sabbath law in 1855, Reverend S. V. Blakeslee wrote a most flattering editorial in which he lavished compliments on its author, James W. Mandeville, a Democrat from Tuolumne. He concluded his gushes of praise with an addendum that contrasted the Sabbath law with

> foul blots on our statute books . . . [that favor] the abandoned who delight in plundering, robbing and murdering the helpless negro, Chinaman and other of those colored races upon whom our laws allow them to prey, if a white man's eye is not upon them.

Mandeville was one of the most adamant opponents of testimony reform. There is no record that this appeal to conscience ever changed his mind.[32]

In 1855, California Negroes began a major effort to revise the testimony law by means of the convention movement. The conditions were ripe for actions embracing a wider sweep of the state. Their churches were achieving greater stability. The economic conditions of blacks were relatively good. More experienced leadership had arrived in the West to add to those already in California, and they had come together through the Atheneum Institute of San Francisco. A new group was slowly entering the activism of the black community. Having gained some economic security, former slaves for the first time were able to look beyond their most pressing needs. By now, too, it was much clearer who were their friends among the whites.

The California political scene in 1855 was cause for some optimism. This was the year in which the American party, also called the Know-Nothings, prepared to capture the state legislature. This party with a national base, which was anti-immigrant (especially Irish) and anti-Catholic, had some adherents in California who were respected by the Negroes. The California Democratic party was notorious for its corruption at all levels. The Whig party had some mildly antislavery men in its ranks, but it was falling apart as a result of its defeat in the presidential election of 1852. A strong wish in the state for a clean-government party sent many voters to the American party, and in particular many moderately antislavery Whigs sought a new political lease on life through this party. California Negroes noted that that part of the state's press which gave cautious support to the aspirations of blacks was going over to the American party camp. Some of the blacks' worst enemies, like David S. Terry, were also jumping on the Know-Nothing bandwagon. However, Negro hopes lay in the significant number of their pro-American party friends, such as the *Alta,* the *Sacramento Daily Union,* and the *Marysville Herald.* In the ranks of this new party's supporters could be found names like E. Gould Buffum, son of a venerable New York abolitionist. When in August 1855 the American party convention nominated J. Neely Johnson for governor, blacks had added reason for straws of hope. Johnson had, just a few years earlier, married the daughter of Joseph Zabriskie, the lawyer who had already shown his friendship to blacks by acting as their attorney in fugitive-slave cases. Therefore the American party seemed to hold some promise for the aspirations of the California Negro. The more antislavery Republican party was virtually nonexistent in the West in those years.[33]

When the first California Colored Convention assembled in November 1855 in Sacramento, the American party had won its victory at the polls and J. Neely Johnson was soon to be governor. Things looked brighter for the testimony campaign. This three-day convention of California Negroes, largely from the northern part of the state and the cities of San Francisco and Sacramento, dealt with a variety of subjects, but its most important objective was the reform of the testimony laws. The convention resolved to conduct a much wider petition campaign and to concentrate on names of white supporters. An executive committee was authorized to direct this work through early 1856 and instructed to present the petition to the spring session of the state legislature.[34]

During the first ten weeks of 1856, the convention movement did a remarkable job of getting white men to sign the petition. Seven hundred in San Francisco alone gave their names to this cause. Sacramento and El Dorado counties also turned in a batch of petitions. While there is no notice of presentation to the state legislature from Yuba County, it is certain that signatures were collected there, because it is known that the publisher of the *Marysville Herald* signed a petition. He was even called an "abolitionist" for doing so.

The petitions were sent to the senate, where, in contrast to the assembly in 1852 and 1853, they *were* officially received. From San Francisco and Sacramento counties, two Democratic state senators presented the petitions that blacks in their areas had sent to them. In El Dorado County an American party senator made the presentation. While politeness prevailed in the senate, the petition fared no better than before. The senate referred these petitions to the judiciary committee, which was dominated by members described as "ultra Southern." Although this effort died in the judiciary committee, the campaign would continue. A momentum had begun that had not yet reached its peak. Of importance, though coming a bit late for the legislature, was the San Francisco grand jury's report that included support for Negro testimony.[35]

The 1857 testimony fight began at the second California Colored Convention in December 1856, again assembled in Sacramento. The convention was the largest gathering of its kind in California up to this time. It took four days in its deliberations, a day longer than the first convention. Although the subject of testimony had to compete for time with the discussions on education and a black press, the testimony question was still at the head of the list of priorities. Again the delegates charged themselves and their executive committee with the heavy work of obtaining petitions with the signatures of whites from the entire state. Seventy-eight men were appointed to do this work, many of them not previously involved in this campaign; and some were from counties not previously represented. Counties such as Sonoma, Napa, and San Mateo were now included. Even Los Angeles County was represented by signature-collector Thomas A. Ricks.[36] A new recruit to this work from a county not previously represented was

Manuel Quivas from Merced. Manuel Quivas was actually Emanuel Quivers, who had been a skilled slave ironworker in Virginia as late as 1849 and had freed himself and his family by purchase from the owner of the Tredegar Iron Works. His involvement in the petition work illustrates his personal victory over the fear that many former slaves undoubtedly still held. In the 1852 California census, Quivers reported himself as born in England, out of fear of the 1850 National Fugitive Slave Law. He may have called himself "Quivas" for this period as a form of protective coloration. During and after the Civil War, Quivers and his family did call themselves by the original name and became quite prominent Negro leaders in Stockton.[37]

Through January and February of 1857 the petitions were circulated throughout the state. In January, a robbery on the streets of San Francisco highlighted the testimony problem. Two black seamen boarding on Sansome Street went for a walk at the invitation of two white former shipmates. Then two white accomplices of the white seamen came along, and the blacks were robbed of their clothing and valuables. The blacks went to the police. The whites were arrested but then were freed because there were no white witnesses.[38]

By the middle of February, an even larger number of white names had been secured than the year before. White press support had increased. Country weeklies like the *Marysville Herald*, the *Shasta Courier*, and the *Placerville American*, as well as the usual big-city newspaper supporters such as the *Alta*, the *Bulletin*, and the *Chronicle* of San Francisco and the *Union* of Sacramento, were on the side of colored testimony. The religious newspaper *Pacific*, which in the past had given more attention to the denial of Chinese testimony, also joined this chorus of support calling for Negro testimony.[39] White self-interest may also have been involved. Some might have read the appeal of one delegate at the second colored convention, in which he said:

> I may see the assassin plunge the dagger to the vitals of my neighbor. . . . I may overhear the robber or incendiary plotting the injury or utter ruin of my fellow-citizen. . . . The robbery may follow, the conflagration may do its work, and the author of the evil may go unpunished because only a colored man saw the act or heard the plot. Under these circumstances who are not really injured and lose by the law? . . . is it not evident that the white citizen is an equal sufferer with us? When will the people of this state learn that justice to the colored man is justice to themselves?[40]

By mid-February the petitions were pouring in. San Francisco contributed nearly 700 names; Sacramento, 455; Shasta, 400; Yuba, 220; and Amador, 200. Amazingly, El Dorado sent in over 1,000 names on a sheet about ten feet long. The Senate journal reveals that more signatures arrived in smaller lists marked, for instance, "sundry citizens of Siskiyou county." In San Francisco, the petition lists read like a "who's who" of prominent businessmen and attorneys of the period. Among the hundreds of entries found on the petition were: Macondray, Stanford, Flint Peabody and Co., Halleck and Co., Levinson, Haskell, William T. Coleman and Co., Colonel J. D. Stevenson, Platt, Wilmerding, H. H. Haight (a future governor), Colonel Edward Baker, Cook Folger and Co., Woodworth and Co. Occasionally a petition signer would write "not Chinamen" or "not Chinese" next to his name, indicating it was not his intention to include the Chinese under a reformed testimony law. There were those whites who felt that since Negroes were part of the Christian tradition of the country, they would understand the solemnity of the oath in court procedure, whereas the Chinese as "heathens" would not.[41]

But while "receiving" these petitions, the state legislature buried them again. Some belated additional public support that year came to the movement. Paradoxically, a lynching of three white men by other whites in Bangor, Butte

County, brought the hitherto hostile *Sacramento Bee* to the position of supporting nonwhite testimony in the courts. The three white men had been robbing and pillaging the Chinese community of Bangor, and while whites and Chinese knew the culprits, they could never catch them when white men might be nearby. And so without benefit of trial, the three whites were lynched by their Caucasian brethren. In the interest of due process for whites, therefore, the *Bee* came around to supporting nonwhite testimony.[42]

In his last message in January 1858, Governor J. Neely Johnson came out openly for the first time in support of the testimony of nonwhites. He called the existing testimony law an "indiscriminate prohibition" and "at variance with the spirit of our constitution." But his call for justice fell on deaf ears; it was actually a recognition of the fact that he had nothing to lose by this humanitarian appeal. It was clear by the end of 1857 that the American party was about to end its short-lived career and that Johnson had little political future left. Johnson had been placed in the unpopular position of having to call out the troops against the famous San Francisco Vigilance Committee, an illegal body born out of a need to prosecute criminals when the established court system failed to do so. Most of his usual political support came from the very people in that city against whom he had to act. They were also the kind of people who tended to support nonwhite testimony. The divisions among the friends of the blacks was an unfortunate development for the blacks.[43]

This new defeat for the effort to democratize testimony was bound to have its demoralizing effects. But 1857 produced yet another blow to the spirits of blacks and gave more moral support to their enemies. This was the year of the Dred Scott decision, which stated that blacks had no claim on American law or rights that white men must respect. It was depressing to blacks from coast to coast.

California Negroes went on to prepare for a third convention and a third effort at changing the testimony laws.

Their continued economic improvement and the continued stability and growth of their population as well as their community institutions made them feel that they had the resources for another round of struggle.[44]

The third convention assembled during the last week of October 1857 in San Francisco. More issues were introduced and the bickering was greater. Again the call for another petition campaign went out. Again the signatures were collected for presentation to the state legislature.[45] The work had hardly begun when the dramatic Archy Lee case broke.

Many blacks probably turned their energies to this case because the testimony struggle seemed so futile and the Archy Lee case held promise of a victory. His owner's case appeared legally hopeless. Negroes in California wanted to chalk up at least one victory, and the courts seemed to hold greater promise than the state legislature. Archy did get his freedom, but the state legislature in 1858 not only buried the testimony petitions once again but drew up new repressive legislation against the small California black minority. Anti-Negro immigration laws were under consideration in the Democrat-dominated state legislature in the spring of 1858. The low morale of blacks on the testimony issue is illustrated by the poor work done on it by the black communities. The executive committee of the Colored Convention complained bitterly on this point and openly discussed the sloppy work of some of its supporters. In the same report the leadership rendered its decision, based on sampling black opinion, that a fourth convention would be pointless and another petition campaign fruitless, given the political composition of the state legislature in 1858. Their only hope for testimony revision seemed to lie with the very small and new Republican party.[46] Yet even in this year of defeat San Francisco never flagged. Eighteen hundred of the city's whites, a larger number than ever, showed their support for equal testimony rights for nonwhites. Nearly one thousand white signatures appeared on the petitions from Yuba, Amador, Sierra, and

Mariposa counties. This legislature rejected the petitions, with only eighteen assemblymen willing to consider them.[47]

While the convention movement temporarily gave up the testimony fight, some of the leaders did not forget their white allies in this cause. Gaven D. Hall, a Democrat from El Dorado County, was one of that small group of courageous Democrats who wished to give judicial justice to blacks. As a result, he lost his seat in the 1857 elections, after serving six years in the state legislature. In that year El Dorado Negroes collected funds in order to present Hall with a testimonial of their appreciation.[48]

A reformed testimony law had to wait until 1863, when, under the impact of the Civil War, a state legislature more favorable to Negro aspirations was elected.[49] To some extent it ratified what was already taking place, at least in San Francisco. As early as January 1857, a Colonel James, in defending a black man in the police court, claimed that an amendment to the testimony law passed in 1855 was so written that Negroes could testify against white men if they were the injured parties. What the 1855 amendment actually contained was an ambiguity through which interpretations could flow. This amendment to the 1850 law stated, "The party or parties injured, shall in all cases be competent witnesses; the credibility of all such witnesses shall be left to the jury as in other cases." This amendment applied so indirectly to the qualifications of persons of color as witnesses that the Colored Convention movement ignored it.[50] James was the first to seize upon it, but it evidently was a weak reed for blacks to lean on, because their most intensive work for reform took place after this amendment was passed. In August 1858, however, Judge Maurice C. Blake, an active Republican, accepted the testimony of a black man who was assaulted and not only referred to the 1855 amendment, but added that it was "in accordance with the common-law, and with the principles of justice and humanity." His position was accepted by the jury, and the black man's assailant was fined $500. A curious ingredient in this case was the fact that the litigants, Pedro Mohica, the injured party, and Jose Gibara, were both Latin-Americans. It was Gibara's attorney who had raised the matter of Mohica's African ancestry by declaring that he was a mulatto and therefore could not testify.[51]

Within three months of this decision, a black woman's testimony in San Francisco was accepted in a case in which she had been struck by a pitcher thrown at her by her white neighbor. Judge Coon took the black woman's testimony and fined the white woman. The cause of the altercation was a complaint by the black woman that her yard was being littered with pieces of coal by the white woman's children. The white woman's response was vituperative and contained racial slurs. In response the black woman hurled some water at her. The white woman then threw the pitcher. The white woman was fined fifteen dollars, but because she was poor the fine was suspended. She was also required to move.[52] A few weeks later, an elderly black in San Francisco won her case against a white man who had beaten her, and this too was on her testimony.[53]

By 1860, the 1855 amendment ambiguity reached the state supreme court in a case involving Albert Grubbs, a Sacramento Negro laundryman who accused a white man named Jim Howard of stealing his watch. A lower court had accepted Grubbs's testimony, but Howard's lawyers carried the case to the supreme court on the contention that Grubbs had no right to present testimony. The supreme court, through Chief Justice Field, declared that the amendment of 1855 was not designed to allow nonwhite testimony where white men were the litigants. Cornelius Cole, as Sacramento's district attorney, protested that the denial of Negro testimony was an invitation to crime. But Field, who was later appointed to the United States Supreme Court by Lincoln, replied:

> It is possible, as suggested by the District Attorney that instances may arise, where upon this construction,

> crime may go unpunished. If this be so, it is only a matter for the consideration of the Legislature.[54]

With this decision, the hopes that blacks had for relief in the courts by local interpretations were blasted. Once more they had to look for more fundamental changes which they did not have the power to direct in nineteenth-century California. Those changes came in sufficient strength to give them testimony rights only after the Civil War began, when many of the opponents to testimony reform had been defeated in the 1862 elections.[55]

Blood had to be shed once more before the statute books were cleared of this undemocratic practice. An incident in October 1861 gave thrust to the testimony petition campaign. It began in a millinery store on the corner of Second and Minna streets, a shop owned by Mrs. George W. Gordon. She was the wife of a black barber whose shop was in the basement of the Tehama House. A white man named Robert Schell walked into Mrs. Gordon's shop in full daylight. Seeing no white persons about, he put his hand in the till, took out eleven dollars, and walked out with it. But Mrs. Gordon and her sister did see him. Mrs. Gordon immediately proceeded to Police Chief Burke and asked for Schell's arrest. The chief told her that although the laws forbade him to take her testimony, he would investigate the charge. He sent out two officers to look into the matter. When Schell learned that the police had been called in, he went to Mr. Gordon's basement barber shop and proceeded to cane him in front of black witnesses. Gordon, knowing the terrible penalties of fighting back at a white man, tried to flee up a flight of steps to the street. At that point Schell drew a derringer pistol and shot Gordon in the chest. Mortally wounded, Gordon still managed to get outside, where he fell dead on Sansome Street. Schell came up after him and began to pistol-whip the dead man. This was seen by white witnesses, who called the police. Schell was arrested, but the court sessions that followed highlighted painfully the handicaps under which Negroes were placed by the existing testimony laws. A witness who was present in the barber shop when the shooting took place was disqualified because two doctors established that he had one-eighth African ancestry. As a consequence, Schell was convicted of not first- but second-degree murder. This tragedy would leave its impression on many whites. The Gordon family, originally from New York, had a very respectable image among a great many whites, and the funeral services that followed intensified this image. One of California's most eloquent and well-reported pulpit preachers, the Unitarian Thomas Starr King, officiated at the services at the Minna Street home of the Gordons.[56]

On 18 March 1863, sixteen and one-half months after George W. Gordon was killed, eleven weeks after the Emancipation Proclamation went into effect, and after one last petition campaign by California blacks in 1862, the state legislature passed an amendment to the testimony law. The relevant portion read, "No Indian, or person having one-half or more of Indian blood, or Mongolian, or Chinese, shall be permitted to give evidence in favor or against any white person."[57] These were the still undemocratic words of victory of the smallest minority of color in California in 1863. The press of their own problems made California blacks unable and unwilling to identify their cause with any other oppressed group at this time.

9 The Three Conventions

During the third week of November 1855, the First State Convention of Colored Citizens of California convened in Sacramento. On 21 November, winds carried ashes from a tule-grass fire in the surrounding countryside and deposited them over the city. Because the first state-wide Negro convention was meeting in Sacramento, the press called this phenomenon "The Colored Snow Storm." Some considered this accident of nature a kind of welcome sign, heralding the event that was taking place in the African Methodist Episcopal Church on Seventh Street.[1]

The three-day convention was the product of immediate as well as long-range factors. By 1855, economic conditions had improved for many blacks. It was a period in which crime was rising in the state and most notably in San Francisco. The same circumstances that gave rise to the second vigilance committee—the increasing crime rate and the resulting threat to life and property—made it more urgent for blacks to seek adequate legal protection. The convention organizers were most impatient with racial discrimination in California, for most of them had lived earlier in the East, where they had formed the political habit of organizational struggle to improve their quality of life.

In the two years prior to this time, a number of events occurred that singly or in concert could have set in motion the processes that produced this convention. In 1854, a meeting of blacks had been held at the St. Cyprian Church in San Francisco to endorse the resolutions of the Colored National Convention held the year before in Rochester, New York. The San Francisco gathering heartily approved of the Rochester program of continuing to fight for their rights in the country of their birth and then went on to declare that they should continue to struggle for those same rights in California. The Rochester conference was especially inspirational for California blacks. Many of the California leaders recognized among the names of Rochester delegates old friends and associates from Eastern civil-rights campaigns. Henry Collins noted the name of his fellow Pennsylvanian, J. B. Vashon; many of the New Englanders saw the names of friends, among them J. B. Sanderson, who would soon be joining them in the West.[2]

The three days of work accomplished by the delegates to this historic convention had been preceded by months of preparation. In January 1855, at a meeting that probably took place in the Atheneum Institute on Washington Street, another event increased the momentum for a state convention. At this gathering, Peter Anderson, black Pennsylvanian, spoke about an emigrationist convention that had taken place in Cleveland the year before, at which a segment of the Eastern black leadership endorsed emigration to Africa or parts of Latin America as a solution to black problems. This was in opposition to the policy of the convention, led by Douglass, that had met a year earlier in Rochester. Anderson urged that a convention in California be called to take a position on this controversy. It also was announced at this meeting that a Sacramento group of blacks had written their San Francisco counterparts, expressing an interest in a state-wide convention. It was agreed to explore the possibilities of holding a California convention, and the San Francisco group set up committees of correspondence to gauge the prevailing sentiment. The results of the survey proved most favorable to the idea of holding a convention. Significantly, however, most blacks in California indicated little interest in emigration or other long-range concerns of Eastern blacks. They overwhelmingly called for the convention to concern itself with equal testimony rights in California.[3]

On the basis of this survey, a call was issued from the Atheneum Institute in September 1855 for a convention to be held in November in Sacramento. The call was signed by J. H. Townsend, Peter Anderson, W. H. Newby, and D. W. Ruggles for San Francisco and James Carter for Sacramento. The call read:

> Brethren—your state and condition in California is one of social and political degredation [*sic*]; one that is unbecoming a free and enlightened people. Since you have left your friends and peaceful homes in the Atlantic States, and migrated to the shores of the Pacific, with hopes of bettering your condition, you have met with one continuous series of outrages, injustices, and unmitigated wrongs, unparalleled in the history of nations.
>
> The Statute Book of the Common Law, the great bulwark of society, which should be to us as the rivers of waters in a dry place, like the shadows of a great rock in a weary land, where the wretched should find sympathy and the weak protection, spurns us with contempt, and rules us from their very thresholds, denying us a common humanity.
>
> Then, in view of the wrongs which are so unjustly imposed upon us, and in the progress of the enlightened spirit of the age in which we live, and the great duty that we owe ourselves and the generations yet to come, we call upon you to lay aside your various vocations, and assemble yourselves together on Tuesday, the 20th of November A.D. 1855, in the city of Sacramento, at 10 o'clock A.M., for the purpose of devising the most judicious and effectual ways and means to obtain our inalienable rights and privileges in California.[4]

This call clearly reflected the mood of American Negro leadership in the middle fifties. While the slave was never forgotten, the convention leaders felt that the needs of the free black called for more attention. Even the national convention of blacks that took place in October in Philadelphia, a month before the California convention, had given most of its attention to the material needs of Northern blacks. California blacks were turning away from national black problems and focusing their attention so strongly on immediate local concerns that very few attended a San Francisco meeting called to discuss the Philadelphia convention.[5]

Jeremiah Burke Sanderson rapped his gavel and called the convention to order at ten o'clock on a Tuesday morning, in the African Methodist Episcopal Church on Seventh Street in Sacramento. With Sanderson presiding, the stage was set for the high visibility of blacks who had had prestigious antislavery careers in the East. Sanderson called Jacob Francis to act as temporary chairman. Francis, a businessman, was well known because of his brother Abner Francis, who had been an antislavery leader in New York and a friend of Frederick Douglass. The two brothers traveled together to California in 1851, but Abner had gone on to Portland, Oregon, where he went into merchandising.

Jacob Francis then conducted routine convention business until the election of William H. Yates as permanent chairman. Possessed of great natural strength and ability, Yates's personal story was impressive. Born a slave, he had held down two jobs, one of them as a custodian in the United States Supreme Court, and owned a business in Washington, D.C., while raising the funds to buy himself, his wife, and their two children. After he came to California in 1851, Yates became one of the best-paid stewards with a line of San Francisco Bay luxury steamers. Some years later, during the last days of the testimony fight in the state legislature, a state assemblyman would rise to support the right of black testimony by mentioning the name of William Yates as a man whose testimony would be as valid as any man's.[6]

With Yates now in the chair, the main business of the convention got underway. Twenty-eight out of the forty-nine delegates came from San Francisco and Sacramento. The rest were largely from the mining counties. Marysville and Grass Valley, although located in mining counties, sent black barbers and businessmen to the convention. Both occupations were well represented in the assemblage, and there were at least four ministers as delegates, three of them from San Francisco.[7]

Before the delegates had concluded their deliberations, it was clear that their most important concern was equal rights of testimony. A temperance resolution by Reverend T. M. D. Ward was rejected as not relevant to the purposes of the convention. An attempt by ex-Philadelphian Peter Anderson to persuade the delegates to take a position on resolutions passed by the recent Negro convention in Philadelphia was turned down. A proposal by another delegate to have blacks look into the possibilities of creating a black banking house was rejected as inopportune. The delegates also showed a keen sense of the problems of public image. More than once the delegates reminded each other that they were being reported in the white press and should be on their best behavior. Sanderson, speaking from the floor, expressed this concern when he said:

> I believe that there are many in this State, this community, who are awaiting the issue of our deliberations with anxiety. There are those too, who think we cannot conduct this Convention with intelligence and ability; they expect scenes of disagreement and confusion; I trust we shall disappoint them.[8]

A remarkable feature of this convention was the degree to which it avoided the appearance of an abolitionist gathering. Given the antislavery backgrounds of people such as Sanderson, Townsend, Anderson, Francis, Gibbs, and Yates, it must have taken much self-discipline. Yates, for instance, had been so active in the Underground Railroad in Washington, D.C., that he had had to leave that city permanently in 1849. The general hostility to "abolitionists" was so apparent in California in this period that even a great many white antislavery men concealed their true views. A brave and bold rhetorical attack on slavery might have read well in the Eastern antislavery papers, but it would have compounded the difficulties of an already uphill effort in California. Therefore, when Mr. Quinn of El Dorado County moved that copies of the proceedings of the convention be sent to the *Liberator* and *Frederick Douglass' Paper,* the motion failed for lack of a majority.[9] However, later on the Eastern antislavery press did get information on the convention—from some of the delegates and from the California press—and did publish it.[10] Of more importance to the delegates was the impression to be made upon the California newspapers, which had considerable representation there. The convention passed a resolution of gratitude to the press and singled out some of the papers for special thanks for their friendly reportage: the Sacramento *Union, Tribune,* and *Journal,* the *Grass Valley Telegraph,* and the *San Francisco Evening Journal.*[11]

There was also controversy over style that reflected differences of opinion about what words to use in front of a white public. Jonas Townsend, in particular, was offended by what he called "crouching" language in the preamble of a convention resolution. At issue seemed to be the reference to the self-interest that whites would have in black testimony. This seemed—to Gibbs as well—too beguiling. Townsend argued that blacks were being denied their testimony rights not because of ignorance of their abilities and achievements, but because of race prejudice.[12] It was Newby who caught the prevailing mood of the convention when he said:

> We are an oppressed people, the subjects of a bitter prejudice, which we are now seeking to overcome. In appealing to our oppressors, we desire to do so in a manner that will have weight.[13]

The problem of language was not to die before one more debate occurred, involving Reverend Moore and again Townsend. Reverend Moore felt that a committee report in which it was said that blacks were "destitute of any protection in person and property" was putting it too strongly and therefore was not quite correct. To this Townsend rose to say:

> I deny that the pitiful support which the law offers can be called protection. . . . There is indeed a semblance of protection, but it is not real.[14]

The serious tone of the convention did not deprive it of some lighter moments. During some self-congratulation about the degree of harmony and decorum that had marked the proceedings to that point, the chairman turned to Reverend Stokes, who was engaged in conversation with a fellow minister, and asked him to change his seat. Yates observed dryly that whenever two preachers of the gospel were seated together he could never keep order. Reverend Stokes moved with good humor, while the delegates exploded with laughter.[15]

Before coming to grips with the practical problem of a petition campaign on the testimony issue, the delegates did express their concerns about education and a Negro press. The problem of exclusion was not yet pressing, in view of the small number of school-age black children in 1855, chiefly in Sacramento and San Francisco. What the convention in effect said was, "Try to get your children into schools where you can; where you can't, organize a school." The matter of a black newspaper was left for continued discussion following the convention in order to determine what support there was for such a venture.[16]

The convention also announced that 4,815 blacks had accumulated $2,413,000 in real and personal estate, not counting those who earned money in California to purchase their freedom. This was a most impressive figure, which was reported in the East and undoubtedly resulted in more black migrants to the West. A rather interesting appeal was made by one committee to the effect that California blacks should turn more actively to agricultural pursuits and not cling to the cities so tenaciously. The great advantages of agriculture in California were pointed out, and it was noted that the average wealth of the few black farmers in the state was greater than that of those in mining or city occupations. But this suggestion was not likely to persuade many blacks, since work on the land had too many negative associations historically. However, the convention's report of successful blacks in agriculture in California was picked up by the *Journal* of Sacramento. It concluded its article with the comment, "It follows that the agricultural regions are the proper places for the negroes of this state." This kind of phrasing would not sit well with many blacks.[17]

The convention concluded with the election of an executive committee empowered to carry on the work of the testimony campaign and to raise the estimated $20,000 required to pay for its costs. Jonas Townsend was appointed a traveling agent for the executive committee to raise funds and, in the course of this work, to bring together the scattered black communities outside of San Francisco and Sacramento.[18]

During the days of planning for this convention, some blacks had negative feelings about its possibilities. Newby, for instance, was gloomy about moral approaches to the white population. He felt that in the American environment the only thing that carried weight was making money and that Negroes should concentrate on getting rich.[19] But once the convention started, the mood of most was optimistic. This was expressed in many ways. The fact that a good deal of the press was friendly was most heartening. In a letter to his best friend, William C. Nell, the black associate of Garrison, Sanderson reported:

> We have got among our young men here the right material for devising and carrying out plans for our

> general good. We anticipated opposition from the press, and this is apt to stir up the baser sort to indulge in some excess. These papers, however, which spoke, did so calmly, and encouragingly in regard to the objects of the convention, (which was mainly to get the right of testimony in the courts,) and though we heard distant grumbling and dark threats, it passed off.
>
> One of our city papers (Know-Nothing) the Daily Tribune, liberally reported our proceedings from day to day. This did us good, and certainly did them good, as they were obliged to strike off many extra copies.[20]

The convention concluded with an eloquent statement directed to the whites of California by J. H. Townsend on behalf of the convention's executive committee. He made reference to the wealth accumulated by California Negroes, their attachement to the American institutions, and to the wars in which blacks fought wearing the United States uniform. He continued:

> We again call upon you to regard our condition in the State of California. We point with pride to the general character we maintain in your midst, for integrity, industry, and thrift. You have been wont to multiply our vices, and never to see our virtues. You call upon us to pay enormous taxes to support Government, at the same time you deny us the protection you extend to others; the security for life and property. You require us to be good citizens, while seeking to degrade us. You ask why we are not more intelligent? You receive our money to educate your children, and then refuse to admit our children into the common schools. You have enacted a law, excluding our testimony in the Courts of justice of this State, in cases of proceedings wherein white persons are parties; thus openly encouraging and countenancing the vicious and dishonest to take advantage of us; a law which, while it does not advantage you, is a great wrong to us. At the same

> time, you freely admit the evidence of men in your midst, who are ignorant of the first principles of your Government—who know not the alphabet. Many colored men, who have been educated in your first colleges, are not allowed to testify! and wherefore? our Divine Father had created us with a darker complexion.[21]

Five thousand copies of the convention *Proceedings,* including the above statement by Townsend, were ordered from the *Sacramento State Tribune.* This presented the *Tribune* with problems when some subscribers threatened cancellation if the paper used its presses for this purpose. The *Tribune* defended the right of Negroes to make their case before the public and said editorially, "He alone is a free man whom the truth makes free."[22]

Although delegates had been generally satisfied with the way the white press reported the convention, this in no way had diminished their enthusiasm for the proposal to start publication of a Negro newspaper. The convention had placed the question in the hand of a committee. Between this convention and the one that occurred a year later, the only California black newspaper of the 1850s, the *Mirror of the Times,* began publication. The newspaper was basically a result of the initiative of two men, William Newby and Jonas Townsend, the latter having had experience editing a paper in New York.

On 19 August 1856, Peter Anderson chaired a public meeting at St. Cyprian's A.M.E. Church in San Francisco on the proposal of starting a newspaper. After the usual discussion, H. M. Collins, the blacks' best money raiser, moved that a committee of five be elected as a publishing committee. The five elected were Collins, Townsend, Newby, Reverend Moore, and Nathan Pointer, all except Pointer delegates to the convention. Another meeting was called for 2 September, where a full proposal was presented and a finance committee established. This committee was composed of Pointer, W. D. Moses, Charles Mitchison, Reverend Barney Fletcher, Charles B. Smith, F. Spotts, and Henry F. Sampson.[23]

Most of these men were new recruits to the general purposes of the convention. This was strikingly illustrated by the presence of Henry Sampson, a man who recently had been an illiterate slave. In his early twenties, Sampson was brought by an army officer to California, where he gained his freedom. He worked for William Tecumseh Sherman's banking firm in San Francisco, earning only $100 a month as a porter. After Sampson persuaded a bank teller named Reilly to teach him to read and write, his services were worth $250 a month. As Sherman recalled it, with this increased income he was able to buy freedom for his brother and family. Some years later, an incident occurred which indicated the measure of the man's self-respect. Sampson had to deal with a drunk one evening as he was closing the doors of the bank. A reporter with a racist sense of humor described the event, giving Sampson's words in dialect. After reading this caricature of himself, Sampson wrote to the paper in perfect English, chiding the reporter for presenting him falsely. During the Civil War, Sampson went to work for the United States Mint and also continued to be active in the Colored Convention movement.[24]

In his closing remarks to the *Mirror*, publications committee chairman Anderson made it clear that the paper would be primarily concerned with the testimony campaign and that slavery "is but secondary in importance." He felt also that the paper should inform white Californians of the attachment and understanding Negroes had for the principles of republican government. Anderson said the new paper should tell Californians that Negroes appreciated and understood those principles more than many of the state's foreigners and illiterates. This last point he was directing at the Irish, who were arriving in the state in great numbers at this time. The general tenor of Anderson's remarks continued the distinctly pragmatic posture of the convention.[25]

The second California Colored Convention took place two months after the *Mirror* published its first issue on 13 September 1856. This convention kept to the policies stated in the *Mirror*, but the hatred of slavery and racism in American life that was never far from the surface occasionally broke through. Just two weeks before the convention began, the *Mirror* was called to task for "intemperate" language by an editorial in the *San Francisco Sun.* The *Mirror* article that upset the *Sun* might have been written by either Townsend or Newby. In this article, the critics of the black testimony campaign were referred to as "liars" and users of "fiendish and hellish expression." The *Sun,* which was not hostile to black testimony aspirations, cautioned the *Mirror*, saying:

> our colored population would consult their best interests, if they would leave such expressions to the use of some of their white allies, by whom they have been made fashionable.[26]

This would not be the last time that blacks would be told that an honest show of rage was counterproductive.

On 9 December 1856, the Second Colored Convention opened in Sacramanto in the A.M.E. Church on Seventh Street. The year just passed had seen California blacks involved in a great struggle to gain signatures for their right-to-testimony cause. These signatures lay buried in legislative committees, but the delegates came together for another effort. The American party, friendly to blacks, was still the dominant party in the state, and the San Francisco Vigilance Committee was active under the banners of law and order. Blacks could hope that the popular support for the work of the Vigilance Committee in the elimination of muncipal corruption might carry over to their own fight for reform of the testimony law. After all, the testimony of people of color could be important in prosecuting the criminal and law-breaker.

Townsend called the convention to order, committees were appointed, and a convention chairman was elected. William Henry Hall, of Butte County, was selected to preside over the sixty-four delegates who came from seventeen counties in central and northern California.[27] Hall had been born free in Washington, D.C. Indeed, three generations of his family had been free. His early education was self-acquired; his early occupation was that of barber. As a young man he already had pride of race, and when the move was initiated to put up a monument in the Capitol in honor of Benjamin Bannekar, the Revolutionary-period black mathematician and almanac editor, Hall was a fund-raising agent for that cause. Before going to New York in 1845, he spent two years at Oberlin College studying for the ministry. In New York he joined the black Masons and engaged in the struggle to remove the property qualifications for Negro suffrage. In 1849, he joined the gold rush, returning to New York in 1851 materially much improved, as noted earlier. He returned with his bride to California in 1854 to reside in Oroville.[28]

While the testimony question was still their main preoccupation, these black leaders spent a considerable amount of time discussing education. It was Newport F. Henry from Tuolumne County who most aggressively pressed the question of education for blacks in California. Initially, he was a bit vague about his concerns. But under interrogation by the other delegates, he made it clear that he wanted them to think about establishing a school along the lines of Oberlin, the interracial and coeducational antislavery college in Ohio.[29] Perhaps his interest in this kind of school was based on the fact that while there were a great many young adults of the right age for Oberlin, elementary school-age black children were still relatively few in California. Henry may also have had a sentimental reason for pushing for a western Oberlin. While still in New York, he had been the "confidential porter" for the anti-slavery Tappan brothers, the New York merchants. In that atmosphere he had heard much about Oberlin, because the Tappans had been great benefactors of the struggling young college.[30] The delegates treated Henry kindly in this matter, but felt that any energies they had left from the testimony fight should be devoted to opening up the public schools to their children.

The delegates were not free of bickering of a pettier sort. Since black men were as capable of the stupidities of regional prejudices as white men, one delegate, E. A. Booth, felt compelled to speak on behalf of unity. He appealed to the delegates to "drive out from our midst all local or sectional prejudices; we are all brothers, whether from Maine or Missouri, from New York or Alabama, . . . let us labor in union for the common good."[31] But the greatest heat was generated over one of the resolutions reported out for the delegates' consideration. This resolution read:

> That we claim our rights in this country, as any other class, not as citizens by adoption, but by the right of birth; that we hail with delight its onward progress; sympathize with it in its adversity; and would freely cast our lot in the fortunes of battle, to protect her against foreign invasion.

It was "freely cast our lot in the fortunes of battle, to protect her against foreign invasion" that stuck in the craw of some of the delegates. Especially did it enrage William Newby, as could have been predicted from his background.

Born in Virginia in 1828 of a free mother, William H. Newby grew up in Philadelphia, where he attended a Negro school. In 1851, he came to California and soon became a leader of the black community. In the fifties he was one of the regular correspondents to *Frederick Douglass' Paper.* His resistance to the above resolution was foreshadowed in one of his letters to that paper. He wrote:

> I apprehend that the free colored people have learned a lesson since the last war. No promises, no flattery, no appeal to patriotism, will induce them to "fly to arms". The removal of all political disabilities, elevation to social equality . . . would be the terms demanded by them, before they would be willing to fight.

The 1856 convention was the last that Newby attended in California. In 1857, the French consul general to Haiti invited Newby to become his private secretary. Newby accepted the flattering offer, and the next time we hear of him he was back in Philadelphia enroute to Haiti. In his home town he was honored at a public gathering before going to his new position. His new post would reflect honor to a black man at a time when black men hungered for nourishment for their self-respect. A reading of his letters to *Frederick Douglass' Paper* reveals that from time to time Newby had mused about the idea of black men migrating to other lands. He may have wanted to see for himself if the much-talked-about Haiti was a suitable place for migration. But when he arrived in Haiti, Newby found that his prospective employer had died suddenly. After Newby returned home to the United States, he suffered from an illness that may have been contracted in Haiti.[32]

On this day in December 1856, Newby rose to address the convention on the resolution calling for black support of the United States in wartime. When he had written to Douglass the year before about his thoughts on the price of patriotism extracted from blacks, he closed his remarks by saying, "But, I must stop this . . . for fear of being considered indiscreet." This time, after the defeat in the fight for testimony rights, Newby was not interested in discretion. He declared,

> Shall we say "we will protect against foreign invasion!" God knows I speak advisedly—I would hail the advent of a foreign army upon our shores, if that army provided liberty to me and my people in bondage; . . . I am influenced by the same motives and spirit which influenced [Patrick] Henry, when he said . . . "give me liberty or give me death!"

Newport Henry then rose to support Newby's sentiments. He said,

> I love my country . . . but I cannot hail with joy her progress; if by progress is meant the acquisition of Territory and the extension of slavery therein. . . . If we are capable of hailing such as progress, . . . we ought to be enslaved. . . . let a different course be pursued—let the whites put away their prejudices, and do a just part by us, and, when they do this, we shall feel that we have a country.

Unfortunately, no contemporary documents provide posterity with an intimate picture of the sense of shock that must have been felt in that Sacramento church on this second morning of the convention. Most of the delegates must have felt the justice of the addresses of Newby and Henry, but many also must have feared the reaction of prejudiced whites. Delegates could have been equally apprehensive of the timidity of some of their white supporters in the face of such militancy. Other delegates, whose mood was more cautious than that of Newby and Henry, soon took the floor either to call for a broader view of the resolution or to put on the record remarks of a more conventionally patriotic flavor. Reverend Moore felt that critics of the resolution were overlooking the fact that progress for blacks would come not because whites were that virtuous, but because it would be in their self-interest to grant justice to blacks. San Francisco barber George W. Gordon rose to warn the delegates that they did not have the power to dictate the style of their appeals. He also said, "Let us not here adopt any language or deportment incompatible with our attitude as petitioners . . . that is likely to prejudice the success of those petitions." Townsend, who was no backslider or "croucher," also commented on the paradoxical character of American development, noting that there were positive ingredients in that development as well as negative, that blacks had shared in both, and that to wish war on the United States was unproductive because "War is a state which suspends all laws except those established for its own efficiency."

Jacob Francis attempted to resolve this painful debate with a motion that would remove the offensive phrase about actual support in war but leave the body of the resolution that wished the country well. What followed was confusing. The motion on Francis's amendment passed. An attempt by Barbadoes to revive the original motion was lost. There is no record of the discussion on this attempt. Then, when the amended motion was put to a vote, it *lost* by two votes; ayes 27, noes 29! A number of the delegates were evidently very torn on this issue and had fluctuated in their mood from one vote to the next.[33]

As a result of the anguish of this session, the delegates voted the next day to suppress "all matters extraneous and foreign to the three great objects set forth in the call of this convention."[34]

However, the 1856 convention did take positions on several issues that had been set aside the previous year. It went on record as seeking the right to vote, something many of the New England and New York delegates had enjoyed in their home states. The delegates also voted to "deprecate" gambling and use of intoxicating liquors, but they treated the subject gently. While Reverend Moore was an advocate of even stronger language in this matter, the delegates must have felt that this was enough of a statement to please their temperance-oriented white friends while not hitting too hard at their black brothers of the

Atheneum Saloon. The delegates also supported a statement urging California blacks to take a greater interest in agriculture and mining.[35]

In the discussion of the wording of the testimony appeal, preparatory to the following year's petition campaign, an interesting debate occurred over the question of whether or not to use the word *white* in the opening paragraphs. Some felt the appeal should be worded as an address to all people in the state, and others said that blacks hardly needed to address it to themselves. Some felt that it was no secret to whom it must be directed because everyone knew who had the power. The delegates, however, were in the mood to point the finger with greater emphasis. The word *white* was left in the public call, although the vote to do so was close.[36]

While attending to the details of the petition campaign for 1857, the convention took up the matter of a press. Many of the delegates had already seen some issues of the *Mirror* that appeared on the initiative of Newby and Townsend. The newspaper's survival, however, depended on the convention approving the proposal to take it over and turn it into its official organ. After much discussion of the details of costs, the convention did agree to do this. It voted to establish a publishing committee to be chosen from among the elected state-wide convention committee. Townsend and Newby were selected to continue as editors. The convention voted to pay the previously unpaid editors $75 a month until it could afford to pay them $100. How Townsend and Newby were to divide the editorial responsibilities is not clear. The problem never arose since Newby was soon on his way to Haiti.[37]

A moment of awkwardness occurred before the convention ended. In the course of the discussion of the wording of the petition introduction, Newby suggested that reference be made to the support for nonwhite testimony by the San Francisco grand jury. As it happened, that statement of support made use of the word "African" together with "Chinese." The debate concerned the use of the exact wording of the grand jury's statement or a general reference to that support. This was sticky because the exact wording would have included "Chinese". The printed convention proceedings does not include the elements of the debate. It seems probable that the delegates felt that reference to the Chinese would make their work more difficult. Some of the white signers of the 1856 petition had taken the trouble to pencil in their opposition to Chinese testimony while signing for Negro testimony. The delegates voted for the use of less specific wording that still referred to grand jury support, and Newby's less pragmatic position was rejected.[38]

The Second Annual Convention closed with an address by Chairman Hall that was punctuated by much applause. Some of his remarks were:

> Brethren, we have initiated a great work, and it seems to be essential that we must not only be superior in mental endowments to those we are to mingle with, but it is also required that we be devoid of other men's vices. Every small folly of our lives, every error of judgment, and every thoughtless, intemperate word of speech is magnified into positive reasons why we are incapable to enjoy the rights we ask. The disadvantages we are compelled to encounter are of such a magnitude that almost any other people would be appalled at its mere contemplation—deprived of protection for the safety of our families, taxed for the support of education and yet the doors of the common schoolhouse closed against our children; denied the exercise of the elective franchise, and subjected to be governed by laws in which we had no hand in framing. Every position of emolument and honor that our country has to bestow our claims as native-born citizens are overlooked, and the ignorant foreigner or the most degraded American citizen is awarded the preference.

In some shrewdly chosen words of advice to the delegates on the tactics of argumentation, Hall added:

> I would urge each one of you to consult and instruct our less favored brothers, both colored and white, remove their prejudices in regard to our condition, induce our colored brethren to cease prattling about being the equals of our oppressors, until they present the mental, pecuniary, and other evidences of being such. Converse with our ignorant white brethren, those who despise the poor negro because he is a negro, and convince them that their social condition and ours are alike degraded, and whatever political measures afflict us, are none the less severe on them.

Hall concluded with an appeal to all delegates to return to their homes and carry with them the resolve to talk to all that they could reach about the objectives of the convention. Not only their black brothers and sisters should be contacted, but whites as well. His remarks had the moral-suasion flavor of the nineteenth-century abolitionist approach to race questions. He said, in part:

> Reason and argue with those who hold power within their fingers upon the injustice with which we are treated. Convince them of our capabilities in a moral and social point of view. Revert their minds back to the days of childhood, when neither (white or black) knew any difference, neither felt any compunctions, but when each heart mingles its grateful emotions in the reciprocity of innocent amusement. . . . appeal to their magnanimity and to their adoration of country, and discover if they are content in the enjoyment of their greatness by compelling us, the equal participators of their troubles, to bear the yoke of servitude.

Knowing the general sophistication of the delegates that Hall was addressing, the reader of his words must wonder if he had his eye on the white reporters in the audience rather than his co-delegates. But his closing words were clearly meant for his fellow delegates. He repeated the call for a turn to agriculture and mining and said:

> educate your children for farmers, mechanics and other industrial pursuits; instill within them the glowing pride of their avocations, and the meanness of menial callings.[39]

The year 1857, the year of the Third Colored Convention, was only three months gone when the fortunes of free Negroes throughout the United States had a dark cloud cast upon them by the Supreme Court's Dred Scott decision. Chief Justice Taney's words, "they [Negroes] had no rights which the white man was bound to respect," would be heard time and time again until the Civil War. The American party in California, with its handful of black supporters, was approaching collapse. An anti-Negro-oriented Democratic party would take control of the state legislature. The Republican party in California was still very small, although it was growing. The California Democrats were experiencing severe internal tensions over the civil war in Kansas, but the tensions were not severe enough to be of any benefit to Negro hopes before the Civil War.

Much of the year until the Colored Convention in October was occupied with making the *Mirror of the Times* a going operation. This black weekly was never free of financial troubles. It was not even able to give employment to black pressmen, since there was no black print shop in California. At one point, during a session of the Second Colored Convention, a delegate had proposed that the convention raise the funds for a press so that they could hire their own skilled printers who were barred from employment because of their color. The convention felt that they did not have the financial resources for that large a venture.[40]

The *Mirror* from the end of 1856 through all of 1857

and the first three months of 1858 put out between fifty and sixty issues. To date, only three issues are known to have survived. It was a four-page paper with advertisements and news of the organized Negro community in California as well as news from the East. Black businessmen in San Francisco, Sacramento, and Marysville advertised their clothing stores, dress shops, hotels, and restaurants in the *Mirror*. Owners of white business firms who felt the black buying market was worth seeking or who had a sympathetic interest in the fortunes of the black community also advertised in the *Mirror*. Sam Brannan of the Vigilance Committee advertised his bank. The California Steam Navigation Company, the largest Bay and river navigation company in northern California, placed its ads in the *Mirror*. Black ministers must have been chagrined at the advertisements for the famous liquor dealers Barry and Patten. Two white doctors and a white dentist also advertised in the paper.[41]

The *Mirror*, unable to sustain itself by subscriptions and advertisements, did its utmost through coverage to spur on the various fund-raising activities being conducted in its behalf. The paper's supporters were urged to organize clubs whose sole purpose was to raise funds. For this purpose Placerville had its Ladies' Club, Stockton its Excelsior Club, and Sacramento its Banneker Society, and even in far-away Siskiyou County, Yreka had its Liberty Club. This last group had only twenty-three members but organized a meeting in August 1857 with some local white friends as guests that raised a record $180. The printers were regularly paid; it was Townsend, the editor, who rarely received his full salary. This would produce bitterness later.

In spite of the depressing developments of the year, the work toward a third convention proceeded. In the month of August, public meetings of blacks began to take place throughout the state for the purpose of having preliminary discussions and electing delegates. These meetings were also used as occasions for futher collections for the *Mirror*. In August, over $300 was turned in for the *Mirror*. With the heightened stimulus of the convention in October, the contribution for the paper that month was $469, the year's largest monthly total.[42]

San Francisco was the location of this third convention. The first morning session opened on 13 October 1857 in the St. Cyprian's A.M.E. Church on Jackson Street and Virginia Place. Townsend called the meeting to order and the convention began its deliberations. William Henry Hall again served as permanent chairman. About seventy delegates were present from eighteen counties, a slight increase in the number of delegates and counties represented.[43] Unfortunately there is no official printed record of this convention. The convention did not publish official proceedings, such as were printed for the two prior conventions. The issue of the *Mirror* which would have given good coverage to the convention has never been discovered. Furthermore, the San Francisco daily press did not cover this convention with anywhere near the thoroughness that the *Sacramento Daily Union* had shown in its reporting of the two earlier conventions held in Sacramento.

It is clear, however, that the testimony cause was still most important. Therefore, another petition campaign was planned for 1858. Again, statistics were called for on material accomplishments of California blacks to buttress their image as a responsible and achievement-oriented people. Although the convention organizers had called upon the blacks in forty-one counties, only seventeen counties responded. The statistics that were provided showed taxable income that came to over a million and a half dollars, The convention leaders estimated that the taxable possessions of the unreported counties were worth about $3 million more and that the true total for the entire state would come close to $5 million in 1858. This could have been true, since Sacramento, with the second largest Negro population in the state, had not reported its statistics.

Likewise, the much smaller black populations in counties like Monterey and Los Angeles, where the 1860 census reveals the sturdy beginnings of a black propertied class, were not included. There is evidence, for instance, that in 1860 Ishmael Williams, a Negro merchant in San Juan township, Monterey County, was worth $10,000.

One of the notable features of this convention was the degree of emphasis given to the taxable properties in mining or agriculture owned by blacks. The pointed reference to this kind of property was in line with an ever-increasing push by the leadership to get their people to turn more sharply to the land. In conjunction with this effort, the convention registered a sharp protest against a United States Land Office decision that blacks could not take advantage of the long-standing preemption laws of the country. These Jackson-period laws had allowed American citizens squatter rights on unsurveyed lands ever since the 1840s, but administrators of the Land Office felt that the Dred Scott decision denied such privileges to blacks.[44]

This Land Office decision brought on a bitter convention resolution that read:

> That to upbraid the free Colored people with servility, to taunt them with proclivity to crowd the cities in their eagerness to fill the most menial positions, and at the same time prohibit them from obtaining respectability and independence as tillers of the soil, is as inconsistent in its conception as it is malignant in its effects, and deserves withering scorn and reprobation of every friend of impartial justice.[45]

Competing with each other for a sense of urgency at the convention were two other issues, education for black children and the *Mirror of the Times.* Each passing year brought more black children closer to school age. Reverend Moore was again their champion at this convention. He called for statistics of school-age black children from each county and a petition to the state legislature for their proportion of school funds. He also called upon black parents to take turns in instructing their children at home where there were no schools. It was his suggestion, too, that night schools and literary societies be organized by young men.[46]

The *Mirror* was the subject of many appeals for support from the delegates. The paper was now about a year old and a source of much pride as well as financial strain. Delegates suggested that every Negro in the state pledge a dollar to this paper, and black businessmen were urged to advertise in it regularly.[47]

Chairman Hall closed the five-day convention, the longest of the three, with a repetition of his earlier call for blacks to turn to farming and mining. He pointed out that mining could yield the seed money for farming. The Land Office might deny preemption rights, but blacks could still buy farm land. He urged blacks to leave bootblacking and other servant occupations. Hall explained he had no personal criticism of such menial work, but felt it was held in low esteem by most people. He said that while people gave lip service to the dignity of all labor, they were actually speaking hypocritically.[48]

In the weeks that followed the convention, letters were written to the *Mirror* discussing the convention and its activities. There were letters of support for the *Mirror* as well as for Hall's proposals about moving out of menial occupations. A postconvention meeting of blacks in Stockton in December came up with some proposals that had not been heard at the convention. Delegate Outley felt that the convention should issue a religious paper along with the *Mirror.* Considering the problems that California blacks had getting adequate funds for the *Mirror,* one can imagine how this suggestion was received. Another proposal at the Stockton gathering would have compelled all persons in the state still holding slaves to pay them an hourly wage for every hour worked since they were brought into the state. Black Stocktonians were particularly conscious of slavery because in the surrounding area many blacks were still kept in a state of servility. The subject of servitude had come up at the recent convention when Sonoma County delegates reported that there were twenty-six black men held as slaves on farms in that thinly populated county.[49]

In January 1858, a dizzying series of events began for California Negroes. They had resolved in the new year to work again for testimony rights, on new efforts for schools for their children, and for a further strengthening of their newspaper. But fate had other plans for their energies. Within ninety days after the new year began, the perspectives of many California blacks were to be drastically altered. In January the Archy Lee case began, and a vicious anti-Negro immigration bill was introduced in the legislature. Two months later came the exciting news that gold had been discovered in the Fraser River country of British Columbia.

These were historic happenings that would frustrate the anticipated work of the Third Colored Convention. While blacks knew that the 1858 legislature was more hostile to their hopes than the previous one, they still proceeded with their work, gathering 1,800 names from San Francisco alone and doing very well in Sacramento. But it soon became apparent that the work was faltering. Out of fourteen counties participating, in only four were the petitions properly prepared. One county sent its petition to the wrong body. As the executive committee of the convention, in a report of this work, later lamented,

> This straggling, imperfect and irritating mode of procedure served to annoy both Houses, at a time when the public mind . . . were laboring under intense excitement, caused by the celebrated Archy case.[50]

The testimony petitions were buried again by the state legislature. But the Archy case was not occupying the thoughts of whites alone in California; blacks were even more deeply involved, and their energies and attention were undoubtedly drawn away from the details of the testimony fight. The legal defense of Archy also took much-needed funds from other activities, such as the *Mirror,* which died in February. While many blacks appreciated the importance of testimony rights, they must have found the work tedious and less compelling than the dramatic element in the struggle for Archy. One finds, for instance, the name of James Riker of the Atheneum Saloon as a central figure in the San Francisco phase of the Archy case, but his name never appears in the work of the three conventions.

The Archy case concluded in April with a victory for the blacks in the courts. But this victory did not balance the rising anti-Negro sentiment in the state. This mood against black people revealed itself a few weeks later, when the state legislature came painfully close to passing an anti-Negro immigration bill. That same month, hundreds of blacks in California would prepare to leave for British Columbia, intending never to return to the United States. Although many blacks remained, this emigration left the Colored Convention movement in California seriously depleted.

In November of the year of the Canadian exodus, the somewhat reduced membership of the executive committee of the convention met in Sacramento to determine what course of action they should suggest to the California Negro community. After their deliberations, they appointed three men to sum up their conclusions in published form. The three were Frederick Barbadoes of Sacramento, C. M. Wilson of Siskiyou, and William H. Hall from Butte. The work of this committee appeared in print the following year as a pamphlet entitled *Address of the State Executive Committee to the Colored People of the State of California.* With an introduction that gave strong intimations of anger at lack of support by blacks during 1858, they reviewed the history of the testimony fight, coupling recognition of valiant efforts with criticism. Without mentioning particulars, this statement spoke out against the personal bickering that had occurred and lamented the false accusations that had been made. Precisely what is meant here can only be divined if one has had the experience of working with human beings in organizations.

The *Address* continued with a lament on the passing of the *Mirror,* and again laid the cause to lack of general black support. It also took the occasion to compliment Jonas Townsend for his devotion to the paper while not receiving his salary. It repeated the theme so often stated in the last two conventions that the American Negro must gain skills in the world of money-making, saying,

> Pecuniary prominence, in a country so diversified as this, takes precedence over intellectual, and it should be our highest aim to seek the end we have marked out, through the mode that has formed a superiority, and left many of us far behind in the business progress of the age.

Touching on a new vein of thought, the *Address* went on to appeal to black pride. This appeal, so familiar in the twentieth century, was put in the following nineteenth-century language:

> The time has nearly arrived, Fellow-Citizens, when the light of experience, pointing back among the smouldering ruins of many ages, collecting the fragments of impartial history, which demonstrates the fact that a race identified with us by complexion, were once distinguished in war, science and art; and the pages of the same history, in prophetic vision, has said that the "first shall be the last, and the last first."

In the body of the *Address,* the executive committee referred to its last meeting, at which the idea of a fourth convention was discussed. The committee ruefully told the readers of its *Address* that they felt that such a convention would be useless. Only a significant change of state administration would warrant such a move. However, the leadership concluded that should the Negro communities evidence an intense desire to have a fourth convention, the executive committee would respond. Otherwise, the committee felt that the best it could do was to remain loosely together as a contingency group awaiting some signs of changing times.[51]

It was not until 1862 that the black leadership group called for united action once again, to renew the testimony rights petition campaign. Their efforts contributed to a victory the following year, when the state administration came into friendly hands. For the first time since 1850 black testimony was placed on an equal footing with white on the statute books of California. But continued interest in education and a renewed interest in voting rights rekindled the convention movement. A Fourth Colored Convention took place in October 1865, six months after the Civil War had ended.

The Colored Convention movement before the Civil War had shown that blacks could organize effectively to work for their common goals. The failure of their efforts was disappointing. In spite of hard campaigning, they had not achieved equal rights of testimony or equal education for their children. The legislature seemed on the verge of imposing even greater handicaps on Negroes. Into this atmosphere of discouragement came the news of gold discovered in British Columbia. For many blacks, tired of fighting the seemingly unalterable prejudices of white society, this provided an answer—to go to a new land where they might find acceptance, equality of opportunity, and equal rights before the law. Thus was born the exodus to British Columbia.

10 The Exodus to Victoria

For California blacks, the month of April 1858 was a bittersweet time. The Archy Lee case was drawing to a dramatic and victorious conclusion, at the same time that a viciously proscriptive immigration law seemed to be moving to inevitable passage in the state legislature. Introduced into a legislature dominated by Democrats, encouraged by the Dred Scott decision, and fueled by the spectacle of masses of blacks working to free a young black brother, the proposed legislation would have placed a mark on California Negroes suggestive of some of the restrictions placed upon Jews in Nazi Germany.

Several prior attempts to impose anti-Negro immigration laws had failed. When the constitution was written in 1849, an effort had been made to include such immigration restrictions.[1] In 1857 an anti-Negro immigration law came close to passage but was finally defeated.[2] In March of 1858, Assemblyman J. B. Warfield of Nevada County introduced a new anti-immigration bill. This time it seemed inevitable that the legislature would pass it. In the course of the debate over the bill, legislators also discussed Chinese immigration, and a bill to bar that was on its way through the legislature. An economic factor in the discussion was the number of unemployed white men to be found at this time, due to the gradual decline of placer mining. But both blacks and Chinese and their alleged inferiority were the main points of debate. The particular viciousness of the anti-Negro bill lay in the requirement that blacks register to prove their residence and then carry such registration papers with them at all times. Also there would have been no protection for blacks enroute to join families in California or returning from business trips. Under the proposed law, blacks who came unwittingly into the state would have had to enter into a kind of slavery to pay their passage back out of the state. The object of the bill seemed to be more vindictive than preventative, for there were very few black immigrants coming into the state at this time. In fact, barely two dozen Negroes had migrated to California in the preceding twelve months.

In the state legislature, the only sure opponents of this bill came from San Francisco. A few other legislators from scattered counties about the state also opposed the bill. The anti-Negro immigration measure passed overwhelmingly in the assembly. In the senate more reservations were evident; reconsiderations and postponements were attempted. The final outcome of this bill's presentation suggests clever maneuvering by some unidentified state senators. On the last day of the legislative session, minor amendments were tacked on to the bill, which then required assembly approval. But by the time the modified document reached the assembly, the celebrating and partially drunk legislators were so anxious to end the session and get home that they failed to act on the bill. "Technicalities" therefore killed the measure during the last week of April.[3]

This attempted legislation contributed to a large-scale exodus of California blacks to Victoria, British Columbia, the most important departure point for the Fraser River gold rush. Naturally many blacks were as interested in the economic opportunity provided by the gold rush as they were in fleeing legislative proscription in California. But pride may have been the prime motivation for the Negro organizers of the emigration movement, who declared that "they will not be degraded by the enactment of such an unjust and unnecessary law against them by their own [American] countrymen."[4]

It must have been painful for the California leadership, but they instructed their executive committee to send out letters to likely places to which blacks might emigrate. Those places most seriously considered were Sonora, Mexico; New Granada, Panama; and Victoria, on Vancouver

Island in British Columbia. As will be seen, some contemplated Haiti, although it was not seriously discussed. A letter sent to a General Bosques in Panama, himself a "colored" man, was not answered until July. When he did reply with apologies for his tardiness, Bosques was quite encouraging and made a point of saying that in New Granada there were no distinctions of color. But by then other plans were well along. The tardy letter of General Bosques produced a minor incident. A reporter from the *Sacramento Union* heard about the letter and attempted to get a copy for his paper. He was rebuffed by C. A. Rodgers, a Sacramento barber and doctor, who was chairman of the Committee on Foreign Correspondence. The friendly *Union* felt hurt by this rejection and publicly said so. In response Rodgers wrote that "he does not wish to treat friends discourteously but the helpless condition of the colored race demands that they should keep their own counsels."[5]

San Francisco blacks debated emigration and expressed their displeasure with the pending anti-Negro immigration bill at three "indignation meetings" held during April 1858. These discussions began in Reverend Moore's Zion A.M.E. Church on Pacific Street. At first, the sentiment seemed to go back and forth between Sonora, Mexico, and Victoria, British Columbia. The strongest advocate of Sonora was Peter Anderson. He claimed that its climate was more congenial and that in Victoria the Hudson's Bay Company might rule with a monarchical hand. Anderson's position was felt to be untenable because of the general belief that the thrust of American expansion would one day soon place Sonora and all of Mexico in American hands, putting blacks right back where they started.[6] While there was a good deal of debate, the discussion over the pros and cons of this migration was generally peaceful. There were times, however, when the debate went beyond words. Two San Francisco black men became so heated over their differences that they came to blows, and one of them was seriously hurt.[7]

The sentiment of the meetings moved more decidedly towards Victoria when the British Captain Jeremiah Naglee of the steamer *Commodore* attended one of the Zion Church meetings and answered questions. He told them of the price and availability of land and of the congenial reception that they would receive. When Anderson tried to get the group to consider Sonora once again, the chairman of the meeting, Jacob Francis, ruled that only discussion of the British possession was in order. The assemblage agreed to this. This was on 17 April. On 22 April, over two hundred men and women, among them Archy Lee, departed for Victoria on the *Commodore*. A farewell address from Mifflin Gibbs included strong urgings that they be sure to buy land.[8]

For Gibbs this must have been a painful moment. Just a few weeks earlier, while the press was full of the pros and cons of the anti-immigration bill, he had written a letter to the *Bulletin*, in response to what he felt was their weak editorial defense of blacks in California. He wrote in part,

> I admit the right of a family or nation to say, who from without, shall be a component part of its household or community; but the application of this principle should work no hardship to a colored man, for he was born in the great American family, and is your black brother—ugly though he may be—and is interested in its weal or its woe, is taxed to support it, and having made up his mind to stay with the family, his right to the benefit of just government is as good as that of his pale face brother who clamors for his expatriation.[9]

But while Gibbs was making a farewell speech to the first group of Victoria-bound emigrants, he was evidently giving serious consideration to following them with the Peter Lester family. The close call of the anti-immigration bill was more than they cared to endure any longer. While the Lesters were doing well financially, they had just had the searing experience of having their brilliant daughter harassed out of the school system. Victoria held promise of relief from this kind of pain.

Certainly the British official attitude at this point toward blacks was a much better one than that of the United States. There were also economic reasons for the hospitality offered by British Columbia. The gold rush to the Fraser River had left Victoria very short-handed in many occupational categories. It was expedient for Victoria officials to assure jobs and land to migrants. The influx of peoples required an expansion of governmental functions and a building program that needed laborers.[10]

In the weeks after the 22 April departure, meetings of those who were contemplating emigration continued to be held in various black churches. The next move seems to have been within the ranks of the Baptist church congregation. Here Peter Anderson spoke again, probably repeating his urgings toward Sonora. Of much more interest to this audience were the letters from the new arrivals in Victoria that were read aloud. Fielding Smithea of Oroville, a convention leader, was in the audience, and he was among those who would soon be won over to the emigration idea. Early in May, plans were drawn for another departure. At a meeting at the Zion Church, there was even talk of buying a boat to carry the migrants, a suggestion which was ultimately rejected, perhaps on the advice of the *Daily Alta California.* The *Alta* informed the emigrants that the amount of money they were considering spending would not provide them with a seaworthy vessel.[11]

The group meeting at the Zion Church felt it was time for a formal organization, and an Emigrant Society was formed with plans for a more orderly removal to British Columbia. At this meeting, the feeling of warmth toward British officials in Victoria was so great that among the resolutions passed was the following:

> That we now unitedly cast our lots (after the toil and hardships that have wrung out sweat and tears for cen-

> turies), in that land where bleeding humanity finds a balm, where philanthropy is crowned with royalty, slavery has laid aside its weapons, and the colored American is unshackled; there in the lair of the lion, we repose from the horrors of the past under the genial laws of the Queen of the Christian Isles.[12]

A black woman poet, Priscilla Stewart, also rose to this occasion, although the exact date of her writing is not certain. In part she wrote:

> God bless the Queen's majesty
>   Her sceptre and her throne
> She looked on us with sympathy
>   And offered us a home.
> Far better breathe Canadian air
>   Where all are free and well
> Than live in slavery's atmosphere
>   And wear the chains of hell.[13]

The San Francisco press gave considerable attention to this emigration. The *Bulletin* styled the emigrants as latter-day Pilgrims and predicted that they would one day have their poet of this event and "The day when colored people fled persecution in California, may yet be celebrated in story." In general, the press recognized this exodus as a protest against the near passage of the anti-immigration bill.[14]

The movement to Victoria received another boost in the form of a series of resolutions passed by a May conference of A.M.E. ministers in San Francisco. In strong terms they said:

> We firmly believe, judging from the past, that the two races can never live together on terms of equality, unless God should change the American heart entirely, which does not seem at all likely.

They went on to describe the developments in British Columbia as "God's rescue" and a signal for Negroes in

California to gather all their resources to make the move financially possible. Their enthusiasm for Victoria was so great that they called upon their black brothers in the Atlantic states to join them in British Columbia. This call of the A.M.E. ministers also went into detail about the great agricultural prospects of Vancouver Island. In spite of this appeal, the only ministers who joined the emigration were Moore and Smithea.[15] Apparently Sanderson, Ward, Stokes, and Randolph of Marysville remained in California.

Since the bulk of the black population of California did not migrate to British Columbia, most of the black ministers undoubtedly felt that at least for the time being their first duty was to remain behind with their parishioners. There were those like Sanderson, of course, who were opposed to migration in principle. However, news of their former parishioners attending integrated church services in Victoria must have given black clergymen the feeling they were not urgently needed in the new land. As Negroes arrived in Victoria, they found that white ministers opened their church doors to them. Reverend Edward Cridge welcomed them very soon after their arrival and invited them to attend the services of the Church of England. The small church that had served adequately before now became overcrowded, with black and white thoroughly intermingled. This caused a decline in white attendance, but Reverend Cridge stuck to his principles. Shortly afterwards, a nonconformist Methodist minister arrived in Victoria who was even more of an antislavery man than Reverend Cridge. Negroes flocked to this church in even greater numbers on Sunday, with the result that it soon became an overwhelmingly black church. This de facto segregation did not sit well with them, and soon many were drifting back to the more aristocratic church of Reverend Cridge. It became clear that the California black migrants were now definitely committed to an integrated church. There is no evidence that after the first day in Victoria Moore or Smithea ever conducted religious services on a regular basis in British Columbia. In fact, Reverend Moore was soon in the gold mining Cariboo region, where he worked as a woodcutter and charcoal burner. He also invested money in a mining company owned by both white and black men. In the years that followed, the religious services offered by black ministers were very poorly attended. In 1862, a letter from Victoria noted that "there is no desire to form a separate and distinct church; it strikes at the root of the principle we desire to maintain. . . . Besides, every church is open freely to us."[16]

This move to Victoria was large enough to include school-age children and it is not surprising that the doors of the schools were open to them as well. When the English Quaker couple Robert and Sarah Lindsay visited Victoria while they were traveling on the Pacific coast early in 1860, they noted in their journal that "We have visited one school where the Indian, African, and white children are upon a level. . . ."[17]

While this migration seems to have been largely from San Francisco, there were a few black migrants from elsewhere in California. In Sacramento, two hotels closed as a result of the exodus. One of them, the Hackett House, was famous for having hidden Archy Lee when he made his break for freedom. Tilghman, the barber from Marysville, and several members of the Booth family who had settled in the mountain counties also departed for Victoria. Some of the West Indian Negroes joined this migration.[18]

While land and jobs were objectives of the migration, some blacks traveled north to go prospecting in this new gold rush. The press was full of the drama of the new gold fever, although it tried to downgrade it so as not to encourage the loss of too many Californians. Playing down the gold rush, of course, had as little effect as the derogatory press comment about California in the Atlantic states ten years earlier. Reportage revealed that blacks were going to the Fraser River and the new gold rush at the Cariboo gold fields. In 1863 there were nearly one hundred Negroes in the Cariboo gold fields on the northern reaches of the

Fraser River, and a year later there were two Negro mining companies and a Negro restaurant that was more prosperous than either of the mining companies.[19]

Within a short time, the skilled black businessmen were doing well in Victoria, one reason being that they were in on the beginning of Victoria's growth and just a bit ahead of the general population growth. Gibbs tells in his autobiography, where he candidly admits giving in to an impulse to boast a bit, that he did exceedingly well in a very short time. With $100 he made a down payment on a lot with a one-story building. Within ten days he received his goods from San Francisco, and fourteen days later he had the funds to pay off 50 percent of his debt of $3,000. Shortly after that, he rented a part of his space for $500 a month. At the other end of the black social spectrum, Archy Lee was reported some years later as a successful drayman and property owner in Victoria. Many other newly arrived blacks found economic opportunity and acceptance as well. Observers in midsummer 1858 concluded that practically all the laboring jobs in Victoria were held by Negroes. They also noted that a good deal of land had been purchased by blacks and that the police force was entirely composed of blacks. Giving added strength to the impression that the dominant government and business agencies of British Columbia were friendly to the Negro was the complaint of one white that the Hudson's Bay Company store clerks gave first service to black men when a white and black entered their store at the same time.[20]

But the idyllic interludes were sometimes followed by rude awakenings. While blacks had access on a democratic basis to schools and churches in Victoria, with the passage of time they found uneven access to public places such as theaters, barber shops, and restaurants. A group charged with practicing discrimination against blacks in British Columbia was the Americans who had joined the gold rush, carrying their prejudices with them. These white Americans charged that the administration showed a great deal of favoritism to the Negro. There was much truth to this, and some of it could be attributed to the antislavery attitudes of local British clergymen. The influx of population found churches severely strained for space during services. Had Anglican church officials, especially Reverend Cridge, been obliging to the American whites, they would have arranged for some kind of segregation, but this they did not choose to do. The result, according to one hostile white observer, was that

> The sexton has repeatedly insulted our people, by crowding negro men into the same seats with white and respectable ladies, and otherwise cast the whites and blacks together in such regular alternation, as made the little chapel resemble a chess board.

Governor Douglass was equally egalitarian in his dealings with the new arrivals. One Canadian historian attributes the governor's fairness in his treatment of the Negroes to the fact that he personally had some African ancestry, derived from the West Indies, on his mother's side. It is not known if his contemporaries knew this or if he was another Leidesdorff. The governor was so committed to integration that when a group of Negroes asked for permission to form a segregated colony on Salt Springs Island, he resisted the idea.[21]

It was inevitable that a confrontation would take place between blacks and those who did not share the governor's attitudes. The outbreak occurred in Victoria's most elegant theater in 1860. Several Negroes purchased the best seats in the Colonial Theatre; whites nearby objected and tried to throw them out. The resistance they met resulted in a general free-for-all, entered into by blacks outside the theater. It was estimated that about one hundred blacks were involved. Very shortly the theater was emptied of all whites. Three of the blacks were arrested and taken into court. When it became apparent that the blacks were not the original aggressors, the court freed them.[22]

In spite of the recurrence of experiences of the kind they had known in the United States, the blacks' appreciation for Canada's more open institutions was strong enough so that many, perhaps most, of the emigrants from California sought citizenship. By 1864, about 150 blacks were believed to be British subjects. In one listing of fifty-four black applicants for citizenship, some of the most prominent of the California Colored Convention leaders were found. On the list were Mifflin Gibbs, Edward A. Booth, and Fielding Smithea as well as Archy Lee. Jacob Francis also became a citizen and unsuccessfully ran for public office in Victoria. Gibbs was elected to the city council in 1866. The black involvement in local politics brought out tensions between the American blacks and the West Indian blacks. West Indian blacks lent their support to a campaign to require that British-born citizens alone be eligible to run for public office. American Negroes believed that the West Indians were jealous of their accomplishments and greater prominence in Victoria.[23]

While large segments of the American black community sank deeper and deeper roots into the Vancouver Island community, spreading out into regions on and near the island, their contacts with San Francisco were never broken. A goodly number of the Victoria Negro community made regular visits back to the Bay area. Peter Anderson wrote during the Christmas season of 1859 that among those who visited with him were John Lewis, now a street contractor in Victoria, and Nathan Pointer, a merchant who, after visiting with Anderson, purchased a large quantity of goods before returning to Victoria. He noted that many visited elsewhere in the northern part of the state before returning to British Columbia.[24] When the new San Francisco-based black weekly, the *Pacific Appeal,* was founded in 1862, it soon had a sales agent in Victoria and printed reports of the black community there as well as elsewhere in British Columbia. In 1864, editor Phillip Bell visited Victoria and reported on the condition of black men and women there in a series of articles in the *Appeal.*[25]

An interesting question one may ask, in light of the size of the movement to Canada, is whether Negroes in California had a history of interest in emigration and colonization. The answer to this is found in the careers of the California leadership in the Eastern states. An examination of their activities in their home states reveals that they were thumpingly against colonization and emigration. A great number of them were associated with Frederick Douglass and William Lloyd Garrison, who despite their differences were both opposed to anything less than full citizenship for Negroes. They were both archenemies of the American Colonization Society, which worked to resettle blacks in Liberia. A considerable number of California blacks came from New Bedford, Massachusetts, which was a thoroughly anticolonization town. In 1853, New Bedford blacks held a series of meetings on the issue and resolved against colonization as a tool of slaveowners. Jeremiah Sanderson was active at that meeting. At the same meeting, California was approved as an exception, but only if settlement were temporary and voluntary. In 1854 Sanderson himself left for California.[26] Public anticolonization positions were taken by Yates in New York and Lester in Philadelphia.[27] Those who had attended Oberlin College had been steeped in an atmosphere of anticolonization and anti-emigrationism. Of all the convention leaders, only Reverend Darius Stokes ever took a position that even mildly supported going to Liberia. In 1852, returning briefly from California, he sponsored a meeting for blacks in Baltimore to discuss the idea. For his pains he was beaten up by angry anticolonization blacks in the hall.[28]

Anti-emigrationist blacks would only condone voluntary moves that did not serve proslavery purposes or emigration under conditions of severe duress. When the anti-Negro riots in Cincinnati in 1829 battered that black community with a virtual pogrom, the normally anticolonizationist black national leadership met the following year to organize relief and support for their migration to Canada.[29] After the passage of the 1850 Fugitive Slave Law, many ex-slaves living in the North fled to Canada, an act that black leadership sanctioned and supported as an emergency measure. But when a national conference of blacks was called in 1854 to take up emigration and colonization as a matter of principle, the majority of well-known black leaders opposed it.[30] Most California black leaders shared this position. In 1858, however, many of these black leaders felt that an emergency situation had been reached in the West.

When the Civil War began, the black communities of Victoria and San Francisco found themselves in an awkward position. Their affection for British rule was strained by the fact that England appeared to be supporting the South. But as time went by and the North's commitment to end slavery became more pronounced and English friendship to the South proved to be insignificant, the concern among blacks relaxed.

Blacks in Victoria did not forget their traditional allegiances, sympathies, and friends. When Colonel Baker, who would soon be off to the battlefields, visited Victoria in 1860, he was given a grand reception by those Negroes who had not forgotten his brilliant defense of Archy Lee two years earlier. During the Civil War years, Victoria blacks kept a close watch on affairs in the United States, and when slavery was abolished in Washington, D.C., they put on a celebration which included their traditional observance of the British Emancipation Act. When President Lincoln issued his Emancipation Proclamation in January 1863, several blacks in their enthusiasm fired off a cannon illegally, earning them a reprimand from a Victoria judge. As the national movement during the Civil War to give material aid to ex-slaves grew, it reached Victoria, where blacks involved themselves in the fund-raising campaigns to aid the "contrabands," as they were called. The fall of the Confederacy was celebrated by a procession of blacks, led by their own Pioneer Rifle Company, at the conclusion of which a mass meeting was held where Mifflin W. Gibbs and the American consul spoke.[31]

After the war, prospects for blacks appeared brighter in the United States. It was not long before a return migration started. Gibbs returned to the East to take various positions with the new Republican administrations. Two of the offices Gibbs held, in a career that covered thirty years, were a federal judgeship in Little Rock, Arkansas, and the position of United States consul to Madagascar. Reverend Moore returned for a period to San Francisco and then went on to church work in the older states. Hundreds of others, including Peter Lester and his family, remained in Victoria. From this 1858 migration, small black communities survived into the twentieth century.

Outside of the successful Victoria migration, estimates of which range from 400 to 800 people, there was no serious move by Western blacks to other countries.[32] The very few who tried it had tragic experiences. John P. Williams, a New Jersey-born black barber from Marysville, went with his wife to Haiti in 1861. Conditions there were so bad that his wife died of a tropical disease and he returned in ill health to New York. He wrote to an Eastern black weekly, warning blacks about Haiti and describing how poorly prepared that country was to receive migrants. He had found that employment opportunities there were nonexistent. Had President Lincoln read Williams's published correspondence, he might not have made his ill-fated attempt to colonize blacks in Haiti in 1864.[33]

There was one last indication of interest in emigration among California blacks. Some time in 1861, a list of 240 names of California blacks was sent to the United States Congress in the form of a petition requesting the financial means to cover the costs of leaving the country. They asked for funds "for their colonization to some country in which their color will not be a badge of degredation [*sic*]." The petition does not single out any preferred land for emigration purposes, indicating that the signers showed interests that included the British West Indies, Haiti, South and Central America, and Africa. The list of names is headed by Leonard Dugged and George A. Bailey, neither of whom was ever noticeably involved in the convention movement. Nothing came of the petition in Congress, and the events of the Civil War undoubtedly overtook it. However, its timing suggests that a considerable number of California Negroes shared Frederick Douglass's despair, that the Civil War would never benefit blacks. In that opening year of the war, Lincoln made it clear that his only objective was to save the Union. In 1861 blacks were depressed when Lincoln removed John C. Frémont as Union Commander of the Department of the West upon his having issued an order of emancipation in Missouri. Besides removing Frémont from his post, Lincoln countermanded the Missouri emancipation order. Under these circumstances, emigration talk rose again among blacks.

A closer examination of the 1861 petition casts some doubt on the validity of the 240 signatures petitioning Congress for funds to emigrate. William Newby's name is on the petition, and he was dead by 1859. There is some question about the meaning of names such as William H. Yates, who had a lifelong hostility to colonization, and Edward Duplex, who was securely established in Marysville in spite of his legal disabilities as a black. Both of these men could have left with the Victoria migration if that was their bent. Politically experienced blacks, and California had as high a percentage of them as could be found anywhere in the Union, knew well from the prior history of state and federal colonization proposals that once their cost became clear, legislators lost interest.[34] The petition was most likely a form of protest against the limited objectives of the Civil War as they appeared in 1861.

The new black subjects of the queen were not in British Columbia long before history, in the shape of the Civil War, thrust new alternatives before them. It is not clear how many remained in British Columbia, how many returned to California, or how many returned to the Eastern states. My impression is that most remained, some came back to California, and a few returned to the East. Those who returned to California rejoined the much larger group of blacks whose lives had continued on as before.

11 The Last Years of the Decade

The 1858 testimony campaign was the last state-wide effort of California blacks on any issue before the Civil War. A proposal in 1860 for another state-wide convention was rejected on the grounds that the times were not right. Although convention proponents could point to the rising tempo of activities by free Negroes in the East, most blacks in the state maintained that the situation was quite different in Democrat-controlled California.[1] The Archy Lee case, the hostile state legislature, the departure of a portion of the state's Negro leadership, and the near-passage of the anti-immigration law left blacks with their political energies temporarily dampened.

Although hundreds of blacks had left for British Columbia, after the exodus more than 4,000 remained in California; for these people, the day-to-day struggles and pleasures of life continued as before. Even as the ships were leaving for Victoria, the first minstrel show of blacks—not black-faced whites—was being performed in the mining town of Columbia. The white reporter of the event felt that the dancing was very good but that the singing was not. Still, he thought the event was worth the dollar ticket.[2] The show would undoubtedly have annoyed many members of the leadership group if it had been presented in San Francisco or Sacramento. They often spoke disparagingly of this kind of entertainment. On another level, later that year, the San Francisco Negro Masons of the Olive Branch Lodge held a celebration in honor of the laying of the Atlantic Cable. This event, much celebrated by all Americans in September of 1858, was separately observed by blacks. At the Masonic banquet held at the quarters of Olive Branch Lodge on Stockton Street, Peter Anderson gave the major address. The press noted that "festivities kept up until a later hour in the evening."[3]

Tuolumne Negroes gathered in August 1859 at an elaborately planned celebration of the West Indian emancipation. This brought together Negroes from Columbia, Angels Camp, and Jamestown. It featured a wide variety of speakers, including a West Indian black as well as James R. Starkey, the orator of the day. Starkey's comments were highly complimentary to England, whereas the West Indian, William A. Ward, spoke favorably of emigration to Central America and Liberia. The appearance of the crowd, however, belied any overwhelming need to seek a better economic environment. At the Tuolumne picnic grounds, called Billy O'Hara's Place, there were about one hundred people, many of whom had arrived in handsome carriages. The event seemed to attract considerable local attention, as there were a good number of white men and women who sat about on the outskirts of the crowd enjoying the proceedings. A reporter who was present said that some of the blacks could pass for whites.[4]

The affluence noted at the West Indian emancipation celebration was matched by the frequent reference throughout the fifties to the fashionable clothing worn by blacks. Phillip Bell's son Zadock, who preceded him to California, once wrote to his father, saying:

> You ask me what I do with my money?–Well, as you judge I put most of it on my back, a young fellow can't live out here and keep his position without dressing well; and you know, sir, clothing here that is good and fashionable, is very expensive, and a young man soon loses caste if he does not dress well.[5]

In San Francisco in May of 1860, a committee was appointed to present a literary festival with dramatic and poetic readings to raise funds for ex-slave and 1849 pioneer George Washington Dennis. Two years earlier, Dennis had signed a note to help finance the Archy Lee legal fund.

But Dennis had been unable to make payment on the note when it was demanded. At the money-raising festival, Reverend Sanderson gave a lecture on phrenology, a topic much in vogue among all classes of Americans at this time. It was of special interest to many antislavery men because of the promise it held for the perfectability of man. The subject had achieved a degree of sensationalism and helped to draw the crowd needed to bring in the money for Dennis.[6]

Dennis's financial troubles started earlier that year, when he and his partner Brown hired two Irishmen, Doyle and Burke, to work in their livery stable, which was one of San Francisco's largest. A quarrel took place between the Irishmen and their black employers. Doyle and Burke were fired. Shortly after that, seven horses in the Dennis and Brown livery stable were found dead from arsenic poisoning. It was discovered that one of the Irishmen had purchased arsenic a few days earlier. The attorney who held the note on the Dennis's property became apprehensive and began to press the livery-stable owner for payment. This placed Dennis in the financial difficulties which prompted the black community to sponsor the festival.

The featured speaker at the festival was a new arrival to California, Phillip A. Bell. Although Bell was middle-aged, his presence represented a fresh infusion of leadership to the black community. A friend of Douglass, Bell had a distinguished background of leadership in the New York Colored Convention movement. He also was associated with the earliest black journalism in the country and would become an editor of the *Pacific Appeal* and the *Elevator.*[7]

Another prestigious new arrival to California's shores in 1860 whose presence would have its encouraging impact on the black community was the already famous white anti-slavery Unitarian minister and orator, Thomas Starr King. Like Bell, King had hardly arrived when he was drawn into the activities of the black community. The twenty-second anniversary of the British West Indies Emancipation Act was celebrated throughout the state on August first in black communities large enough to get a crowd together. In San Francisco, the Pacific Gardens was packed with festive blacks. Here King spoke to an adoring audience, who applauded him vigorously when he spoke such words as:

> The greatest day of the last hundred years was not when Adams and Jefferson were first fired with the spirit of liberty nor when our heroes met in Philadelphia to sign the Declaration of Independence; but that day when the British nation laid its millions of money on the table of the House of Commons, in reverence for a principle that had only been taught before as an abstract truth.

And:

> The almighty had a great mission for this nation. Here the church was to proclaim the equality of the races.

At the end of the speech, many of the older blacks applauded with tears streaming from their eyes.[8]

There was some difference of opinion over ways to conclude the day's celebration. When it was announced that there would be dancing after the speeches concluded, a number of the more straightlaced members of the assemblage went to Russ Gardens, where Reverend Sanderson, Reverend Fletcher, and Peter Anderson, critics of the frivolous, held forth. However, according to reports, a good time was had by everyone at this gathering as well as at the more boisterous one at the Pacific Gardens.[9]

Other Negro gatherings to celebrate this event took place in Sacramento and at Sutterville. At Sutterville, blacks came together from Placerville, Auburn, Oroville, Napa, and Sonoma, and some people even came from San Francisco. Convention leader William Hall came from the Bay area to be the major speaker for the Sutterville event.

Thus, not only did blacks outside the major metropolitan areas observe their cherished holiday, but they also kept in touch with one another.[10]

Although two of the biggest black-owned shops were closed, the post-Victoria-migration period found the San Francisco black business community largely intact. Lester and Gibbs were no longer occupying their well-known boot shop on Clay just below Kearny, and two blocks away Nathan Pointer's clothing store, on Kearny near Jackson, was closed and marked "Gone to Victoria." But Henry Cornish and his furniture store, George Smith and his saloon, William H. Hall and his billiard parlor and saloon, Peter Anderson and his used-clothing house and tailor shop, George Washington Dennis and his livery stable, as well as scores of black barbers were still conducting their day-to-day lives as usual in San Francisco.[11]

In Marysville, the black barber community remained virtually intact, and its outstanding representative Edward P. Duplex, the New Haven-born Colored Convention leader, must have felt especially secure in his position. In 1859 he left for the East to bring his mother, Adaline Duplex, a New Haven dressmaker, back to California with him. Mrs. Duplex joined her twenty-nine-year-old son and his young family, resuming her trade as dressmaker. Duplex's position remained secure in Marysville, as in nearby Wheatland where he later moved. In 1888 he achieved the distinction of becoming the first black mayor of a California city, when the board of trustees of Wheatland in Yuba County elected him to that position.[12]

The black business scene in Sacramento also remained largely intact, with the exception of the Hackett House, whose black owners had gone to British Columbia, and the shoe shop of bootmaker John Wilson, a Colored Convention leader, who had left for Jamaica. But Wilson's emigrationist mood was evidently of short duration. By August of 1860, when the San Francisco black community was celebrating the British West Indies Emancipation Act,

Wilson was back in California and on hand to give an eloquent introduction for the main speaker, the recently arrived Reverend Thomas Starr King.[13]

In the years just prior to Reverend King's arrival in California, blacks experienced a bleak political climate. Race was still a political issue in the state, but now it was more intensely than ever a national problem. Members of the dominant party, the Democrats, were becoming more deeply split over events in Kansas, nearly half a continent away. In Kansas, civil strife was taking place between the free-soil forces and the proslavery forces. While the evidence in 1858 was overwhelming that most Kansans wanted their territory to become a free state, Democratic President James Buchanan was using all his power and influence to make it become a slave state. In Congress, Democrat Stephen Douglas from Illinois was splitting with his party leader over this issue. He and the Democratic senator from California, David Broderick, opposed Buchanan because they believed that Kansas should be allowed its preference. In California, pro-Broderick Democrats were therefore at odds with pro-Buchanan Democrats. The language of the quarrel involved the Kansas proslavery constitution drawn up at the town of Le Compton. Democrats who were opposed to it were called anti–Le Compton Democrats. In the state legislature of California, the pro–Le Compton Democrats predominated between 1858 and 1861. While the very young Republican party in 1858 made great strides in the Northern states east of the Mississippi River, a similar growth did not take place in California. The Republican party labored unsuccessfully under the charge of being "abolitionist." Democrats in California in the latter years of the decade were becoming increasingly opposed to the addition of any more slave states to the Union, but moral hostility to slavery had few political adherents in the state. In other words, the political picture in California near the end of the decade offered little hope to blacks.[14]

Some of the events of this watershed year, 1858, illustrate new moods among whites as well as blacks. The attack on blacks that the state legislature attempted with its anti-Negro immigration bill had its counterpart in the lynching of a black man named Aaron Bracy in the town of Auburn in Placer County. Bracy was one of that small handful of Negroes who went into agriculture. He farmed a piece of land by himself about a mile from Auburn. In the course of an altercation with a white man named Murphy, from whom he had purchased some adjoining land, he struck Murphy in the head with a pick, wounding him mortally. Bracy walked to Auburn and turned himself in to the police. Upon learning the details, men from town then went out to bring in the injured white man. A wave of rage rose against Bracy, and while he was in jail awaiting due process, a mob prepared to lynch him. There seems to have been a special hate for Bracy by white townsmen, perhaps because he was a very independent and hot-tempered man. Within a few days, the jail was stormed by the mob, and Bracy was taken out to be hanged. A Catholic priest attempted to persuade the mob to allow the courts to deal with the case. His pleas were to no avail. The hanging was viewed by San Francisco newspapers as outrageous, especially since Murphy was not yet dead. The fever and avarice of the mob continued for some weeks after the event. They plundered the lynched man's house and then burned it down. When Bracy's brother, Henry Bracy of Marysville, came to claim his brother's land, he found it occupied and he was driven away.[15]

One San Francisco newspaper suggested that the Auburn outrage occurred because the mob felt that the state supreme court decision to give Archy Lee back to his alleged owner gave them license to do what they pleased. Other Negroes living in or near Auburn were also victimized by the unpunished mob. In July, six months after the Bracy lynching, an Auburn mob attacked three homes occupied by black men and destroyed hundreds of dollars of their property without provocation. The victimized black men were locally considered peaceable, quiet men, and some Auburn whites felt legal action should have been taken against the mob. There is no record that justice was ever done.[16]

A probable casualty of the Canadian migration and temporary decline of political and intellectual activity was the Atheneum Institute. The Atheneum Institute, once the cultural center of the black community with its debates, lectures, and leadership meetings, had been replaced by a new restaurant. Although former convention chairman W. H. Hall now owned the property, it was no longer used for educational pursuits. Peter Anderson, in reporting this change, lamented, "The taste for literature among our young men, once so encouraging in this city seems to have died out."

St. Cyprian Church, where the Third Colored Convention took place, was now abandoned except for the basement, where Reverend Sanderson conducted the black public school. Peter Anderson noted that the main floor of the church was now being used by blacks who were practicing and performing minstrels and other "Jim Crow nonsense." He observed sadly, "Truly we have an uphill road in endeavor to elevate some of our people."[17] In matters musical, Anderson found other areas in which to be critical of his people. The A.M.E. Zion Church congregation planned an outing by boat to Sausalito in the fall of 1859 and did it in style. They hired a boat and a band for this all-day event. What annoyed the race-proud Anderson was that an all-white group of musicians was hired. He wrote, "a sufficient number of colored musicians could have been obtained, and in the opinion of many, would have been more appropriate . . . for reasons I need not explain." Anderson was quite right about the availability of a black band. Samuel Groomes had been leading a band of Negro musicians in the Bay area since 1854.[18]

Two funerals in 1859 were given more than usual attention by the San Francisco black community. The first was that of William Newby, who in 1858 had returned to the state where he had participated most actively in causes dear to him. He arrived sick and dying. In reporting his death, the press reminded its readers that Newby had been an editor of the *Mirror of the Times.* There were about thirty carriages in his funeral procession, making it one of the largest ever conducted by the San Francisco black community. As a Mason, he was given the full Masonic honors. He was buried in Lone Mountain cemetery.[19]

The other funeral was that of David Broderick, the anti-slavery-expansion Democrat and leader of that wing of his party in California. In a famous duel with David Terry, a state supreme court justice and a proslavery leader of the California Democrats, Broderick was mortally wounded. The struggle between these two wings of the California Democrats, a contest that on the national level would set the stage for the Civil War, boiled to a head with the events leading up to the duel between the two men. Broderick's subsequent death was deeply lamented by most Democrats in California, and even his political opponents in the young Republican party recognized the loss to the antislavery movement. One of the most important leaders of the Republican party in California, the man who had been the principal attorney for Archy Lee, Colonel Edward E. Baker, gave the funeral oration and paid his respects to Broderick's struggle for the rights of free labor. A number of blacks who had not forgotten Broderick's contribution attended the funeral services.

Blacks had been deeply divided over their feelings about Broderick. Many of them could not swallow his political label; "Democrat" in the nineteenth century stood for everything that freedom-loving blacks detested. In commenting about the Terry-Broderick quarrel before the duel occurred, a black reporter wrote, "Between two devils there is little to choose." When Broderick was killed, some some of the black leadership discussed the idea of putting up a monument to him. They must have remembered how, during the early fifties when Broderick was in the state senate, he did all he could to oppose the 1852 Fugitive Slave Law. Perhaps those who remembered his work best had gone to British Columbia, because the group gathered to decide on the monument idea tabled it for lack of enthusiasm. At a meeting at the A.M.E. Zion Church, resolutions were passed expressing sorrow at his death.[20]

A few months after Broderick's death, the news of John Brown's raid on Harper's Ferry reached San Francisco. The very first reports of the event left the impression that a significantly large group of white and black Northern abolitionists were rushing to give assistance to a large-scale slave uprising in the South. At that point, the Western correspondent of the *Weekly Anglo-African* reported that some San Francisco blacks were ready to volunteer their services in the cause of freedom. But when, some hours later, it became apparent that the numbers involved at Harper's Ferry were insignificant, those about to volunteer lost interest. The San Francisco correspondent to the newspaper wrote,

> Osawatomie Brown and his adherents had taken very foolish steps to accomplish their objects. . . . it is not believed by reasonable persons that the Abolitionists and the free colored persons of the North would so imprudently array themselves against the South.[21]

The willingness displayed by some California blacks to travel to fight slavery was matched by the readiness of others to travel for economic improvement. The great 1859 silver discoveries across the mountains in Nevada produced another mining rush of all classes and colors. A few California blacks led the way to the Nevada silver rush, returning with pieces of the metal that they exhibited to friends. By the next year, many more headed for the silver mines to make their fortunes. At least forty-five were in Nevada by 1860. A Virginia City agent was required in

1862 when the San Francisco-based Negro weekly, *Pacific Appeal,* began publication.[22]

Among those seeking material improvement, a number of leading black businessmen came together in 1859 to organize in California a Savings and Land Association. The convention leadership was prominent in this new endeavor. H. M. Collins was the president, Peter Anderson the vice president, and E. R. Johnson the secretary. Convention leader William Hall was on the board of directors. Edward Cain, Thomas Bundy, Benjamin Harris, Thomas Taylor, and the well-known George Washington Dennis were also on the board. The object of the association was to issue four hundred shares of stock at $25 a share in order to collect $10,000 within one year. The long-range objective was to accumulate $100,000 for land speculation. Some black business leaders in San Francisco were so committed to this kind of venture that they said they would put money into it even though there was a chance of failure.[23]

The organization of this association led Peter Anderson, convention leader and future editor of the *Pacific Appeal,* to muse about the long-range possibilities of this kind of effort. His imagination took in the whole of the free Negro population in the United States, and he thought if they could be brought together in a a national project,

> for the ostensible object of acquiring territory, either by conquest or purchase . . . what a powerful fund could be raised. Then we could send our McCune Smiths, our Douglass', our Garnetts, and many others who have labored in our common cause . . . not begging . . . but respectfully asking or demanding an interview with the Governments of Mexico or the United States or of any other government that might have territory to dispose of. By those means we could at least obtain land enough, however small or insignificant to organize a republic, or at least a state, somewhere on this continent.

Anderson felt that if all went well in this effort at nationhood, it would succeed, because foreign nations would feel sympathetic toward the new republic and the United States would be "shamed" into giving it attention. If nothing else, wrote Anderson, the very effort, "Lilliputian" though it would be, would compel more respect from Americans than they had heretofore given. At the same time, he counseled that the usual colonization thoughts that from time to time preoccupied black Americans were bankrupt and demeaning. He had no objection to black Americans as individuals going to Africa but was opposed to it as an organized movement. He also recommended a temporary abandonment of the struggle against slavery. This thought he offered five days after he knew the details of the John Brown effort at Harper's Ferry. "In short," he wrote, "we must let the slave sit for a while, as being too heavy a load for us to carry at present."[24]

While Anderson contemplated black liberation in sweeping terms, most blacks looked upon opportunity in California more mundanely. In 1855, before he moved west, Bell received a letter from a Detroit black friend then in California. It read, "The day for making rapid fortunes in California is passed unless by some lucky hit in speculation." But he added:

> As in the Eastern States, money can only be made by actual manual labor, or by shrewd business capacity. True, more money can be made here than there, in a given time."[25]

Four years later, in 1859, Jonas Townsend repeated this upbeat theme in a letter to his friends who edited the *Weekly Anglo-African.* He wrote, in the course of describing racism in the California schools, that "Notwithstanding all these disabilities, we are rapidly progressing in intelligence and wealth, in this new state of the far West."[26]

The fact that black people faced common problems did not eliminate conflicts among them. By the end of the decade, the tensions between West Indian blacks and American blacks had become discernible. Occasionally a glimpse of this conflict appears in a police arrest story in which the combatants are black, one from the West Indies and the other from the United States. At times this sort of discord appeared within the black organizations. At a Zion Church fund-raising festival held in San Francisco in 1860, a difficulty arose between some West Indian blacks and the others. Unfortunately, the issue involved was not given by the reporter of the event, who felt that at the bottom of the matter were the resentments the West Indians held toward the American Negroes. Of interest here was the reporter's insight into the West Indians' perception of the American black. First he claimed that the West Indians, especially the Jamaicans, felt that they were socially superior to the American black. Then he presented their view of the various kinds of black Americans:

> Of the New Yorkers . . . they are too proud; of the Philadelphians, they are too isolated and Quaker-like; of the Bostonians, they are too ultra [meaning radical]; of the Baltimoreans, they are too vain in the admiration of their females; while the Washingtonians are too gay, the Southern people in general too polite, the Western people too independent, and so on.

The reporter concluded that the "equality" that blacks achieved by sharing the discriminations of white society kept them working together. However, no evidence has been found that any of the delegates to the three California Colored Conventions of the 1850s was of West Indian origin.[27]

The West Indian element in the California black community was not very large. There were probably no more than 200 West Indian blacks throughout all of California by 1860. In San Francisco, where the largest West Indian group resided, there were over 60, and at least 40 of them were from Jamaica. This put the West Indians at about six percent of the black population of that city. In Sacramento, the West Indians were 10 in number and 5 of them were from Jamaica. West Indian blacks arrived in very small numbers during the first months of the gold rush. Most of them came later in the decade and worked at first on the railroad that was built across the Isthmus of Panama. When that was completed, many of them went to California. By 1865 they were numerous enough to organize their own associations.[28]

The black population in northern California as the Civil War decade opened totaled close to 5,000 persons. In the cities and towns, Negroes tended to live in well-defined areas without necessarily being segregated. In San Francisco, Sacramento, Stockton, and Marysville, pronounced clustering took place near or along the waterfront, in the oldest parts of town where seamen found their lodgings. In San Francisco the wards most heavily occupied by blacks were in the areas known today as Chinatown or North Beach. Nearly a fourth of the city's blacks lived in the first and ninth wards that fronted the Bay at both ends of the ever-expanding wharf system. This was also the area where the very considerable black maritime population clustered. More than one-third of the city's Negroes lived in the second ward, one of the most densely populated wards in the city. Many also lived in the fourth ward. There were several dozen black families in each of the other wards. These were the newer city wards, representing growth to the south and west of the city. Here could be found some of the more affluent members of the black community, such as George Washington Dennis and Abner Francis who had moved down from Portland, Oregon.[29]

While legal segregation did not exist in San Francisco, there were some places in the city where doors were either partly or totally closed to blacks. Blacks had to sit in the cheapest seats in the city's famous Maguire Opera House. It was there that Edward E. Ayer, who later achieved business fame in Chicago, as a young man heard the great actor Joseph Jefferson. Ayer recalled that he was seated in the pit in the company of Negroes as well as Chinese and Hawaiians.[30] If black citizens wished to use a library, they had real difficulties. The three libraries that were established in the fifties, the Mercantile Library, the Mechanics Institute, and the Odd Fellows Library, were barred to blacks. The Atheneum Institute had established its own library in an attempt to remedy this situation.[31]

During the last half of the fifties, the black population grew at a very slow rate. It is possible to record the arrival of prominent free blacks but not others. With the exception of Archy Lee in 1858, there is no evidence of other slaves brought into California. A Georgia slaveowner freed all his slaves in 1857 and at the same time provided for their transportation to either California or Liberia. Which they chose is not known. In 1859 an Eastern black weekly reported that a Mississippi slaveowner freed nearly twenty slaves, gave them $1,000 to divide between them, and paid for their transportation to California. Whether they ever arrived in the West is not reported. The arrivals from the East were few during the Civil War decade and were probably balanced by departures.[32] Not until 1880 was there a discernible though modest growth of the black population in California. In that year, the census records 6,018 blacks in the entire state. However, by 1890 the Negro population of California had nearly doubled. The census reports 11,322. This growth paralleled the overall growth in California's population. The most dramatic growth took place in southern California, and it is most striking in the case of Los Angeles, where the black population in 1880 was only 188 and by 1890 had increased tenfold to 1,817.[33]

The roughly 5,000 blacks who came to California in the gold rush decade were in many ways exceptional and represented a higher degree of initiative, aggressiveness, and tenacity than most Americans, black or white. For men and women like George Washington Dennis and

Henry Sampson, who both purchased their freedom in California; Emanuel Quivers and James R. Starkey, who bought their freedom shortly before leaving for the West; Isaac Sanks, who gained his freedom when his master died in the mines; and Archy Lee and Biddy Mason, who struck for freedom in California, the strong desire they held for liberty surmounted the effects of the institution of slavery. These black men and women came through the slave experience with their psychic strength and sense of self-worth sufficiently intact to enable them to make the great effort for freedom and go on to use that freedom constructively. Once again, it is evident that historians cannot generalize about all blacks. In a recent study of slavery, John Blassingame wrote,

> The inescapable conclusion which emerges from an examination of several different kinds of sources is that there were many different slave personality types. Sambo was one of them. But, because masters varied so much in character, the system was open at certain points, and the slave quarters, religion and family helped to shape behavior, it was not the dominant slave personality.[34]

In the spectrum of types of slave personalities shaped by the American South, blacks who came to California stood at the opposite end from "Sambo."

While many black Californians continued after the Civil War to improve the quality of their lives, it would be dangerous to make broad comparisons between them and the millions of ex-slaves who remained in the South. This relatively small group of California blacks lived and worked in a state that was experiencing almost constant growth through the rest of the century. The ex-slaves in the South coped with not only a short-lived and uneven Reconstruction but also a collapsed cotton economy. Fearful whites in the South also heaped severe repression upon them. While white racism continued in California, it lacked the degree of fear of blacks present in the South. California blacks were too few in number to evoke it.

The overwhelming majority of California blacks had known freedom in the Northern states for most if not all of their lives. Many of them had participated earlier in the intellectual and organizational leadership of black causes in the East. It was from this group that most of the leadership, the talent, and the financial support came for the organized activities of the black community in the West. While they took pride in and were more informed about their African heritage than most blacks, their life patterns in the West revealed that they had been heavily influenced by Puritanism and Quakerism. And they were pragmatists. They demanded what they thought was achievable in conservative and racist California, only tempering their style when they realized that there were few New England white antislavery people present to applaud them. Not that there were no white Philadelphians, New Yorkers, or Massachusetts men and women of sympathy to black causes in California. Some there were, but they had taken on protective coloration, and many of them had vanished into the conservative Western woodwork.

The materialistic culture of California and its remoteness from the dramatic scenes of the antislavery struggles in the East reinforced the decision by the black leadership to concern itself primarily with local issues. They would revive earlier passions and hopes during the Civil War. Some of the earlier rhetoric was heard again and some new activities serving wartime purposes were undertaken. This was short-lived. A handful of blacks, who wanted to play a part in the making of the new era they thought they saw on the horizon, left California for the older states North and South. But the vast majority of blacks who had migrated earlier now called California their home. Post-war California slowly mitigated some of its anti-Negro racist practices and allowed some of them to slumber, to re-emerge later under new conditions and in new ways.

An important factor favoring California blacks in the gold rush era was the weakness of the organized labor movement. White organized labor in the East had already gained enough strength to threaten the job opportunities of free Negroes. The weakness of the Western organizations of white labor in this same period was a boon to black workers, who were not to become the objects of white labor's hostile attentions for many years to come. Also, large numbers of California blacks found work in trades that in those years were not of any interest to labor organizers, such as service trades, inland navigation, and the domestic-service trades, which white labor often viewed as "nigger work." The employing classes in these businesses were often paternalistic whites who combined mild antislavery views with their wish to avoid the more independent white workers. The Irish, who were the main job competitors of the Negro in the nineteenth century in the East, were not yet in California in large numbers, and when their numbers did increase they found themselves much more in conflict with the Chinese. Thus for a generation the black one percent of the California population found itself in a generally benign economic environment, in contrast to its Eastern brethren.

This gold rush generation of black migrants made its mark on history by being the first major voluntary migration of Afro-Americans to travel this distance for self-betterment. For a despised and oppressed minority group successfully to match their energies against nature and their wits against hostile human forces in this effort was no small accomplishment. Had the Civil War and the Reconstruction period that followed not held out the hope of a new era of racial democracy in the East, many more Negroes would have come to California in the sixties and seventies. But there was a brief period of hope in the older states which resulted in the Western black population remaining relatively small, until the coming of the railroad brought new economic development and spurred new migration.

Back in 1849, many delegates to the California Constitutional Convention had predicted that free Negroes would become a dissolute and profligate part of the population of the new state and that they would be a burden on the community. History has given proof that they were overwhelmingly wrong.

Notes

CHAPTER 1: BEFORE THE GOLD RUSH

1. J. F. Rippy, "The Negro and Spanish Pioneers in the New World," *Journal of Negro History* 6(1921): passim.

2. Morris, Bishop, *The Odyssey of Cabeza de Vaca* (New York, 1933), passim.

3. George Parker Winship, *The Coronado Expedition* (Chicago, 1964), p. 90.

4. Jack D. Forbes, "Black Pioneers: The Spanish-Speaking Afro-Americans of the Southwest," *Phylon* 27(1966):233–46.

5. Henry R. Wagner, *Sir Francis Drake's Voyage Around the World* (San Francisco, 1926), pp. 32, 99, 281, 344, 381.

6. Ibid., pp. 236, 241, 244.

7. *The Works of Hubert Howe Bancroft* (San Francisco, 1888), 19:230–31; 34:283–84.

8. Santa Barbara Mission Book, Bancroft Notes, Bancroft Library, University of California, Berkeley, Calif.; *Works of Bancroft,* 19:393; ibid., 20:178; John Alfred Swann, "A Trip to the Gold Mines in 1848," Bancroft Library.

9. Letter to the alcalde of San Jose from Monterey, 7 May 1832, H. H. Bancroft Collection, Bancroft Library.

10. Alvarado to Light, 27 January 1839, Hayes Documents, part 2, San Diego Archives, transcript, Bancroft Library; Adele Ogden, *The California Sea Otter Trade* (Berkeley, 1941), pp. 113, 131; William Henry Ellison, ed., *The Life and Adventures of George Nidever* (Berkeley, 1947), passim.

11. Charles Raymond Clar, "Pioneer Among the Argonauts," p. 16, transcript, Bancroft Library; Henry Fowler, dictation, Bancroft Library; Theodore H. Hittell, *History of California* (San Francisco, 1898), 2:426.

12. Alan K. Brown, *Sawpits in the Spanish Redwoods* (San Mateo, Calif., 1966), p. 24; James Peter Zollinger, *Sutter, the Man and His Empire* (New York, 1939), pp. 120, 134; H. D. Pierce, journal, Bancroft Library.

13. Dale Morgan, *Jedediah Smith and the Opening of the West* (Indianapolis, 1953), pp. 195, 278.

14. Morgan, *Smith,* p. 177; Horace Bell, *Reminiscences of a Ranger* (Los Angeles, 1881), pp. 281–82; George W. James, *Heroes of California* (Boston, 1910), pp. 111–13; Owen C. Coy, *The Great Trek* (Los Angeles, 1931), pp. 186, 192; *Daily Evening Bulletin,* 21 March 1860; *Marysville Herald,* 13 August 1853.

15. *Works of Bancroft,* 22:443; John Bigelow, *Life and Services of John C. Frémont* (New York, 1856), pp. 152–54.

16. *Works of Bancroft,* 22:24.

17. M. A. De Wolfe Howe, ed., *Home Letters of General Sherman* (New York, 1909), p. 109; Sherman to Ord, 28 October 1848, Beinecke Library, Yale University, New Haven, Conn.

18. Walter Colton, *Three Years in California* (Stanford, Calif., 1949), p. 235.

19. *Californian,* 5 December 1846.

20. San Jose, California Archives, microfilm, Bancroft Library.

21. *Californian,* 7 October 1847.

22. One of the Mormon efforts to colonize the West resulted in the formation of the New York company which was headed by Sam Brannan. This group arrived in San Francisco in July 1846, bringing with it two non-Mormon Negroes, a male cook and a stewardess. Leo J. Muir, *A Century of Mormon Activities in California* (Salt Lake City, 1951), 1:30–31.

23. *Californian,* 28 August 1847.

24. Zoeth Skinner Eldredge, *The Beginnings of San Francisco* (San Francisco, 1912), 2:526–29; *Californian,* 15 and 25 September, 13 December 1847, 25 March 1848.

25. *California Star,* 20 May 1848.

26. M. E. W. Sherwood, *An Epistle to Posterity* (New York, 1897), p. 73.

27. Jacob Wright Harlan, *California '46 to '88* (San Francisco, 1888), pp. 109, 158.

CHAPTER 2: BLACKS JOIN THE GOLD RUSH

1. *New York Journal of Commerce,* cited in *New Bedford Mercury,* 21 December 1848.

2. *Albany Argus,* 18 January 1849.

3. *North Star,* 30 November 1849.

4. *Liberator,* 15 February 1850, 21 December 1849.

5. *New Bedford Mercury,* 22 August 1849.

6. *New York Tribune,* 21 November 1849; *Daily Alta California,* 31 January 1850.

7. *Tribune*, 17 August 1849; *Mercury*, 21 August 1849; Benjamin Quarles, *Black Abolitionists* (New York, 1969), p. 21; I. Garland Penn, *Afro-American Press* (Springfield, Ill., 1891), p. 30.

8. Eugene H. Berwanger, *The Frontier Against Slavery* (Urbana, Ill., 1967), passim.

9. Ronnie C. Tyler, "Fugitive Slaves in Mexico," *Journal of Negro History 57* (January 1972):1–12.

10. *National Anti-Slavery Standard*, 14, 21 December 1848; *North Star*, 25 May, 8 June, 16 November 1849; *Liberator*, 8 February, 27 April, 24 August 1849.

11. *Standard*, 28 June 1849.

12. *Liberator*, 9 November 1849.

13. Mifflin Wistar Gibbs, *Shadow and Light* (Washington, D.C., 1902), p. 37.

14. *North Star*, 21 December 1849; *Liberator*, 21 December 1849.

15. T. Johnson to William McLain, 5 February 1849, American Colonization Society Papers, Library of Congress; *North Star*, 23 March, 25 May, 8 June, 10 August, 12 October, 16 November 1849.

16. *Mercury*, 8 August 1849.

17. *Tribune*, 16 August 1849; *Standard*, 29 August 1850; *National Era*, 28 November 1850.

18. *Mercury*, 18 January 1849.

19. Ibid., 30 March 1849.

20. *Tribune*, 27 June 1849.

21. By the end of 1848 sixteen whalers from New Bedford were already reported as abandoned by their crews in San Francisco harbor; *Mercury*, 2 December 1848.

22. *Pennsylvania Freeman*, 12 May 1852.

23. C. F. Hovey to May in Boston, 14 June 1852, Samuel May Collection, Boston Public Library.

24. *Mercury*, 7, 18 March 1851.

25. *Marysville Appeal*, 25 April 1901.

26. *New Bedford Standard*, 15 August 1854.

27. *Elevator*, 30 March 1866, 17 June 1870.

28. William Still, *Underground Railroad* (Philadelphia, 1872), pp. 746–47; *Christian Recorder*, 6 February 1864; *Appeal*, 5 December 1863.

29. Howard L. Scamehorn, *Buckeye Rovers in the Gold Rush* (Athens, Ga., 1965), pp. 5, 136.

30. Jesse B. Frémont, *A Year of American Travel* (New York, 1878), p. 114.

31. Owen to Durbin, 9 July 1851, Isaac Owen Correspondence, Bancroft Library; *Alta,* 4 November 1884.

32. *Elevator,* 27 October 1865; 30 March 1866.

33. *Frederick Douglass' Paper,* 1 April 1852; *Appeal,* 29 August 1863.

34. *Freeman,* 25 March 1852.

35. Walker D. Wyman, ed., *California Emigrant Letters* (New York, 1952), p. 160; Leonard Kip, *California Sketches with Recollections of the Gold Mines* (Los Angeles, 1946), p. 51.

36. P. Brown to Alley Brown, December 1851, California-Oregon Collection, Missouri Historical Society, St. Louis, Mo.

37. *Douglass' Paper,* 1 April 1852.

38. Howard H. Bell, ed., *Minutes of the Proceedings of the National Negro Conventions: Colored National Convention, October 16, 17, 18, 1855, in Philadelphia* (New York, 1969), p. 16.

39. Howard H. Bell, ed., *Minutes and Proceedings of the Second Annual Convention for the Improvement of the Free People of Color* (Philadelphia, 1832), p. 16.

40. *Douglass' Paper,* 31 March 1854.

41. Martin R. Delaney, *The Condition, Elevation, Emigration and Destiny of the Colored People of the United States* (Philadelphia, 1852), p. 185; Frémont, *American Travel,* p. 22.

42. Manuscript of the reminiscences of Alvin Coffey is in the archives of the Society of California Pioneers in San Francisco; see pp. 46–52.

43. G. W. Read and R. Gaines, eds., *Gold Rush: The Journals of J. Goldsborough Bruff* (New York, 1944), 1:252; "The Journal of John Lowery Brown of the Cherokee Nation en Route to California in 1850," *Chronicles of Oklahoma* 12(1934):183; *Era,* 9 August 1849.

44. *North Star,* 27 July 1849; L. C. McKeeby, memoirs, typescript copy, Beinecke Library.

45. Octavius T. Howe, *Argonauts of '49* (Cambridge, Mass., 1923), p. 42; Read and Gaines, *Gold Rush,* 2:819; George Mifflin Harker, "Morgan Street to the Old Dry Diggins 1849," Missouri Historical Society, St. Louis, 6:52; Eva Turner Clark, ed., *California Letters of William Gill* (New York, 1922), p. 34; Richard Dillon, ed., *The Gila Trail* (Norman, Okla., 1960), p. 78; Read and Gaines, *Gold Rush,*

2:797; Charles Camp, ed., *John Doble's Journal and Letters from the Mines* (Denver, 1962), p. 115.

46. Hagerstown Mining Company Proceedings, Archibald B. Knode Collection, Indiana State Historical Society, Indianapolis.

47. Read and Gaines, *Gold Rush,* 1:491; Almarin B. Paul, "My First Two Years in California," *Quarterly of the Society of California Pioneers* 4(1927):37; Alonzo Delano, *Across the Plains and Among the Diggings* (New York, 1936), pp. 76-77; Irene D. Paden, *Journal of Madison Berryman Moorman* (San Francisco, 1948), p. 1; P. F. Castleman, diary, transcript, Beinecke Library.

48. Helen S. Giffen, *Diaries of Peter Decker* (Georgetown, Calif., 1956), p. 102; Delano, *Across the Plains,* p. 77; Charles A. Kirkpatrick, journal, Bancroft Library; Dillon, *Gila Trail,* p. 83.

49. James W. Evans, journal of the year 1850, pp. 51-52, Bancroft Library.

50. Mabelle Eppard Martin, ed., "From Texas to California in 1849," *Southwestern Historical Quarterly* 29(July 1925):202.

51. *New Orleans Picayune,* 17 June 1849; Castleman, diary, p. 30; Paden, *Moorman,* p. 51.

52. Castleman, diary, pp. 3, 24; George W. Groh, *Gold Fever* (New York, 1966), p. 94.

53. "Journal of John Lowery Brown," p. 209; Finley McDiarmid, letters, 5 June 1950, Bancroft Library.

54. Harker, "Morgan Street," p. 45.

55. Amos Batchelder, journal, 31 August 1849, Bancroft Library.

56. Margaret Frink, *Adventures of a Party of California Gold Seekers* (Oakland, Calif., 1897), p. 92.

57. Joseph Alonzo Stuart, "Notes on a Trip to California," 14-16 September 1849, Beinecke Library.

58. John G. Ellenbacker, *The Jayhawkers of Death Valley* (Marysville, Calif., 1938), p. 24; Carl I. Wheat, "The Forty-Niners in Death Valley," *Historical Society of Southern California* 21(1939):112.

59. Benjamin Hayes, *Pioneer Notes* (Los Angeles, 1929), pp. 34-35; Mary E. Foy, ed., "By Ox Team from Salt Lake to Los Angeles," *Annual Publication of the Historical Society of Southern California* 14(1930):286; William B. Lorton, diaries, transcript, Bancroft Library.

60. Dillon, *Gila Trail* p. 83.

61. G. P. Hammond and E. H. Howes, eds., *Overland to California* (Berkeley, 1950), pp. 95-96.

62. Stanislaus Lasselle, diary, Indiana State Library, Indianapolis.

63. John Walton Caughey, ed., *Rushing for Gold* (Berkeley, 1949), pp. 28, 31.

64. *New Orleans Picayune,* 7 August 1849.

65. Glenn S. Dumke, ed., *Mexican Gold Trail* (San Marino, Calif., 1945), p. 45.

66. David Demarest, diary, 29, 30 April 1849, Bancroft Library. I can't resist the thought that this might have been a confidence game perpetrated by an enterprising white Texan and his black cohort.

67. Henry F. Dobyns, ed., *Hepah, California* (Tucson, 1961), p. 36.

68. Ralph P. Bieber, ed., "Diary of a Journey from Missouri to California in 1849," *Missouri Historical Review* 23(1928):35.

69. Edmund Green, "Reminiscences of a Pioneer," p. 17, Bancroft Library.

70. Franklin Walker, *San Francisco's Literary Frontier* (New York, 1939), p. 60; John Clark, "The California Guide," 28 August 1852, transcript, Beinecke Library.

71. Giffen, *Diaries,* p. 75; "Dr. Charles Elisha Boyle Diary," Columbus Dispatch, 17 October 1949.

72. *New Orleans Picayune,* 7 August 1849; Lorton, diaries, p. 251.

73. Bayard Taylor, *El Dorado* (New York, 1854), p. 48; *National Era,* 4 July 1850.

74. *San Francisco Evening Picayune,* 7 August 1851; W. Augustus Knapp, "An Old California Pioneer's Story," *Overland Monthly* 10(1887):400.

75. Hayes, *Pioneer Notes,* p. 71.

76. Douglass S. Watson, ed., *The Santa Fe Trail* (San Francisco, 1931), pp. 92, 121, 136, 169.

77. Leroy R. Hafen, ed., *Journals of Forty-Niners* (Glendale, Calif., 1954), 2:52-53, 108, 285; Lorton, diaries, p. 236.

78. *Sacramento Transcript,* 23 September 1850; *New Bedford Mercury,* 8 November 1850; *New Orleans Picayune,* 6 November 1850.

79. William G. Doolittle, statement, p. 6, Bancroft Library.

80. *New York Tribune,* 21 November 1849.

81. Gibbs, *Shadow,* p. 38.

82. Wendell Phillips to Thomas Starr King, Boston, 18 November 1857, Archives, Society of California Pioneers, San Francisco.

83. *Elevator,* 31 December 1869.

84. William H. Chipman, journal, February 1850, typescript, Dwinelle Papers, California Historical Society, San Francisco.

85. Delilah L. Beasley, *The Negro Trail Blazers of California* (Los Angeles, 1919), pp. 115-16.

86. *Douglass' Paper,* 16, 23 October 1851.

87. Ibid., 27 May 1852.

88. Anthony Serna and Allison Serna, eds., *The Wanderings of Edward Ely* (New York, 1954), pp. 126-27.

89. *New Orleans Picayune,* 3 April 1849.

90. For further examples see ibid., 19 January, 21 March, 15 April, 28 June, 14, 20 July, 16 October 1849.

91. Amelia Ransome Neville, *The Fantastic City* (Boston, 1932), p. 29.

92. *Panama Herald,* 28 April 1851; *New Orleans Picayune,* 26 June 1850.

93. Elizabeth W. Martin, ed., "Hulbert Walker Letters," *California Historical Society Quarterly* 36(1957):142.

94. Read and Gaines, *Gold Rush,* 2:987.

95. A. P. Hannum and J. B. McMaster, eds., *A Quaker Forty-Niner* (Philadelphia, 1930), p. 384; *Douglass' Paper,* 27 May 1852; Daniel Fletcher, reminiscences, pp. 67-68, Bancroft Library.

96. Forbes Parkhill, *Mister Barney Ford* (Denver, 1963), pp. 56-57.

97. *Panama Herald,* 27 October 1851; *San Francisco Picayune,* 17 November 1851; J. P. Jones and W. W. Rogers, eds., "Across the Isthmus in 1850," *Hispanic-American Historical Review* (1961): 535.

98. *New York Tribune,* 13 August 1849.

99. C. E. Grunsky and Clotilde Grunsky, "From Europe to California," *Quarterly of the Society of California Pioneers* 10(1933):20.

100. John E. Minter, *The Chagres* (New York, 1948), pp. 250-51; Albert Edwards, *Panama* (New York, 1911), pp. 416-17.

101. *Panama Star,* 21 July 1853.

102. Peter J. Barber, diary, 10 March 1852, Bancroft Library.

103. *Douglass' Paper,* 16 October 1851; "The Diary of John W. Dwinelle," *Quarterly of the Society of California Pioneers* 8(1931):

143. Dwinelle Hall on the Berkeley campus of the University of California is named after him.

104. Hiram Dwight Pierce, *A Forty-Niner Speaks* (Oakland, Calif., 1930), p. 20; J. D. Borthwick, *Three Years in California* (Oakland, Calif., 1948), p. 16.

105. Cowan to Derby, 10 March 1852, Foreign Office 55-100, Public Records Office, London. See also Perry to Palmerston, 22 December 1849, Foreign Office 55-84, no. 32, Public Records Office, for early signs of this concern by the British officials in Panama. Perry wrote, "I regret to observe a bad feeling growing between them [the Americans] and the black population of the Isthmus."

106. *New Orleans Picayune,* 19 October 1850, 11 March 1851; John M. Letts. *California Illustrated* (New York, 1852), p. 164.

107. *New Bedford Standard,* 26 July 1854; *Era,* 10 August 1854. This report of the bombing of Greytown cites a New York Times interview with John C. Frémont, an eyewitness observer of the event, who testified to its racist features; Parkhill, *Ford*, p. 62.

CHAPTER 3: IN THE MINES

1. *A Compendium of the Ninth Census* (Washington, D.C., 1872), p. 29.

2. Population Schedules, Seventh Census, California.

3. *Governor Bigler's Message and Report of the Secretary of the Census of 1852* (published by California State Printers).

4. Erwin G. Gudde, *California Place Names* (Berkeley, 1969), p. 219.

5. William Redmon Ryan, *Personal Adventures in Upper and Lower California in 1848-9* (London, 1850), 2:104-10; Thomas Robertson Stoddart, *Annals of Tuolumne County* (Sonora, Calif., 1963), p. 62.

6. P. Sioli, *History of El Dorado County* (Oakland, Calif., 1883), p. 201; *The Works of Hubert Howe Bancroft* (San Francisco, 1888), 23:352, n. 3; *Daily Alta California,* 12 February 1850; *New Bedford Mercury,* 17 March 1852.

7. Sioli, *El Dorado County,* pp. 201-02; Newton C. Miller, letters, 26 December 1854, Bancroft Library; James M. Hutchings, diary, p. 66, Bancroft Library.

8. Hutchings, diary, p. 67; *Marysville Daily Herald,* 6 November 1856.

9. *Works of Bancroft,* 35:391-92; *Calaveras Chronicle,* 18 Octo-

ber 1851; *Alta,* 1 December 1851; Charles Peters, *Autobiography* (Sacramento, 1915), p. 14.

10. Andrew S. Hallidie, "Moquelomne Hill-Vamos-Prince Lib," Hallidie Collection, California Historical Society, San Francisco.

11. *San Francisco Picayune,* 17 November 1851; Edna Bryan Buckbee, *The Sage of Old Tuolumne* (New York, 1935), p. 329; *Alta,* 4 August 1853, 20 February 1854; *San Francisco Evening Bulletin* 4 March 1859.

12. *Alta,* 22 February 1858.

13. J. D. Borthwick, *Three Years in California* (Oakland, Calif., 1948), p. 134.

14. Ibid., 164-65; Louis J. Stellman, *Mother Lode* (San Francisco, 1934), p. 71.

15. A P. Hannum and J. B. McMaster, eds., *A Quaker Forty-Niner* (Philadelphia, 1930), p. 289.

16. Census returns, 1850, El Dorado County, California.

17. William W. Miller, diary, 6, 28 October 1849, Beinecke Library.

18. Ibid., 31 October 1849; 8 February 1850. Garrison's Hawaiian wife and children were on the family farm in Hawaii at this time.

19. Hannum and McMaster, *Quaker Forty-Niner,* pp. 289-90.

20. William Downie, *Hunting for Gold* (San Francisco, 1893), pp. 27, 34-35, 51.

21. *New Orleans Picayune,* 2 May 1851.

22. *The Pioneer,* official organ of the Santa Clara County Pioneers, 9 March 1878, 2:1.

23. *Frederick Douglass' Paper,* 31 August 1855.

24. Benjamin Bowen, journal, pp. 2, 8, 50-51, 55, Bancroft Library.

25. Howard Mitcham, ed., "A Mississippian in the Gold Fields," *California Historical Society Quarterly* 35(1956):215.

26. Hallidie, "Moquelomne Hill."

27. John Simpson, ed., *Joseph Batty—Over the Wilds to California* (Leeds, England, 1867), p. 43.

28. William F. Terry, diary, 12, 13, 22, 31 March, and 1, 12 April 1850, Bancroft Library.

29. Sherlock Bristol, *The Pioneer Preacher* (Chicago, 1898), pp. 172-75.

30. Heinrich Leinhard, memoir, folio 138, Bancroft Library.

31. Amos Batchelder, journal, 15 August 1850, Bancroft Library.

32. Anna Lee Marston, ed., *Records of a California Family* (San Diego, 1928), pp. 211, 235. While in California Mrs. Gunn subscribed

to the *Pennsylvania Freeman*, a Philadelphia antislavery weekly. Mrs. Smith was active in black abolitionist organizations in Philadelphia.

33. Returns, 1850, Tuolumne, Yuba, and Calaveras counties, California.

34. *Alta*, 15 February 1858.

35. Hutchings, diary, p. 67.

36. "Edmund Booth—Forty-Niner," *San Joaquin Pioneer and Historical Society* (Stockton, Calif., 1953), p. 21.

37. *Alta*, 4 May 1850.

38. *San Francisco Picayune*, 9 April 1852.

39. *New Orleans Picayune*, 23 November 1850.

40. Horace Bell, *On the Old West Coast* (New York, 1930), p. 21; *Works of Bancroft*, 35:722.

41. *Alta*, 28 July 1854, quoting the *New Orleans Picayune*.

42. Ibid.; Hinton Helper, *Land of Gold* (Baltimore, 1855), p. 278.

43. *New Bedford Mercury*, 22 July 1850, quoting the *New York Journal of Commerce; New Bedford Standard*, 19 August 1851, quoting the *New York Tribune*.

44. *Era*, 2 May 1850, quoting the *Cherokee Advocate*.

45. George Murrell, letters, 1 July, 24 August, 28 December, 8 November, 5 December 1850, Huntington Library, San Marino, California.

46. *Alta*, 5 February 1856.

47. John Steele, *In Camp and Cabin* (Lodi, Calif., 1901), p. 49.

48. *Mercury*, 22 July 1850.

49. Helen T. Catterall, ed., *Judicial Cases Concerning American Slavery and the Negro* (Washington, D.C., 1929), 2:232.

50. Buckbee, *Saga*, p. 290; returns, Tuolumne County, California.

51. Coffey, reminiscences, pp. 50–52, Archives, Society of California Pioneers, San Francisco.

52. George H. Tinkam, *Men and Events* (Stockton, Calif., 1915), p. 134, n.

53. Sarah Bixby-Smith, *Adobe Days* (Cedar Rapids, Iowa, 1926), p. 52; Waldemar Westergaard, ed., "Diary of Dr. Thomas Flint," *Publications of the Historical Society of Southern California* 12 (1923):62.

54. Benjamin Drew, *The Refugee* (Boston, 1856), p. 123.

55. *Alta*, 18 September 1851, quoting the *New York Commercial*

Advertiser; New Bedford Standard, 19 August 1851, quoting the *New York Tribune.*

56. "The Story of a Gold Miner: Reminiscences of Franklin Morse," *California Historical Society Quarterly* 6(1927):223.

57. David Cosad, journal, 6 October 1849, California Historical Society, San Francisco.

58. William Ellis, letters, 9 March 1850, Beinecke Library.

59. P. V. Fox, diary, p. 42, Beinecke Library.

60. *Era,* 2 May 1850.

61. *Pioneer,* 9 March 1878.

62. William D. Marmaduke, letters, 6 March 1850, California Historical Society, San Francisco.

63. George Johnson, notes, nos. 10, 14, Bancroft Library.

64. Daniel Woods, *Sixteen Months at the Gold Diggings* (New York, 1851), p. 155.

65. *Grass Valley Telegraph,* 4 December 1855; Lionel U. Ridout, "The Church, the Chinese and the Negroes in California 1849-1893," *Historical Magazine of the Protestant Episcopal Church* 28(1959).

66. Joseph E. Roy, *Pilgrim Letters* (Boston, 1888), p. 64.

67. *Alta* 4 May 1850.

68. William Henry Ellison, *A Self-Governing Dominion* (Berkeley, 1950), pp. 169-78.

69. *New Bedford Mercury,* 3 September 1850.

70. Edmund Kinyon, *The Northern Mines* (Grass Valley, Calif., 1949), pp. 60-63; Ralph Friedman, "They Came as Bonded," *Fortnight* (October 1955):39.

71. Thompson and West, *History of Los Angeles County* (Oakland, Calif., 1880), p. 90; *Pennsylvania Freeman,* 27 June 1850; returns, 1850, Mariposa County, California; Carvel Collins, ed., *Sam Ward in the Gold Rush* (Stanford, Calif., 1949), p. 28; Henry W. Splitter, "Los Angeles in the 1850's," *Historical Society of Southern California Quarterly* 31(1949):118; Charles Davis, letters, 6 January 1854, Beinecke Library; Delilah L. Beasley, *The Negro Trail Blazers of California* (Los Angeles, 1919), p. 84. Newell Chamberlain, in his *Call of Gold* (Mariposa, Calif., 1936), p. 143, incorrectly stated that Thorn freed his slaves when he heard that California was a free state.

72. "Sherman Was There," *California Historical Society Quarterly* 23(1944):349-69.

73. Borthwick, *Three Years in California*, pp. 134–35; *Colville's Marysville Directory* (San Francisco, 1855), p. vi.

74. Murrell, letters, 15 October 1849, 24 August 1850.

75. Leonard Kip, *California Sketches with Recollections of the Gold Mines* (Los Angeles, 1946), p. 51.

76. Borthwick, *Three Years in California*, p. 165.

77. Dale Morgan, ed., *In Pursuit of the Golden Dream* (Stoughton, Mass., 1970), pp. 101, 107.

78. Borthwick, *Three Years in California*, p. 177; William T. Ellis, *Memories* (Marysville, Calif., 1939), p. 60.

79. B. Meder, letters, 23 January 1852, Bancroft Library.

80. Friedrich Gerstaecker, *California Gold Mines* (Oakland, Calif., 1946), p. 89.

81. George H. Beach, "My Reminiscences," *Quarterly of the Society of California Pioneers* 9(1932):239–41.

82. Returns, 1850, Yolo County, California; Raymond Rossitter, *Statistics of Mining* (Washington, D.C., 1875), vol. 7(1874), pp. 91, 96.

83. Jasper Hill, letters, 5 July 1851, Beinecke Library; Mary E. Foy, ed., "By Ox Team from Salt Lake to Los Angeles," *Annual Publication of the Historical Society of Southern California* 14(1930): 330.

84. William C. Ellis, letters, 25 November 1851, Beinecke Library.

85. Carl I. Wheat, "Journals of Charles E. De Long," *California Historical Society Quarterly* 10(1931):169.

86. Bowen, journal, passim.

87. Bowen, journal, 29 October 1854.

88. *Alta*, 27 July 1854.

89. *Sacramento Union*, 15 March 1860.

90. Coffey, reminiscences, p. 49.

91. William I. Morgan, "Log of a Forty-Niner," p. 81, Bancroft Library.

92. William H. Townsend, "Experiences in California," 11 July 1849, transcript, Bancroft Library.

93. Ezra Bourne, "Diary of an Overland Expedition to California in 1850," Bancroft Library; John W. Caughey, ed., *Six Months in the Gold Mines* (Los Angeles, 1959), pp. 65–67.

94. Carl I. Wheat, ed., *The Shirley Letters* (New York, 1949), p. 169.

95. *Alta,* 17 April 1850, 1 May 1853; *San Francisco Picayune,* 3 October 1851; *Alta,* 26 June 1854.

96. Baker Whitcomb, letters, 15 August 1856, Bancroft Library; "Adventures of William Ballow," p. 2, Bancroft Library; Joseph Henry Jackson, *Bad Company* (New York, 1949), pp. 61, 64, 77.

97. Steele, *In Camp and Cabin,* pp. 40–47; *Union,* 13 April 1852.

98. *Union,* 9 March 1858; *New Bedford Mercury,* 8 October 1850, quoting the *Sonora Herald; Alta,* 1 November 1852; *Grass Valley Telegraph,* 24 November 1853.

99. G. W. Read and R. Gaines, eds., *Gold Rush: The Journals of J. Goldsborough Bruff* (New York, 1944), 2:894; Bayard Taylor, *El Dorado* (New York, 1854), p. 76.

100. A. J. Bledsoe, *Indian Wars of the Northwest* (San Francisco, 1885), pp. 299-31.

101. *San Andreas Independent,* 14 May 1859.

102. *San Francisco Evening Bulletin,* 27 July 1858; *San Francisco Herald,* 31 March 1856; *Alta,* 29 July 1858.

103. Paul C. Phillips, ed., *Scenery of the Plains, Mountains and Mines* (Princeton, N.J., 1932), p. 151; Douglas S. Watson, ed., *The Santa Fe Trail to California* (San Francisco, 1931), p. 247.

104. Gaines and Read, *Gold Rush,* 2:827; *Alta,* 4 December 1852.

105. *Union,* 18 October 1860; *Weekly Placer Herald,* 3 September 1853.

106. *Marysville Herald,* 11 October 1855.

107. Mitcham, "A Mississippian," p. 215; *Alta,* 23 February 1858.

108. Returns, Eighth Census, California, passim; Eugene H. Berwanger, *The Frontier Against Slavery* (Urbana, Ill., 1967), p. 25, n.

109. Returns, Eighth Census, El Dorado and Tuolumne counties, California.

110. *California Reports* (San Francisco, 1877), 1875–77, pp. 120–25.

111. *Grass Valley Telegraph,* 31 October 1854.

112. John Carr, *Pioneer Days in California* (Eureka, Calif., 1891), pp. 156, 224-25.

113. Frederich F. A. Windeler, journal, 9 October 1852, 4 July 1853, Beinecke Library.

114. Miller, diary, 25 December 1849, 1 January 1850.

115. Woods, *Sixteen Months,* p. 65.

116. *Alta,* 27 October 1854; Edwin F. Bean, *History and Directory of Nevada County* (Nevada City, Calif., 1867), p. 193.

117. *Alta,* 15 February 1858.

118. Colored American Joint Stock Quartz Mining Company records, Bancroft Library.

119. Richard Dillon, ed., "Mother Lode Memoir," *Journal of the West* 3(1964):358; Beasley, *Trail Blazers,* p. 114; journal of the Washington Mining Company; p. 205, Bancroft Library.

CHAPTER 4: IN THE CITIES

1. *Liberator,* 15 February 1850.

2. Darius Stokes, *Elevation of the People* (pamphlet, San Francisco, 1853), p. 2.

3. Vincent Perez Rosales, *California Adventure* (San Francisco, 1947), p. 17; F. Gerstaecker, *California Gold Mines* (Oakland, Calif., 1946), p. 106; Albert Williams, *A Pioneer Pastorate* (San Francisco, 1879), p. 62; Hinton Helper, *Dreadful California,* ed. Lucius Beebe and Charles M. Clegg (Indianapolis, Ind., 1948), p. 56; Mary E. Foy, ed., "By Ox Team from Salt Lake to Los Angeles," *Annual Publication of the Historical Society of Southern California* (1930):317; Henry L. Byrne and Dolores Waldorf Bryant, eds., "San Francisco, 1850," *Quarterly of the Society of California Pioneers* 2(1925):203.

4. Census returns, 1850, Sacramento County, California; James H. Carson, *Recollections of the California Mines* (Oakland, Calif., 1950), p. 68.

5. Jonas Winchester to wife, 8 July, 5 August 1849, Jonas Winchester Collection, California State Library, Sacramento.

6. California State Census, 1852, microfilm, compiled by the Daughters of the American Revolution from the original fading census reports. These statistics are roughly accurate in spite of the errors that crept into the laborious work of the D.A.R. committee that compiled them.

7. M. W. Gibbs, *Shadow and Light* (Washington, D.C., 1902), pp. 43-44; Gibbs to J. C. Frémont, 1 October 1902, Frémont Papers, Bancroft Library.

8. Clarkson Crane, ed., *Last Adventure, San Francisco in 1851* (San Francisco, 1931), p. 10; Pringle Shaw, *Ramblings in California* (Toronto, 1857), pp. 16-17; J. D. Borthwick, *Three Years in California* (Oakland, Calif., 1948), p. 38; *Daily Alta California,* 1 February 1851.

9. Gibbs, *Shadow,* p. 40; *Alta,* 22 June 1850; *Pacific Appeal,* 15 October 1870.

10. *Colville's San Francisco Directory for 1856-1857* (San Francisco, 1856), p. 213; *Alta*, 19 September 1853, 13 March 1854.

11. Gibbs, *Shadow*, pp. 44–45; *Pennsylvania Freeman*, 16 February 1854; *National Anti-Slavery Standard*, 25 February 1854; *North Star*, 10 November 1848.

12. D. L. Beasley, *The Negro Trail Blazers of California* (Los Angeles, 1919), p. 120; *Colville's Directory*, p. 71.

13. Martin R. Delaney, *The Condition, Elevation, Emigration and Destiny of the Colored People of the United States* (Philadelphia, 1852), pp. 104-05; *Elevator*, 27 June 1874; *Appeal*, 27 June 1874, 1 August 1863.

14. William T. Sherman, *Recollections of California* (Oakland, Calif., 1945), pp. 131-32; Anthony Tasheira to wife, 14 June 1854. Tasheira Collection, California State Library, Sacramento. Tasheira was a white employee of Drexel, Sather, and Church.

15. *Daily Evening Bulletin*, 4 November 1858; *Alta*, 22 September 1851.

16. *Alta*, 23 July, 30 December 1853; Helen Holdredge, *Mammy Pleasant* (New York, 1953), p. 44.

17. *Appeal*, 20 June 1863; *Colville's Directory*, p. 5.

18. *Alta*, 23 July 1853, 17 July 1854; *Pacific*, 21 July 1854; *Appeal*, 20 June 1863.

19. *Appeal*, 20 June 1863.

20. *Frederick Douglass' Paper*, 18 May 1855.

21. *Alta*, 8 February 1857; *Mirror of the Times*, 12 December 1857.

22. *Douglass' Paper*, 17 August 1855; *Mirror*, 13 December 1857.

23. *Alta*, 7 April 1854.

24. Ibid.

25. *The Works of Hubert Howe Bancroft* (San Francisco, 1888), 33:181; Rosales, *California Adventure*, p. 82; *Alta*, 11 October 1849, 22 March, 8 July 1850, 30 November 1852; Dorothy Huggins, ed., *Continuation of the Annals of San Francisco* (San Francisco, 1939), pp. 26, 27; Bryne and Bryant, "San Francisco, 1850," p. 201.

26. Bryne and Bryant, "San Francisco, 1850," p. 203; *Alta*, 14 February 1851, 8 November 1854.

27. *California Chronicle*, 4 May 1858.

28. *Douglass' Paper*, 22 September 1854.

29. Returns, 1860, San Francisco County, California.

30. *Alta*, 27 January, 3 February 1851; *Mirror*, 22 August, 12 December 1857.

31. *Bulletin,* 6 February 1858; *Morning Globe,* 2 October 1856; *Alta,* 15 January 1857.

32. *Alta,* 25 October 1849, 1 April 1851, 13 March 1854, 23 May 1857.

33. Mary F. Williams, ed., *Papers of the San Francisco Committee of Vigilance* (Berkeley, 1919), pp. 115–23, 266–68; *Alta,* 1 July 1851.

34. *Alta,* 23 November 1854.

35. Ibid., 2, 3 December 1851; *San Francisco Picayune,* 3 December 1851.

36. Anthony Tasheira to wife, 14 June 1854.

37. *California Chronicle,* 20 November 1855.

38. *Douglass' Paper,* 14 May 1854; *Appeal,* 12 April 1862.

39. California State Census, 1852; census returns, 1860, San Francisco and Sacramento counties, California.

40. Thompson and West, *History of Sacramento County* (Oakland, Calif., 1880), p. 105.

41. Returns, 1850, Sacramento County, California; an impression of where Sacramento Negroes tended to live was culled from a variety of news notices in which addresses were mentioned. See *Alta,* 26 May 1853; *Mirror,* 22 August 1857; *Sacramento Daily Union,* 26 March, 19 November 1860.

42. *Mirror,* 22 August 1857.

43. Returns, 1860, Sacramento County, California; H. J. Bidleman, *Sacramento City Directory,* 1861–62 (Sacramento, 1861).

44. John Vance Cheney, "Mose the Black Pioneer," *Californian* 1(January–June 1880):287.

45. Returns, 1860, Sacramento County, California; *Union,* 19 November 1855.

46. Returns, 1860, Sacramento County, California; *Union,* 19 November 1855.

47. *Minutes of the Seventh Anniversary of the San Francisco Baptist Association* (San Francisco, 1857), p. 22.

48. *Bulletin,* 26 July 1858, quoting the *Sacramento Mercury.*

49. *Union,* 9 November 1851, 6 November 1855.

50. Returns, 1860, Yuba and San Joaquin counties, California.

51. William C. Ellis, letters, 17 April 1852, Beinecke Library; returns, 1860, Yuba County, California.

52. *Marysville Herald,* 17 August 1853; *Amy's Marysville Directory for 1858* (Marysville, Calif., 1858); returns, 1860, Yuba County, California.

53. *Amy's Directory*; returns, 1860, Yuba County, California; *Marysville Democrat* 21 August 1858.

54. *Amy's Directory*; returns, 1860, Yuba County, California.

55. *Amy's Directory; Colville's Marysville Directory* (San Francisco, 1855); returns, 1860, Yuba County, California.

56. *Amy's Directory.*

57. Richard G. Stanwood, journal, 7 January 1855, Bancroft Library; *Marysville Appeal,* 8 February, 8, 30 March 1860.

58. *Amy's Directory*; returns, 1860, Yuba County, California.

59. *Marysville Herald,* 3 June 1857.

60. *Alta,* 8 August 1853.

61. J. P. Bogardus, *Stockton City Directory, 1856* (San Francisco, 1856); returns, 1860, San Joaquin County, California.

62. Bogardus, *Directory.*

63. *San Joaquin Republican,* 25 February 1858.

64. *Bulletin,* 27 May 1858, quoting *San Joaquin Republican; San Francisco Herald,* 28 May 1858; *Alta,* 31 May 1858.

65. *Proceedings of the First State Convention of the Colored Citizens of California* (Sacramento, 1855); *Proceedings of the Second State Convention of the Colored Citizens of California* (San Francisco, 1856). This may be partly explained by the fact that travel from Marysville to Sacramento was cheaper because the route was entirely by water.

66. Bogardus, *Directory* pp. 42, 65; returns, 1860, San Joaquin County, California.

67. Returns, 1860, San Francisco, Sacramento, Yuba, and San Joaquin counties, California. The data given is based on the legible returns in the microfilm manuscript census. For hundreds of names of persons who were undoubtedly Negro, the state of origin was either not noted by the enumerator or unreadable. I believe that the enumerators failed to record many blacks partly because of slipshod census work and partly because some blacks were hiding out due to real or imagined fears.

68. *The Population of the United States, Eighth Census* (Washington, D.C., 1864), pp. 28, 30, 31, 32.

CHAPTER 5: SOUTHERN CALIFORNIA

1. Census returns, 1850 and 1860, Los Angeles County, California.

2. Harris Newmark, *Sixty Years in Southern California,* 3d ed. (Boston, 1930), pp. 30-31.

3. Mayme R. Krythe, ed., "First Hotel of Old Los Angeles," *Historical Society of Southern California* 33(1951):45; Newmark, *Sixty Years*, p. 330; Benjamin Hayes, *Pioneer Notes* (Los Angeles, 1929), pp. 87–88; Horace Bell, *Reminiscences of a Ranger* (Los Angeles, 1881), p. 22.

4. *Historical Sketch of Los Angeles County* (reprint, Los Angeles, 1936), p. 82.

5. Hiram A. Reid, *History of Pasadena* (Pasadena, Calif., 1895), p. 386; Newmark, *Sixty Years*, p. 138; returns, 1860, Los Angeles County, California.

6. Kate B. Carter, *The Negro Pioneer* (Salt Lake City, 1965), pp. 8, 16, 20, 31, 33, 44; returns, 1850, Los Angeles County, California.

7. Delilah L. Beasley, *The Negro Trail Blazers of California* (Los Angeles, 1919), p. 90; *National Anti-Slavery Standard*, 5 April 1856, quoting the *Los Angeles Star*.

8. Thompson and West, *History of Los Angeles County* (Oakland, Calif., 1880), p. 90.

9. Bilderback to Coutts, 23, 31 December 1861, 8 November 1866, Cave Coutts letters, Huntington Library, San Marino, Calif. In 1864, Bilderback was arrested for saying that he wished the Confederates to kill every black Union soldier and every white officer of a black military unit. Newmark, *Sixty Years*, p. 330.

10. John Wells Brier, "The Death Valley Party of 1849," *Out West* 17(1903):463–64; Jessie H. Coopman, ed., *Overland in 1849* (Los Angeles, 1961), pp. 53–54.

11. Bell, *Reminiscences*, 284–86.

12. Hayes, *Pioneer Notes*, pp. 90, 104; returns, 1860, San Diego and Santa Barbara counties, California.

13. R. P. Putnam, journal, 7 October 1858, Bancroft Library; returns, 1860, San Diego County, California.

14. W. A. Chalfant, *The Story of Inyo County* (n.p., 1933), pp. 154, 180; returns, 1860, Tulare County, California. After this skirmish, Tyler was never seen again.

15. Hayes, *Pioneer Notes*, p. 206; returns, 1860, San Diego County, California.

16. Hayes, *Pioneer Notes*, p. 171.

17. Affidavit, 6 July 1860, Justices' Court, County of San Diego, Huntington Library, San Marino, Calif.

18. *Proceedings of the California State Convention of Colored Citizens* (San Francisco, 1865), pp. 3–4; *A Compendium of the Eleventh Census* (Washington, D.C., 1892), p. 477.

CHAPTER 6: SLAVERY AND THE FUGITIVE SLAVE IN CALIFORNIA

1. *Californian,* 3 March 1848.
2. *Daily Alta California,* 25 January, 22 February, 22 March 1849.
3. *Alta,* 26 July 1849.
4. *New Orleans Picayune,* 29 September 1849; *Liberator,* 28 September 1849; Arthur Woodward, ed., "Benjamin David Wilson's Observations on Early Days in California and New Mexico," *Annual Publication of the Historical Society of Southern California* 18 (1934):125.
5. *New Orleans Picayune,* 13 October 1849.
6. *New Orleans Picayune,* 8 December 1849; J. Ross Browne, *Report of the Debates in the Convention in California on the Formation of the State Constitution* (Washington, D.C., 1850), p. 456.
7. Browne, *Report,* pp. 144, 148; *Alta,* 26 July 1849.
8. Browne, *Report,* pp. 331–40.
9. *The Works of Hubert Howe Bancroft* (San Francisco, 1888), 23:313; Theodore H. Hittell, *History of California* (San Francisco, 1898), p. 2:806.
10. *New Orleans Picayune,* 9 June 1849.
11. Robert Givens, letters, 10 September 1852, typescript, Bancroft Library.
12. *Liberator,* 29 June 1849; *New Orleans Picayune,* 30 June 1849.
13. "Grandma Bascom's Story of San Jose in '49," *Overland Monthly* 9(1887):543.
14. *Sacramento Transcript,* 1 April 1850, cited in Ira Cross, *History of the Labor Movement in California* (Berkeley, 1935), p. 295.
15. First Magistrate records, 22 October 1849, Sacramento County, California State Archives, Sacramento, Calif.; William C. Ellis, letters, 4 July 1852, Beinecke Library.
16. *Thomas Eads vs. B. Miller,* Sacramento State Archives; *National Era,* 1 November 1849; Dorothy H. Huggins, ed., "Diary and Letters of Thomas B. Eastland and Joseph Eastland," *California Historical Society Quarterly* 18(1939):244. See also pp. 78, 148 in this text on Rheubin and Archy Lee who were hired out.
17. *Alta,* 29 May 1850.
18. *California Chronicle,* 16 December 1857.
19. *National Era,* 11 July 1850.
20. *New Bedford Mercury,* 4 December 1849; *New Orleans Picayune,* 30 November 1849.

21. *Alta,* 29 May 1850; *Mercury,* 11 July 1850; *Liberator,* 19 July 1850.

22. *Alta,* 16 February 1850.

23. Richard Ness, "Account of Overland and the Mines," 1 May 1850, Beinecke Library.

24. *Liberator,* 30 August 1850.

25. *Pacific,* 4 January 1851; *Alta,* 20 July 1851; *San Francisco Picayune,* 19 July 1851.

26. Frederick Law Olmstead, *The Cotton Kingdom* (New York, 1862), 2:136.

27. *Pennsylvania Freeman,* 5 December 1850.

28. Ruth Frye Axe, ed., *Bound for Sacramento* (Claremont, Calif., 1938), p. 144.

29. *Alta,* 30 October 1851.

30. *Alta,* 31 March, 1 April 1851; *San Francisco Herald,* 1 April 1851; *California Courier,* 31 March 1851; *Liberator,* 9 May 1851; *Era,* 29 May 1851.

31. *Journal of the Proceedings of the Assembly,* Third Session, San Francisco, 1852, pp. 95, 146, 147; *Journal of the Proceedings of the Senate,* Third Session, San Francisco, 1852, pp. 257–85; *Union,* 6 February, 9 April 1852.

32. *Weekly Placer Herald,* 16 April 1853; *Alta,* 20 April 1853.

33. *Pacific,* 25 August 1854; *Columbia Gazette,* 2 September 1854; E. B. Buckbee, *The Saga of Old Tuolumne* (New York, 1935), p. 211; Carlo M. De Ferrari, "Stephen Spencer Hill," *Quarterly of the Tuolumne County Historical Society* (January-March, 1966): 162–63.

34. *California Christian Advocate,* 20 May, 3 June, 8 August 1852; *Pacific,* 25 June 1852; Caleb Fay, statement, pp. 18–21, Bancroft Library; B. F. Alley, *History of San Mateo County* (San Francisco, 1883), p. 318.

35. *Union,* 3, 9 June 1852; *Advocate,* 8 August 1852.

36. *Memoirs of Cornelius Cole* (New York, 1908), p. 94.

37. *Pacific,* 11 June, 2 July 1852; *Advocate,* 17, 24 June 1852.

38. *Frederick Douglass' Paper,* 6 July 1854; Benjamin Quarles, *Black Abolitionists* (New York, 1969), p. 166.

39. Pratt to Cole, 30 June 1852, Cornelius Cole Papers, Library of the University of California at Los Angeles.

40. Simonds to Cole, 8 June 1852, ibid.

41. *Douglass' Paper,* 1 June 1855.

42. *California Reports* 2, 1852 (Philadelphia, 1854), pp. 424–59.

43. Ellis, letters, 26 October 1852, Beinecke Library.

44. *Advocate,* 1 July 1852; Cole Papers, undated notes, Library, University of California at Los Angeles.

45. *Columbia Gazette,* 22 April 1854; *Union,* 13 April 1854.

46. *Statutes of California* (Sacramento, 1854), p. 30.

47. *Union,* 25 April 1855; *Douglass' Paper,* 1 June 1855.

48. See chapters 8 and 9 on Colored Conventions for further explanation.

49. *Union,* 8, 9, 11, 25 January 1858; *Daily Evening Bulletin,* 9, 11, 28 January 1858.

50. *California Reports* 9, 1858 (Sacramento, 1858), p. 171; *Union,* 16, 18 February 1858; *Alta,* 14 February 1858; *San Joaquin Republican,* 13 February 1858.

51. *Alta,* 5 March 1858; *Chronicle,* 8 March 1858; *San Francisco Herald,* 6 March 1858; *Bulletin,* 5 March 1858.

52. Oscar T. Shuck, ed., *Eloquence of the Far West* (San Francisco, 1899), p. 307.

53. *Alta,* 18 March 1858.

54. *Alta,* 18 March 1858.

55. *Bulletin,* 17 March 1858; *Herald,* 18 March 1858.

56. *Herald,* 18 March 1858; *Alta,* 18 March 1858; *Chronicle,* 18 March 1858.

57. *Chronicle,* 19, 20 March 1858; *Herald,* 20 March 1858; *Alta,* 20 March 1858.

58. *Alta,* 15 April 1858; *Chronicle,* 7, 15, April 1858.

59. *Herald,* 15 April 1858; *Bulletin,* 14, 16 April 1858; *Union,* 23 April 1858; D. L. Beasley, *The Negro Trail Blazers of California* (Los Angeles, 1919), p. 83.

60. *Bulletin,* 27 March 1858.

61. *Alta,* 30 March 1857; *Pacific,* 15 January 1857.

62. *Alta,* 21, 22 January 1859; *Bulletin,* 20, 21, 22 January, 8 February 1859.

63. *Bulletin,* 8 July 1859; *Weekly Anglo-African,* 20 August 1859.

64. For a more complete account of the Archy Lee case, see Rudolph M. Lapp, *Archy Lee, A California Fugitive Slave Case,* Book Club of California Publication 131 (San Francisco, 1969).

CHAPTER 7: CHURCHES AND SCHOOLS

1. Daniel Woods, *Sixteen Months at the Gold Diggings* (New York, 1851), p. 65; Clifford M. Drury, ed., "Timothy Dwight Hunt and His

Wedding Records," *California Historical Society Quarterly* 27(1949): 289-96; Thompson and West, *History of Sacramento County* (Oakland, Calif., 1880), p. 105; *Frederick Douglass' Paper,* 30 October 1851.

2. John Hope Franklin, *From Slavery to Freedom* (New York, 1967), pp. 162-63.

3. Owen to Durbin, 9 July 1851, 24, 25 July 1852, Reverend Isaac Owen, letters, Correspondence 54; Bancroft Library; Thompson and West, *Hsitory of Sacramento County,* p. 105.

4. *Colville's San Francisco Directory for 1856-1857* (San Francisco, 1856), p. 148; *Langley's Directory* (San Francisco, 1859), p. 374; *Pacific Appeal,* 6 June 1863.

5. *Langley's Directory,* p. 374; Rudolph M. Lapp, "Jeremiah B. Sanderson: Early California Negro Leader," *Journal of Negro History* 53(1968):324.

6. *Colville's Directory,* p. 148; *Weekly Anglo-African,* 5 November 1859; *Pacific,* 24 March 1854.

7. *Proceedings of the California Baptist State Convention* (San Francisco, 1867), pp. 11, 36; *Pacific,* 8 December 1854.

8. *Proceedings of the Baptist Convention,* pp. 11, 20; *Pacific,* 26 February 1857; *Mirror of the Times,* 12 December 1857.

9. *Proceedings of the Baptist Convention,* p. 20; *Appeal,* 9 November 1872.

10. *Proceedings of the Baptist Convention,* pp. 11, 20.

11. Ibid., p. 11; *Minutes of the Tenth Anniversary of the San Francisco Baptist Association* (San Francisco, 1860), p. 20; *Journal of the Third Annual Convention of the African Methodist Episcopal Church* (San Francisco, 1863), p. 19.

12. Thompson and West, *History of Sacramento County,* p. 107; *Baptist Circular* (Sacramento, 1859); *Union,* 27 December 1860; *Minutes of the Tenth Anniversary,* p. 22.

13. *Proceedings of the Baptist Convention,* p. 22; *Pacific,* 14 May 1857; *Minutes of the Tenth Anniversary,* p. 11; *Illustrated History of San Joaquin County* (Chicago, 1890), pp. 169-70; V. Covert Martin, *Stockton Album* (Stockton, Calif., 1959), p. 179.

14. *Amy's Marysville Directory* (Marysville, Calif., 1869), p. 98; *Marysville Herald,* 2 November 1853, 29 July, 7 October 1857; *Mirror,* 12 December 1857.

15. Edwin F. Bean, *History and Directory of Nevada County* (Nevada City, Calif., 1867), p. 193; *Pacific,* 14 September 1855, 28 February 1856; *Daily Alta California,* 27 October 1854.

16. *Union,* 8 August 1860; *Alta,* 19 January 1858; *San Joaquin*

Republican, 19 January 1858; *California Chronicle,* 9 March 1858; *Union,* 8 March 1858.

17. Lionel U. Ridout, "The Church, The Chinese and the Negroes in California 1849–1893," *Historical Magazine of the Protestant Episcopal Church* 28(1959):132; George R. Crooks, *Life of Bishop Simpson* (New York, 1890), p. 315.

18. The Pallier family of San Francisco were Louisiana-born black Catholics.

19. Walton Bean, *California* (New York, 1973), p. 194.

20. John Swett, *History of the Public School System of California* (San Francisco, 1876), p. 205; *Alta,* 1 March 1851.

21. *Colville's Directory,* pp. 148, 193.

22. Ibid.; *San Francisco Municipal Report for 1863–64* (San Francisco, 1864), p. 271.

23. *Douglass' Paper,* 18 May 1855; *Chronicle,* 29 September 1855; *Message of the Honorable Stephen P. Webb, Mayor of San Francisco* (San Francisco, 1855).

24. *San Francisco Herald,* 23, 24 January 1855; *Douglass' Paper,* 6 April 1855.

25. Roy W. Cloud, *Education in California* (Stanford, Calif., 1952), p. 44; *Douglass' Paper,* 18 May 1855; *Daily Evening Bulletin,* 6 June 1857; *Chronicle,* 23 November 1857.

26. *Bulletin,* 1 May 1858; *Langley's Directory,* p. 3.

27. *Chronicle,* 20 February 1858.

28. *San Francisco Herald,* 28 January 1858.

29. *Bulletin,* 18, 24 February 1858; *San Francisco Herald,* 19 February 1858; *Chronicle,* 20 February 1858.

30. *San Francisco Herald,* 11 February, 11 March 1858; *Chronicle,* 20 February 1858.

31. *Chronicle,* 12 March 1858; *Bulletin,* 4 March 1858; *Alta* 25 March 1858.

32. *San Francisco Herald,* 19 February 1858.

33. Leon Litwack, *North of Slavery* (Chicago, 1961), pp. 143–50.

34. *Bulletin,* 24 February 1858.

35. Lester to Still, 4 June 1858, Peter Still Papers, Leon Gardiner Collection, Historical Society of Pennsylvania, Philadelphia.

36. *Alta,* 25 March, 27 May 1858; *Bulletin,* 21 October 1858.

37. *Pacific,* 31 January 1861.

38. *Report of the Superintendent of Common School, San Francisco, 1860* (San Francisco, 1860), p. 64; *Weekly Anglo-African,* 25 February, 31 March, 14 April, 5 May 1860.

39. Handwritten page tipped in between pp. 36–37, *Rules of the*

Board of Education (Stockton, Calif., 1873), Sanderson Collection, Bancroft Library.

40. *San Francisco Municipal Report for 1863–64* (San Francisco, 1864), p. 271.

41. *Appeal,* 27 September 1862.

42. Cloud, *Education,* p. 44; D. L. Beasley, *The Negro Trail Blazers of California* (Los Angeles, 1919), p. 174.

43. *Liberator,* letter from Sanderson to Nell, 25 January 1856; *Union,* 9 October 1855.

44. Thompson and West, *History of Sacramento County,* p. 113; *Union,* 8 April 1858.

45. D. S. Cutler, *Sacramento City Directory* (Sacramento, 1859), p. xxii; *Union,* 20 November 1856, 2 January 1860.

46. *Union,* 23 April, 18 August, 17 December 1860; J. J. Bidleman, *Sacramento City Directory 1861–1862* (Sacramento, 1860); Leonard Mears, *Sacramento Directory* (Sacramento, 1863); H. S. Crocker, *Sacramento Directory* (Sacramento, 1871).

47. Thompson and West, *History of Sacramento County,* p. 113.

48. *Columbia Gazette,* 31 March 1855; *Weekly Anglo-African,* March (no date given) 1859.

49. *Marysville Herald,* 1 November 1855, 8 November 1857; Marysville City Council, minutes, 9 November 1857, microfilm, Marysville Public Library; *Amy's Marysville Directory for 1858,* pp. xvii, xviii.

50. *Tuolumne Courier,* 30 July 1859; H. Carroll to wife, 3 June 1860, Huntington Library, San Marino, California.

51. Census returns, 1860, Tulare County, California.

52. *Appeal,* 11 October 1862; Lapp, "Sanderson," pp. 329–30.

53. Cloud, *Education,* pp. 44–45.

54. *Elevator,* 16 July 1869; *California Reports,* 1874 (San Francisco, 1875), 48:36–57.

55. *Appeal,* 25 November 1871, 17 February 1872.

56. *California Reports,* 1874, p. 48.

57. *Appeal,* 7 August 1875.

58. *California Reports,* 1890, 82:588–95.

59. *Appeal,* 3 January 1863, 7 September 1872; *Elevator,* 26 October 1865.

60. Beasley, *Trail Blazers,* p. 177; Cloud, *Education,* p. 44.

61. Santa Cruz Historical Society, *News and Notes* (April 1955); *Elevator,* 2 July 1869.

CHAPTER 8: THE BACKGROUND OF THE CONVENTION MOVEMENT

1. J. H. Franklin, *From Slavery to Freedom* (New York, 1967), pp. 236-37; *Constitution of the American Society of Free Persons of Colour* (Philadelphia, 1831), pp. 9-10; Howard H. Bell, *Minutes of the Proceedings of the National Negro Conventions* (New York, 1969).

2. Leon Litwack, *North of Slavery* (Chicago, 1961), passim; Benjamin Quarles, *Black Abolitionists* (New York, 1969), passim.

3. *North Star,* 30 November 1849.

4. *Frederick Douglass' Paper,* 6 November 1851. By this date Douglass had changed the name of his paper.

5. Carter Woodson, ed., *Mind of the Negro as Reflected in His Letters* (Washington, D.C., 1926), pp. 76-81.

6. *Douglass' Paper,* 24 June, 1 July, 22 October, 10 December 1852, 21 January, 22 May, 9 September 1853, 30 June, 6 October, 1, 15 December 1854.

7. Ibid., 1 July 1852, 21 September 1855.

8. Philip S. Foner, *The Life and Writings of Frederick Douglass* (New York, 1950), 2:48-66.

9. *Douglass' Paper,* passim.

10. R. M. Lapp, "Jeremiah B. Sanderson: Early California Negro Leader," *Journal of Negro History* 53(1968):326. Even Douglass made a contribution to this fund.

11. *Douglass' Paper,* 27 July 1855.

12. *Douglass' Paper,* 16 February 1861.

13. *National Anti-Slavery Standard,* 16 February 1861.

14. Ibid., 2 May, 9 September 1852; 7 July 1860.

15. *Pennsylvania Freeman,* 12 February 1862.

16. *Douglass' Paper,* 22 September 1854; Lapp, "Sanderson," passim.

17. Letter from Kenneth P. Blake, Librarian, Colby College Library, 12 March 1973; Oberlin College Catalogue and Record of Colored Students, Cowles Papers, Oberlin College Library, pp. 7, 9, 19.

18. *Statutes of California, 1850,* (Sacramento, 1850), p. 230; *Statutes of California, 1851* (Sacramento, 1851), p. 114.

19. M. W. Gibbs, *Shadow and Light* (Washington, D.C., 1902), p. 46.

20. *People vs. W. R. Potter,* December 1850, Sacramento Court of Sessions, California State Archives, Sacramento.

21. *Argus* (Melbourne, 15 March 1855. Signed letter from "Homo."

22. *Daily Alta California,* 18 January 1851.

23. Oscar T. Shuck, *A History of Bench and Bar in California* (Los Angeles, 1901), p. 1117.

24. *Daily Evening Bulletin,* 27 April 1858; *Pacific,* 26 February, 1857.

25. Petition 44, California State Archives, Sacramento.

26. Gibbs, *Shadow,* p. 47.

27. [G. E. Montgomery], "Lost Journals of a Pioneer," *Overland Monthly* (January 1886):77, census returns, 1860, Sacramento County, California.

28. *Journal of the Proceedings of the Assembly* (Sacramento, 1852), 20 March 1852, p. 395; *Union,* 23 March 1852; Theodore H. Hittell, *History of California,* 4:97, 98; *Liberator,* 23 July 1852.

29. *Alta,* 13, 14 March 1853; *Union,* 15 March 1853; Hittell, *History of California,* 4:112; *California Reports* 4 (San Francisco, 1868), *People vs. Hall,* pp. 399–405.

30. *Douglass' Paper,* 13 April 1855.

31. *Alta,* 26 March 1854; *Douglass' Paper,* 1 June 1855.

32. *Pacific,* 27 July 1855.

33. Edward C. Kemble, *A History of California Newspapers,* edited by Helen Bretnor (Los Gatos, Calif., 1962), pp. 96, 97, 120, 180; H. Brett Melendy and Benjamin F. Gilbert, *The Governors of California* (Georgetown, Calif., 1965), p. 68.

34. *Proceedings of the First State Convention of Colored Citizens of the State of California* (Sacramento, 1855).

35. *Union,* 10 December 1856; *Bulletin,* 11 December 1856; *Grass Valley Telegraph,* 18 March 1856; *Marysville Herald,* 25 January 1856; *Journal of the Proceedings of the California State Senate* (Sacramento, 1856), pp. 488–496, 559.

36. *Proceedings of the Second Annual Convention of the Colored Citizens of the State of California* (San Francisco, 1856), p. 27.

37. Ibid.; Luther P. Jackson, *Free Negro Labor and Property Holding in Virginia,* 1830–1860 (New York, 1942), pp. 198–99; California State Census, 1852, microfilm.

38. *Alta,* 6 January 1857.

39. *Chronicle,* 24 November, 25 December 1857; *San Francisco Call,* 13 February 1857; *Marysville Herald,* 23 January, 25 February 1857; *Pacific,* 19 February 1857.

40. *Proceedings, Second Annual Convention,* p. 9.

41. *Journal of the Proceedings of the State Senate,* Eighth Session, 1957, pp. 285, 294, 337; Secretary of State Petitions to the State Legislature, California State Archives; *Pacific,* 5 March 1857, *Marysville Herald,* 30 January 1857.

42. *Marysville Herald,* 10 April 1857.

43. *Union,* 9 January 1858; Melendy and Gilbert, *Governors of California,* 67-78.

44. *Mirror of the Times,* 22 August 1857.

45. *Address of the State Executive Committee to the Colored People of the State of California, 1859,* passim.

46. Ibid.

47. *Union,* 2 February 1858; *San Francisco Times,* 2 February 1858.

48. *Elevator,* 28 May 1869, quoting the *Mirror,* 16 May 1857.

49. *Statutes of California, 1863,* p. 69.

50. *Marysville Herald,* 30 January 1857, quoting the *San Francisco Herald; Statutes of California, 1855,* p. 106.

51. *Bulletin,* 24 August 1858; *Alta,* 25 August 1858; Shuck, *Bench and Bar,* p. 551.

52. *Bulletin,* 3 November 1858; *Alta,* 4 November 1858.

53. *Bulletin,* 9 December 1858.

54. *California Reports* 17(San Francisco, 1872), pp. 64-67; *Union,* 10 September 1860.

55. *Statutes of California, 1863,* p. 69; *Appeal,* 13 September 1862.

56. *Alta,* 31 October 1861; *Bulletin,* 29 October 1861; *Appeal,* 5 April 1862.

57. *Statutes of California, 1863,* p. 69.

CHAPTER 9: THE THREE CONVENTIONS

1. *Union,* 21 November 1855; *Grass Valley Telegraph,* 27 November 1855.

2. *Pacific Appeal,* 18 July 1874; *Proceedings of the Colored National Convention, 1853* (Rochester, N.Y., 1853), reprinted in Howard Holman Bell, ed., *Proceedings of the National Negro Conventions 1830-1864* (New York, 1969), passim.

3. *Frederick Douglass' Paper,* 16 February 1855.

4. *Appeal,* 12 April 1862.

5. *Douglass' Paper,* 26 October 1855.

6. *Proceedings of the First State Convention,* (Sacramento, Calif., 1855), pp. 1, 6; *Appeal,* 1 August 1863; *Daily Evening Bulletin,* 22 March 1862.

7. Proceedings, First State Convention, pp. 3, 4.

8. Ibid., pp. 6, 15, 19, 21.

9. Ibid., p. 22.

10. *Liberator,* 11, 25 January 1856; *National Anti-Slavery Standard,* 12 January 1856.

11. *Proceedings, First State Convention,* pp. 7, 8, 15, 16.

12. Ibid., pp. 10, 11.

13. Ibid., p. 11.

14. Ibid., pp. 18, 19.

15. Ibid., p. 20.

16. Ibid., p. 25.

17. Ibid., pp. 18, 26; *Union,* 21 November 1855; *Democratic State Journal* (Sacramento), 24 November 1855.

18. *Proceedings, First State Convention,* p. 15; *Appeal,* 19 April 1862.

19. *Douglass' Paper,* 28 September 1855.

20. *Liberator,* 25 January 1856.

21. *Proceedings, First State Convention,* p. 27.

22. *Ibid.,* p. 22; *Liberator,* 18 January 1856.

23. *Appeal,* 7 June 1862.

24. William Tecumseh Sherman, *Recollections of California* (Oakland, Calif., 1945), pp. 131–32; *Bulletin,* 8 May 1858; *Elevator,* 6 October 1865.

25. *Appeal,* 7 June 1862.

26. *California American,* 26 November 1856.

27. *Proceedings of the Second Annual Convention of Colored Citizens of the State of California* (San Francisco, 1856), pp. 3, 4, 5.

28. *Appeal,* 29 August 1863.

29. *Proceedings, Second Annual Convention,* p. 24.

30. See chap. 2, n. 6; James H. Fairchild, *Oberlin: the Colony and the College* (Oberlin, Ohio, 1883), p. 65.

31. *Proceedings, Second Annual Convention,* p. 9.

32. Ibid., p. 13; *Appeal,* 20 June 1863; *Douglass' Paper,* 16 March 1855; *Anti-Slavery Standard,* 10 October 1857; *Bulletin,* 22 March 1859.

33. *Proceedings, Second Annual Convention,* pp. 14–19.

34. Ibid., p. 20.
35. Ibid., pp. 13, 19, 23, 44.
36. Ibid., pp. 28–29.
37. Ibid., pp. 29–38.
38. Ibid., pp. 41–42.
39. Ibid., pp. 43–44.
40. Ibid., p. 33.
41. *Address of the State Committee to the Colored People of the State of California* (Sacramento, 1859), p. 19; *Mirror of the Times,* 22 August, 12 December 1857.
42. *Address of the State Committee,* p. 19; *Mirror,* 22 August, 12 December 1857.
43. *Bulletin,* 13 October 1857.
44. *Bulletin,* 26 October 1857; *California Chronicle,* 27 October 1857; census returns, 1860, Monterey County, California.
45. *Appeal,* 3 May 1862.
46. *Chronicle,* 27 October 1857; *San Joaquin Republican,* 31 October 1857.
47. *Union,* 20 October 1857.
48. *Mirror,* 12 December 1857.
49. Ibid., *Chronicle,* 27 October 1857.
50. *Address of the State Committee,* p. 10.
51. Ibid., passim.

CHAPTER 10: THE EXODUS TO VICTORIA

1. See chap. 6, "Slavery and the Fugitive Slave."
2. *Journal of the Proceedings of the Assembly,* 1857, p. 824.
3. *Journal of the Proceedings of the Assembly,* 1858, pp. 342, 408, 444–45, 462, 489–500; *Journal of the Proceedings of the California State Senate,* 1858, pp. 661, 663–64; *Daily Evening Bulletin,* 8, 15, 23, 27 April 1858; *Daily Alta California,* 20 April 1858; *Union,* 27 March 1858.
4. *Bulletin,* 15 April 1858.
5. *Address of the State Committee to the Colored People of the State of California* (Sacramento, 1859), p. 5; *Union,* 22 July 1858; *Bulletin,* 24 July 1858.
6. *Bulletin,* 15, 17, 21 April 1858; *Alta,* 16 April 1858.
7. *Alta,* 15 May 1858.

8. *Alta,* 17, 20, 21 April 1858; *Bulletin,* 21 April 1858; *Union,* 16 April 1858.

9. *Bulletin,* 5 April 1858.

10. James W. Pilton, "Negro Settlement in British Columbia," unpublished manuscript, chap. 2, Library, University of British Columbia, Vancouver.

11. *Bulletin,* 6 May 1858; *Alta,* 12 May 1858.

12. *Bulletin,* 12, 13 May 1858.

13. D. L. Beasley, *The Negro Trail Blazers of California* (Los Angeles, 1919), p. 263.

14. *Union,* 16 April 1858; *Alta,* 20 April 1858; *Bulletin,* 21 April 1858; *San Francisco Herald,* 6 June 1858.

15. *Bulletin,* 13 May 1858.

16. *Bulletin,* 7 May, 1 September 1858; Mathew Macfie, *Vancouver Island and British Columbia* (London, 1865), pp. 389–90; *Pacific Appeal,* 16 August 1862, 17 October 1863.

17. Elizabeth Galloway (ed.) *Travels of Robert and Sarah Lindsay,* London, 1886, p. 149.

18. Edgar Fawcett, *Some Reminiscences of Old Victoria* (Toronto, 1912), pp. 216, 217; *Alta,* 5 July 1858.

19. *Appeal,* 11 July 1863, 20 February 1864.

20. M. W. Gibbs, *Sadow and Light* (Washington, D.C., 1902), pp. 61–62; *Appeal,* 6 February 1864; *Bulletin,* 7, 15, 20 July 1858.

21. *Bulletin,* 8 September 1858; Robin Winks, *The Blacks in Canada* (New Haven, 1971), pp. 274–75; Robert W. O'Brien, "Victoria's Negro Colonists 1858–1866," *Phylon* 3(1942):15–18.

22. *Union,* 23, 30 November 1860, quoting the *Portland* (Oregon) *Advertiser; Bulletin,* 30 November 1860.

23. *Appeal,* 6 February, 5 March 1864; Fawcett, *Old Victoria,* pp. 217–18, Winks, *Blacks in Canada,* pp. 284–85.

24. *Weekly Anglo-African,* 31 December 1859.

25. *Appeal,* through January and February 1864.

26. *Frederick Douglass' Paper,* 30 September 1853.

27. *Appeal,* 1 August 1863; *Pennsylvania Freeman,* 2 May 1850.

28. *Freeman,* 28 August 1852; *National Era,* 12 August 1852.

29. Howard Holman Bell, *Negro Convention Movement 1830–1861* (New York, 1969), pp. 12–16.

30. Ibid., p. 160.

31. *Union,* 9 August 1860; *Appeal,* 12 July 1862, 3 January, 25 April 1863; *Elevator,* 21 April 1865.

32. Macfie, *Vancouver Island,* p. 388; Fawcett, *Old Victoria,* p. 215.

33. *Appeal,* 7 June 1862.

34. Memorial of Leonard Dugged and George A. Bailey Miscellaneous Document no. 31, Thirty-seventh Congress, Second Session (Washington, D.C., 1862).

CHAPTER 11: LAST YEARS OF THE DECADE

1. *Weekly Anglo-African,* 14 April, 26 May 1860.
2. *Tuolumne Courier,* 11, 24 April 1858.
3. *Daily Evening Bulletin,* 28 September 1858.
4. *Tuolumne Courier,* 6 August 1859.
5. *Frederick Douglass' Paper,* 31 August 1855. See also Helen F. Giffen, *Diaries of Peter Decker* (Georgetown, Calif., 1856), p. 254; John McCrackan, letters, 21 March, 23 September 1851, Bancroft Library.
6. *Weekly Anglo-African,* 2, 23 June 1860.
7. Frederick Douglass, *Life and Times* (Hartford, Conn., 1882), p. 253; Charles Wesley, "The Negroes of New York in the Emancipation Movement," *Journal of Negro History* 24(1939):78–79, 83, 85; *Weekly Anglo-African,* 8 October 1859, 7 July 1860; *Elevator,* 1 September 1865.
8. *Bulletin,* 1, 2 August 1860.
9. Ibid.
10. *Union,* 2 August 1860.
11. Census returns, 1860, San Francisco County, California.
12. Returns 1850, New Haven County, Connecticut; *Weekly Anglo-African,* 3 March 1860; *Marysville Appeal,* 14 April 1888.
13. *Weekly Anglo-African,* 17 December 1859.
14. Walton Bean, *California* (New York, 1973), pp. 174–75.
15. *Bulletin,* 19, 20 February, 15 March 1859; *San Francisco Times,* 23 February 1858.
16. *California Chronicle,* 23 February 1858; *Bulletin,* 12 July 1858.
17. *Weekly Anglo-African,* 19 November 1859.
18. Ibid.; Indiana-born Sam Groomes was listed in the 1860 census as a musician.
19. *Bulletin,* 22 March 1859; *Weekly Anglo-African,* 5 November 1859.
20. *Weekly Anglo-African,* 20 August, 22 October, 19 November

1859; David A. Williams, *David C. Broderick* (San Marino, Calif., 1969), p. 245.

21. *Weekly Anglo-African*, 17, 31 December 1859.

22. *Weekly Anglo-African*, 3 March 1860; *A Compendium of the Ninth Census* (Washington, D.C., 1872), p. 73.

23. *Weekly Anglo-African*, 26 November 1859.

24. Ibid.

25. *Douglass' Paper*, 31 August 1855.

26. *Weekly Anglo-African*, March 1859.

27. *Bulletin*, 8 September 1859; *Weekly Anglo-African*, 17 March 1860.

28. Returns, 1860, San Francisco and Sacramento counties, California; *Weekly Anglo-African*, 17 March 1860.

29. Returns, 1860, San Francisco County, California.

30. Frank Lockwood, *The Life of Edward E. Ayer* (Chicago, 1929), p. 33.

31. Hugh S. Baker, "Public Libraries in California," *California Historical Society Quarterly* 38(1959):303–04.

32. Helen Tunncliff Cattarall, *Judicial Cases Concerning American Slavery and the Negro* (Washington, D.C., 1932), 3:53; *Weekly Anglo-African*, 30 July 1859.

33. *A Compendium of the Eleventh Census* (Washington, D.C., 1892), Population, p. 477.

34. John W. Blassingame, *The Slave Community* (New York, 1972), p. viii.

Bibliographical Essay

The materials for this study are as thinly scattered throughout the usual research resources as the imagination can conceive. They appear usually in small fragments in a wide variety of sources, and to date no single collection of letters, journals, or diaries has been found that might be called an "Afro-American Gold Rush Collection." One soon, however, gets accustomed to small yields in each case. Fortunately, the pay dirt does accumulate as the great collections are panned. Data on the Afro-American experience gradually materialized out of the two great Western history collections in the United States—the Bancroft Library at the University of California in Berkeley and the Beinecke Library at Yale University in New Haven, Connecticut. Useful fragments were also found in the manuscript collections in the Huntington Library in San Marino, California, as well as in the California State Library in Sacramento. There will be no attempt, however, in this essay to list all items discovered in all libraries searched. They are in the footnotes. I have no doubt that buried in manuscript collections around the country there are still undiscovered choice single nuggets of information that could further deepen our knowledge of the experience of the black argonauts.

One of the subjects that remained elusive in this research is the subsequent careers of those Negroes who returned to the South as slaves after working for their masters in California. They numbered in the hundreds. My comment to this point is made with the hope that subsequent scholarship may produce a unique story. When the Civil War came, most of these blacks were persons of broader experience than their plantation-slave colleagues, and my hypothesis is that from this group may have emerged some of the black leadership of the Civil War and Reconstruction periods.

With few exceptions, the manuscript materials useful for this study were written by whites. Their primary concerns were their health, the weather, the dullness or excitement of the journey, the presence of Indians, problems with their fellow travelers, or their own homesickness. Fortunately, some of these chroniclers and letter-writers noted the black people they saw about them, albeit too often without naming them, and made some passing comment or observation. In this their perceptions varied widely, and it must be said that New Englanders, New Yorkers, and Pennsylvanians were more literate and more sensitive to blacks than were persons from other states.

Everything stated above holds true for material about the mining experience of Afro-Americans. Also, it must be added, manuscript materials were most rewarding for information they provided about the journey to the gold fields and life in the mines. As the concerns of this book move to urban life and the stabilization of black communities, manuscripts decline sharply as a source of information.

A second valuable source of data on the black experience enroute to California and in the mining country is the press. Conventional Eastern newspapers in New York and New England as well as some of the California papers yielded important information in their California columns. The antislavery papers were also useful, especially the *North Star,* which later called itself *Frederick Douglass' Paper,* because Douglass took a more favorable view of black migration to California than did the white antislavery press. Because New Orleans was a very important embarkation point for so many gold hunters taking the Panama route, the *Picayune* reportage was quite useful.

A legion of published diaries, journals, and collected letters was read for this study, and only about a fifth of them had something worthwhile on blacks. The vast majority of these had at the most three to four references. Most had only one reference. About two-thirds of the published materials were in books, about one-third in historical journals. One must be eternally grateful to the journal editors who published these contemporary materials too short or limited in appeal for book publication.

The one and only book-length work covering the gold rush Negro is Delilah Beasley's *The Negro Trail Blazers of California,* published in 1919. It carries the subject of blacks in California into the twentieth century. This was a labor of love for this black woman, but the work is marred by poor editing and mug-book characteristics. The book must be read with care, but it must be read, for Miss Beasley did talk to many who still remembered their families' experiences in the gold rush era. When Carter Woodson, the founder of the *Journal of Negro History,* reviewed the book, he wrote, "As it is, it is so much of a hodge podge that one is inclined to weep like the minister who felt that his congregation consisted of too many to be lost but not enough to be saved" (*J.N.H.* 5, 1920, pp. 128–29).

As a debate, the issue of slavery in California had a short career, and most of the material on that debate can be found in the 1849 *Report of the Debates* of the Constitutional Convention. What is of greater interest in these debates, and the subject that was of greater concern to the delegates, was the controversy over the free Negro. In this debate and in the general hostility to free blacks, there is the foreshadowing of the subsequent California laws denying civil rights to blacks. The two pre–gold rush newspapers, the *Californian* and the *California Star,* which combined shortly before the gold rush to become the *Daily Alta California,* are also of some interest for the way they switched their highly moral antislavery sentiments to an antislavery position based on anti-Negro grounds after the gold rush began.

The fugitive-slave issue that marked the first half of the decade of the 1850s is best documented in the newspapers and in the state supreme court reports for the two cases that came to that body. For only these were there any fragments of information in manuscript materials. More fragments of information about California fugitive-slave cases of modest importance appeared in the Eastern anti-slavery papers. California literature on the fugitive slave is singularly bereft of the publication of reminiscences and reports that marked the same kind of story in the East.

As this study moved into the more stabilized period of the gold rush era, newspapers and government documents became more important as data sources, although manuscript materials continued to yield occasional surprises. In this period, Negro churches and schools were organized, blacks went into business, took jobs, and organized civil rights groups, and as a result, blacks became increasingly visible in the records. The 1850 and 1860 federal censuses published under the title, *A Compendium of the Ninth Census,* became important, as did *Governor Bigler's Message and Report of the Secretary of Census of 1852.* With all of their imperfections, these did provide many names and did give a profile of population trends. Another validation of the black presence by name is the 1852 manuscript petition gathered largely by San Francisco Negroes in the course of their work for testimony reform. The later petitions for the same cause appear to contain solely names of white supporters. These unpublished petitions are in the California State Archives.

In easily overlooked positions in the California press, especially in the San Francisco, Sacramento, Marysville, and some mountain-county papers, black activities or individual blacks made their appearance from time to time. The low survival rate of small mountain papers is a real loss to California Negro history as well as to the state's history in general. But from time to time an item on blacks from a small paper whose issues are no longer extant was reprinted in a larger surviving paper. These bits of reporting can be found as far east as New York, where some transplanted Easterner sent a mountain paper back to his hometown newspaper for amusement or to fulfill a promise. Some Eastern newspapers would report on one of their former black townsmen with an item about his being murdered or on his demise in the gold fields and, unfortunately, with little else said.

Some of the most significant materials are the correspondences between the politically seasoned California Negroes and the black and antislavery press in the East. While one reads with disappointment that more letters were sent than were printed in *Frederick Douglass' Paper* and other antislavery papers, one is grateful for what was printed. In these reports the ideological currents of the California leadership became evident as well as the specific activities of the California Colored Convention movement. Scattered segments of this correspondence also appear in Herbert Aptheker's *Documentary History of the Negro People* and in Carter Woodson's *The Mind of the Negro as Seen in His Letters.* I was fortunate to become acquainted with Miss Kate Grases, nonagenarian granddaughter of Reverend Jeremiah B. Sanderson, a schoolteacher and convention leader, and thus was able to rescue several pieces of correspondence between him and his good friend William C. Nell, the black Boston abolitionist leader. Shortly after this correspondence was acquired, Miss Grases's two-story Oakland, California, home burned down. The rescued letters are now in the Bancroft Library, with copies in the Howard University Library.

Of considerable importance among journalistic sources is the religious press, especially the Congregationalist *Pacific.* While they were most concerned about the Chinese, they more than any other denomination were also concerned about Negroes and especially about their decade-long struggle for the right of equal testimony in the courts.

The struggle for their testimony rights and the three conventions that California Negroes conducted in the 1850s were reported unevenly in the Sacramento and San Francisco papers; the best sources for these activities are the published convention proceedings reports. An additional source for this struggle is the two existing numbers of the otherwise all-but-vanished black weekly of 1856–57, the *Mirror of the Times*. The loss of the other issues is slightly mitigated by the fact that two Negro weeklies, the *Pacific Appeal* and the *Elevator*, were published in San Francisco in the 1860s, and they from time to time reprinted some of the material in the *Mirror*. More light on the 1850s can be found in these two later papers, because nearly all of the California leadership was still alive and references by them to the earlier period frequently appeared in the papers' columns in the post–Civil War period. More information on the earlier period appears as the obituary columns report the deaths of these men and dwell on their past activities. The only autobiography of a black who lived in California during the gold rush era is Mifflin Wistar Gibbs's *Shadow and Light* (1902), in which he devoted two out of thirty-three chapters to California. He wrote the book at an advanced age, and his memory was a bit clouded about earlier events. However, the work has much that is sound and it is an excellent example of the ideology of one kind of black abolitionist, who in later years became a stalwart Republican office-holder.

The Journal of the Assembly and *The Journal of the Senate* for the seventh, eighth, and ninth sessions are valuable for their material on the response of legislators to the efforts of the Colored Conventions to get equal rights in the state courts. A further etching out of this response is available in the columns of the press, especially the *Sacramento Union*, a daily that was sympathetic to the aspirations of California Negroes and covered legislative activities thoroughly. A very useful book about the press that was written by a contemporary is Edward C. Kemble's *A History of California Newspapers* (new edition edited by Helen Bretnor, 1962). It is a guide to the politics of the California press in the fifties which in turn assists the scholar in determining which papers might have had more of an inclination to note the existence of blacks in anything more than the "mayhem" columns. Generally speaking, Whig and Know-Nothing party papers were the friendliest to the California black community.

Of considerable importance as sources for churches, schools, occupations, and even addresses are the city directories for San Francisco, Sacramento, Marysville, and Stockton. Less reliable are such sources for the mining counties because of the fluidity of populations in those areas. Two additional sources are also useful in this regard. A publication of the San Francisco African American Historical and Cultural Society entitled *A Walking Tour of the Black Presence in San Francisco* (1974), by Elizabeth Parker and James Abajian, locates many of the black-owned businesses of the gold rush decade. A useful alphabetical listing of names culled from contemporary sources can be found in the unpublished manuscript of Ernest V. Siracusa, Jr., called "Black 49'ers." A copy is in the Bancroft Library.

Additional valuable data about the early black church can be found in the several published proceedings of the California Baptist state conventions and in the American Missionary Association letters for California now on microfilm. Of especial value are the letters of Reverend Isaac Owen, who was assigned to work with Negro Methodists when he came to Sacramento. Some black church history can be found in local and county histories outside of San Francisco. Of particular use is the series of Thompson and West county histories.

Except in the *Pacific Appeal* and the *Elevator,* information about the Eastern background of the gold rush era black leadership was difficult to find in California sources. One must scour the recollections, memoirs, biographies, and autobiographies of Eastern antislavery men to piece together some of the facts on the lives of these blacks. The reports of black-sponsored events in the antislavery press were most useful. Similarly, the conventional Eastern press was useful where there were large free black communities. Again the obituary columns of the California Negro press come to the scholar's aid. Some of these men were active in the convention movements in the East, and Howard H. Bell's *Proceedings of the National Negro Conventions 1830–1864* (1969) has done scholarship a real service in bringing these data together.

By now the reader may wonder why no mention has been made of the seven volumes of California history in the massive *Works of Hubert Howe Bancroft.* I did explore these volumes and found some items early in this study, but as the research progressed, I realized that I was getting most of the same material elsewhere in greater amounts and from more reliable sources. Bancroft was not particularly interested in the Afro-American (although his father was an antislavery man) but limited his concerns about minorities to the Chinese and the Indians. He shared this attitude with most of the White Californians of his generation. Some of the unpublished "statements" gathered by Bancroft and his small army of interviewers of "old-timers" were of some value to this study. To these late nineteenth-century scribes, however, the black old-timer in California was of no interest.

There are three excellent contemporary studies that present regional descriptions of the antebellum free Negro. The first of these is Leon Litwack's *North of Slavery* (1961), which presents the legal discrimination suffered by blacks in the nonslave states. Jay Berwanger's book, *The Frontier Against Slavery* (1967), concentrates on the same discrimination in the Western states and is more a description of prejudice than an antislavery study. Finally, Ira Berlin's *Slaves Without Masters* (1974) is a comprehensive study of blacks in the slave states that deals with the legal disabilities placed upon them in that region but also dwells considerably on their social and cultural condition. Berlin's study gives more time to the colonial and revolutionary periods than the other two studies.

Index